BEYOND FEMINIST AESTHETICS

Beyond Feminist Aesthetics

Feminist Literature and Social Change

Rita Felski

Harvard University Press
Cambridge, Massachusetts

Library of Congress Cataloging-in-Publication Data

Felski, Rita, 1956–
    Beyond feminist aesthetics : feminist literature and social change
    Rita Felski.
        p.   cm.
    Bibliography: p.
    Includes index.
    ISBN 0-674-06894-7 (alk. paper).—ISBN 0-674-06895-5 (pbk. :
alk. paper)
    1. Feminist literary criticism.   2. Literature—Women authors—
Aesthetics.   3. Social change in literature.   4. Social history in
literature.   I. Title.
PN98.W64F35   1989   88-34460
809'.89287—dc19   CIP

To the memory of my mother

Acknowledgments

This book was conceived and written while I was at the Department of German, Monash University, Victoria, Australia, and most of what it contains was learned during my time there. I owe a particular debt to two individuals. David Roberts read all of the manuscript in several drafts and was an unfailingly perceptive and challenging critic who constantly forced me to rethink my most basic assumptions; the book would not have been possible without him. Leslie Bodi has been an inspiring and generous source of encouragement, wisdom, and advice ever since we first met.

The following people read parts or all of the manuscript in various stages and have my deep gratitude for their advice and encouragement: Terry Eagleton, Marie Maclean, Andrew Milner, Judith Ryan, Elaine Showalter, and Philip Thomson. I am particularly indebted to Jean Franco and John Frow for detailed and helpful criticisms and to Alison Lewis and Herbert Meier for help with knotty translations. Una Snell helped to prepare the final manuscript.

Thanks to all the friends who cheered me along, in particular to Peter Nelson for many years of friendship and support.

Early versions of parts of Chapters 2, 4, and 5 have been published in *Theory, Culture and Society, Southern Review* (Australia), and *Postmodern Conditions*, ed. Andrew Milner et al. (Melbourne: Centre for General and Comparative Literature, 1987).

Contents

possibly
relate to
ZN H ?

Contents

BEYOND FEMINIST AESTHETICS

Introduction

This book has a dual focus. First, it investigates the reasons for the emergence of a large and distinctive body of feminist literature in the last two decades, elucidating its social meanings and functions by linking genre analysis to a consideration of the ideological frameworks shaping the production and reception of recent women's writing. Feminist fiction can be understood as both a product of existing social conditions and a form of critical opposition to them, and this dialectic can be usefully interpreted in conjunction with an analysis of the status of feminism as a social movement within advanced capitalism. The emergence of a second wave of feminism in the late 1960s justifies the analysis of women's literature as a separate category, not because of automatic and unambiguous differences between the writings of women and men, but because of the recent cultural phenomenon of women's explicit self-identification as an oppressed group, which is in turn articulated in literary texts in the exploration of gender-specific concerns centered around the problem of female identity.

Second, such an analysis raises broader theoretical questions which require a critical engagement with existing paradigms within feminist literary and aesthetic theory. This metacritical dimension of the argument does not simply develop alongside the analysis of feminist literary genres, but is intended to interweave closely with it. If literary theory can be used to illuminate contemporary feminist writing, it is also the case that aspects of women's current literary practices can be drawn upon to problematize the more abstract and speculative claims of feminist literary theory. Thus one of the main contentions developed in these pages is the impossibility of a feminist aesthetic, defined as a normative theory of literary or artistic form that can be derived from a feminist politics, and I attempt to expose some of the contradictions resulting from existing efforts to develop such a unifying theory, efforts themselves reminiscent of similar unresolved debates in the domain of Marxist aesthetics. The chimera of a "feminist aesthetic" has tended to hinder any adequate assessment of both the value and limitations of contemporary feminist writing by measuring it against an abstract conception of a "feminine" writing practice, which in recent years has been most frequently derived from an antirealist aesthetics of textuality. I suggest in contrast that it is impossible to speak of "masculine" and "feminine" in any meaningful sense in the formal analysis of texts; the political value of literary texts from the standpoint of feminism can be determined only by an investigation of their social functions and effects in relation to the interests of women in a particular historical context, and not by attempting to deduce an abstract literary theory of "masculine" and "feminine," "subversive" and "reactionary" forms in isolation from the social conditions of their production and reception.

Sexual and Textual Politics

In arguing such a position, I part company from some of the more established approaches in feminist literary theory, which have recently been surveyed in Toril Moi's *Sexual/Textual Politics*.[1] I am in full agreement with Moi's critique of the limitations of what she refers to as "Anglo-American" feminist criticism, insofar as this tends to rely upon a reflectionist theory of literary meaning and is unable to theorize adequately the significance of modernist and avant-garde texts in the context of the development of literary form. Moi's discussion of the work of Hélène Cixous, Luce Irigaray, and Julia Kristeva also indicates some of the inadequacies of their positions from the standpoint of a feminist politics, although my own analysis of "French feminism," by which I mean the influential theories of gender and language associated with the works of the above writers, takes a more overtly critical stance toward what I perceive as its theoretical and political limitations. Moi's survey of the main currents in feminist literary theory can be drawn upon to provide an introductory illustration of aspects of my general thesis. It shows that both French and Anglo-American theories raise issues of central importance to literary analysis, but simultaneously makes it apparent that

note Marxist influence (in ans.)

each fails in itself to provide an adequate basis for a feminist literary theory. This conflict between different feminist approaches to the literary text does not simply constitute an as yet unresolved state of affairs which will be transcended at some future date by the emergence of a superior feminist theory which will overcome all contradictions, but needs to be recognized as a social and historical problem rather than a purely theoretical one, a consequence of existing tensions as well as interrelations between literary and political domains which problematize attempts simply to collapse the one into the other. Feminist literary theory in fact offers a reenactment of an ongoing dispute between what can be described as "instrumental" and "aesthetic" theories of the text, with many points of comparison to the earlier debate between realism and modernism within Marxist aesthetics in the 1930s.[2]

One possible option in developing a feminist aesthetic is the position discussed by Moi in her survey of Anglo-American criticism: an instrumental theory of the literary text which emphasizes its pragmatic political use-value. Good art is defined in this context as requiring a sympathetic depiction of female experience or feminist ideology: "Politics is a matter of the right content being represented in the correct realist form."[3] Perhaps the appropriate theoretical equivalent in the case of Marxism would be the doctrine of socialist realism,[4] with Lukács developing a far more sophisticated version of a realist aesthetic defined in terms of a formally mediated knowledge of the objective contradictions of the social totality, which cannot be defined as instrumental in the same sense. While the investigation of the ideological dimensions of literary representation remains an important element of textual analysis, which feminism has usefully emphasized in opposition to the formalism that continues to characterize much literary criticism and theory, this kind of purely instrumental aesthetic does not provide an adequate basis for a theory of literature or art by dint of its overt reductionism. As Moi points out, a feminist aesthetic grounded in reflection theory is most appropriate in analyzing examples of realist texts, which easily lend themselves to thematic interpretation in terms of their positive or negative images of women, and it is least relevant in identifying the significance of more experimental literature, which often foregrounds the process of literary production rather than communicates an unambiguous content. It fails to demonstrate the possibility that literary texts may to varying degrees transform or rework rather than simply replicate

3

given ideological positions. The insufficiencies of such an aesthetic theory are particularly apparent in the case of nonrepresentational media where a semantic content cannot be easily identified; in what sense can one evaluate the feminist standpoint of abstract painting, music, or other similar forms? A purely content-based feminist aesthetic which argues that texts can be adequately understood in terms of their mimetic and utilitarian function remains blind to questions of artistic form and technique and is unable to account for the pleasure gained from literature and art in cases where the ideologies of text and feminist reader cannot be said to coincide.

The second possibility is to approach the problem of synthesizing the interests of politics and art from the opposite direction; instead of equating the literary text *with* ideology, it is distinguished *from* ideology, and the "specificity" of the text as a literary construct is endowed with political significance as a subversive or oppositional force. The complex structure of literary form and language is perceived to undermine, distance, or otherwise call into question the fixed meanings of ideology. This position frequently draws upon a dualistic schema in which the subversive "literariness" of certain high culture texts is contrasted to more popular works, which are assumed to function as transparent bearers of dominant ideologies. The concept of the specificity of the literary text constitutes, broadly speaking, the basis for a number of Marxist aesthetic theories, although the nature and degree of critical knowledge resulting from this relative autonomy varies according to the standpoint of the theorist.[5] It reappears in the feminist position which hypostatizes the "feminine," subversive quality of the polysemic text that undermines the linguistic conventions of a phallocentric symbolic order. Although poststructuralist feminist theory tends to speak of the text rather than the work of art, and to foreground notions of desire and *jouissance* rather than cognition, its identification of the (usually experimental) text as a privileged site of resistance to patriarchal ideology by virtue of its subversion of the representational and instrumental function of symbolic discourse bears significant similarities to the position of Marxist theorists of modernism such as Adorno.[6] In both cases the text acquires an exemplary importance as a locus of indeterminacy which undermines fixed meanings and authoritarian ideological positions, which in the one case are explained in terms of the totally administered world of modern capitalism, and in the other are attributed to an entire Western cultural and philosophical tradition rooted in patriarchal interests, a tradition that has sought to control meaning and repress difference. *L'écriture féminine* and Kristeva's theory of the semiotic constitute two models of a "revolutionary" writing practice which have received extensive coverage in recent feminist literary theory. Both stress the radical implications of a rupture and fragmentation of symbolic discourse, which is defined as repressive and fundamentally phallo-centric through reference to the writings of Derrida and Lacan.[7]

This second option, however, offers an equally unsatisfactory basis for a comprehensive feminist theory of the text. Although it is undeniably the case that some texts are characterized by a greater formal complexity and ability to generate multiple meanings than others, and that this polysemic capacity, in modernity at least, is regarded as an important constitutive feature of literature and literary language, this does not adequately solve the problem of the relation-ship between literature and feminist politics. It is impossible to make a convincing case for the claim that there is anything inherently feminine or feminist in experimental writing as such; if one examines the texts of *l'écriture féminine,* for example, the only gender-specific elements exist on the level of content, as in metaphors of the female body. The attempt to argue a necessary connection between feminism and experimental form, when not grounded in a biologistic thinking which affirms a spontaneous link between a "feminine" textuality and the female body, relies on a theoretical sleight-of-hand that associates or equates the avant-garde and the "feminine" as forms of marginalized dissidence vis-à-vis a monolithic and vaguely defined "patriarchal bourgeois humanism" which is said to permeate the structures of symbolic discourse. The problem with defining linguis-tic subversion as "feminine" is that it renders the term so broad as to become meaningless—almost any example of experimental literature in the last hundred years can be seen as "feminine"—and this conflation of questions of modern literary style with an ideology of the feminine as quintessentially marginal and outside the symbolic order is of little help in theorizing the historically specific locations of women in culture and society. Furthermore, this kind of vague argumentation by analogy begs the question of whether experimental writing can in fact any longer be defined as marginal or subversive, and conspicuously fails to offer any analysis of the broader ideological constructs and institutional locations framing the process of textual production and reception. In this context, it can be argued that French feminism reveals an overestimation of the radical effects of linguistic indeterminacy which has not come to terms with the contemporary realization of the political limitations of modernism. Such a position, moreover, tacitly if not explicitly limits an oppositional culture to the reading and writing practices of an intellectual elite, and fails to offer any adequate explanatory account of the relationship between the subversion of internal formal structures and processes of social change. Any such abstract conception of a feminine text cannot cope with the heterogeneity and specificity of women's cultural needs, including, for example, the development of a sustained analysis of black women's or lesbian writing, which is necessarily linked to issues of representation and cannot be adequately addressed by simply arguing the "subversive" nature of formal self-reflexivity.[8]

Current approaches in French and Anglo-American feminist literary theory thus exemplify alternative possibilities in developing an oppositional political aesthetic within contemporary society: an aesthetically self-conscious experimental writing which challenges stylistic conventions and calls into question established modes of representation but which as a result of this esotericism remains accessible only to a minority, or an instrumental aesthetic which seeks to relate literature to the lives of large numbers of women, stresses the issue of political content, and consequently fails to address the specificity of forms of literary signification. Neither in itself constitutes an adequate solution to the problem of a feminist aesthetics, as Moi herself is forced to concede. While discussing Anglo-American feminist criticism, she rejects the opposition of aesthetics and politics as unsatisfactory, arguing that a Kristevan analysis would enable a more sophisticated understanding of Woolf, "locating the politics of Woolf's writing *precisely in her textual practice.*"[9] Yet this project is revealed as problematic when Moi comes to analyze Kristeva's position in more detail and admits that there exists no obvious relation between the subversion of language structures and the processes of social struggle and change: "It is still not clear *why* it is so important to show that certain literary practices break up the structures of language, when they seem to break up little else."[10] The defamiliarizing capacity of literary language and form does not in itself bear any necessary relationship to the political and social goals of feminism. This is not to counterpose literature and politics as antithetical opposites in an undialectical way, or to imply that literature should be reduced to a narrowly utilitarian function in advancing specific and identifiable political goals. Feminism does not after all merely address immediate social and political problems, but is deeply conscious of the importance of effecting changes in the cultural and ideological spheres, where the complex perspectives generated by literary texts may well have a part to play in that process. However, a link between literature and feminism can only be established if a text addresses themes in some way relevant to feminist concerns; multiplicity, indeterminacy, or negativity are not in themselves specifically feminist, or indeed specifically anything.

Feminist literary theory must also consider the various ideological implications of this isolation of the literary text as a supposedly privileged space, rather than assume that this can in itself provide an unequivocal answer to the problem of a feminist theory of the text. The hypostatization of the text as a site of negation, heterogeneity, indeterminacy, and so on, runs the risk of ignoring the question of the symbolic functions of literature in the broader context of social life. Here I would argue that Moi's analysis of American criticism needs to proceed more dialectically by recognizing that its interest in a literature which articulates female experience is a legitimate cultural need of an oppositional movement that cannot simply be dismissed out of hand. Literature does not merely constitute a self-referential and metalinguistic system, as some literary theorists appear to believe, but is also a medium which can profoundly influence individual and cultural self-understanding in the sphere of everyday life, charting the changing preoccupations of social groups through symbolic fictions by means of which they make sense of experience. This social function of literature in relation to a relatively broad-based women's movement is necessarily important to an emancipatory feminist politics, which has sought to give cultural prominence to the depiction of women's experiences and interests. Its significance is obscured by the assertion that experimental writing constitutes the only truly "subversive" or "feminine" textual practice, and that more conventional forms such as realism are complicit with patriarchal systems of representation, a position which maps onto gender what are in fact class questions and thus avoids any examination of the potentially elitist implications of its own position. In other words, whether the feminist critic wishes it or not, existing attempts to develop a feminist literary theory bring to light issues that are not explainable in gender terms, such as existing divisions between "high" and "popular" culture, which have also confronted Marxism and which cannot be resolved by means of a unifying aesthetic theory.

7

Literature, Ideology, and the Feminist Public Sphere

It can be concluded that feminist literary theory, as surveyed in *Sexual/Textual Politics,* reveals some of the difficulties which are involved in theorizing a relationship between the political and the symbolic, between sexual and textual politics, in such a way as to avoid both reductionism and a reliance upon inadequate homologies. To simply read literary texts in terms of their fidelity to a pregiven notion of female experience or feminist ideology is in effect to deny any specificity to literary language and meaning, rendering literature redundant by reducing it to a purely documentary function as a more or less accurate reproduction of an already existing and unproblematically conceived political reality. Equally clearly, Moi's discussion reveals the insufficiencies of a "metaphysics of textuality"[11] which relies upon a vague homology between literary structures and social and political structures (such as realism and patriarchy), thereby assuming that the disruption of forms of literary signification bears some necessary relationship to changes in patriarchal structures and institutions. To suggest that both of these conclusions are unwarranted is not to deny the intermeshing of literature and politics, but to argue for the necessity of moving beyond either a polarization or a simple conflation of political and aesthetic spheres. A feminist textual theory cannot simply move from text to world; it must be able to account for the levels of *mediation* between literary and social domains, in particular the diverse and often contradictory ideological and cultural forces which shape processes of literary production and reception. In other words, a feminist literary theory is dependent upon a feminist social theory, which can relate texts to changing ideological structures as they affect women as social subjects. Such an approach makes it possible to address the historically and culturally diverse relations between politics and literature, and to consider the possibility that literary forms may take on quite different social and political meanings in relation to changing cultural perspectives and struggles over meaning and interpretation.

Rather than aiming at the construction of a single, comprehensive feminist literary theory (a problematic project given the shifting status and meanings of both gender and literature throughout history), the present analysis offers a historically specific account of some major developments in contemporary feminist writing as shaped by ideological changes initiated by the women's movement in the last two decades. This analysis seeks to establish links between literature and the broader realm of social practice while avoiding the presuppositions inherent in a reflectionist aesthetic; feminist literature is understood as a form of meaning production, a construction of gendered identity which draws upon intersubjective cultural and ideological frameworks rather than a more or less truthful representation of an unproblematically given female reality.

In investigating the conditions of possibility for the recent appearance of a large body of feminist writing, the model of a feminist counter-public sphere can be drawn upon as a means of theorizing the complex mediations between literature, feminist ideology, and the broader social domain. Defined as an oppositional discursive arena within the society of late capitalism, structured around an ideal of a communal gendered identity perceived to unite all its participants, the concept of the feminist public sphere provides a key to analyzing the distinctive yet often diversified political and cultural practices of the women's movement. It offers an appropriately dialectical means of thinking about feminism as a force for social change which is able to move beyond simplistic oppositions between "idealism" and "materialism." The model acknowledges the relative autonomy of the cultural and ideological spheres and the importance of affecting changes in the way male-female relations are conceptualized and represented, and as a result it avoids the economist tendencies of traditional forms of Marxism which have often worked against attempts to link feminist and socialist theory. Simultaneously, however, the model of a public sphere draws attention to the communicative networks, social institutions, and political and economic structures through which ideologies are produced and disseminated and thus avoids the formalism and subjectivism of some feminist literary and cultural theory, which attempts to extrapolate grand political consequences from micrological textual excavations without any systematic account of the relationship between the two. It becomes possible to link textual and theoretical analysis to a historically specific examination of the constitution of the feminist public sphere, an examination that can address the diverse ways in which the politics of the women's movement is itself influenced and constrained by external social processes. In the following chapters, this idea of a discursive community grounded in a necessary yet often problematic commitment to a shared gendered identity is revealed as a central factor underlying the discursive presuppositions and the formal and thematic structures of the literary genres under analysis. The model receives its fullest articulation in the last chapter, where I move beyond the confines of textual analysis to offer a broader elaboration of the distinctive features of the feminist counter-public sphere in relation to the cultural and social institutions of late capitalism.

The justification of this methodological approach to the analysis of feminist literature will be undertaken in the pages that follow, but it may be helpful to summarize some of its potential benefits.

First, simplistic homologies between text and gender are avoided. The emphasis shifts from a purely internal thematic or formal analysis which ascribes a political value to particular textual features to an examination of the historically specific frameworks of textual production and reception generated within the feminist public sphere, allowing for an account of the interrelations between literature and feminist politics, which avoids the problems inherent in the theories of feminist aesthetics discussed above. As Peter Bürger points out, "works of art are not received as single entities, but within institutional frameworks and conditions that largely determine the function of the works."[12] The focus of attention is thus directed at an investigation of the specific ways in which feminist approaches to literature both problematize and are influenced by existing ideologies of art. It becomes possible to examine the specific ways in which the women's movement has served to repoliticize reading and writing practices without the need to resort to a functionalist and reductionist aesthetic theory that simply collapses literary meaning into its current use-value for a feminist politics.

Second, the feminist public sphere can be understood as both ideal and real, as both a utopian ideology and a determinate set of cultural practices governed by given political and socioeconomic conditions; as such, it provides a model capable of addressing the reasons for contradictions and tensions within the women's movement. The feminist counter-public sphere cannot be understood as a unified interpretative community governed by a single set of norms and values; in reality, women are never only feminists but also many other things as well, resulting in a diversity of standpoints influenced by other forms of affiliation in relation to class, nationality, race, sexual preference, and so on. A sociologically based model of feminist theory and practice which grounds its analysis in a recognition of the empirically diverse constitution of this feminist public sphere rather than in an abstract model of a gendered identity or a

10

gendered text is thus able to account for the plurality of feminist practices as shaped by the conflicting interests of its members. For example, it becomes possible to see that the debate between "experiential" and "poststructuralist" feminism does not lend itself to simple resolution by adjudicating their respective validity as theories, but springs from conflicting ideological interests: on the one hand a populist position which seeks to link texts to everyday life practices in the hope of affecting direct social change, on the other the emergence of an academic feminism with often quite different affiliations and a professional commitment to more rigorous and intellectually sophisticated, and hence necessarily more esoteric, forms of analysis.[13] It should be stressed that a recognition of the real diversity of feminism does not validate an uncritical pluralism which values all positions equally, and does not absolve the theorist from engaging in a critique of the more dubious elements of particular feminist ideologies. It is possible, however, to move beyond a crude form of taking sides for or against particular theories as "more" or "less" feminist by recognizing the embeddedness of theory in differing ideological and social interests which cannot be transcended simply by means of a unifying idea of the female self or the feminine text.

Finally, and perhaps most important, the category of a feminist public sphere is able to engage with and account for the historical significance and specificity of contemporary feminism as a vehicle of ideological and social transformation, offering a flexible analytical framework for investigating the diverse, changing, and often contradictory influences upon feminism as a complex network of cultural and social practices. Abstract theories of text and gender, particularly those grounded in psychoanalytical models, are conspicuously unable to account for feminism as distinct from femininity and frequently seek to ground a theory of resistance in characteristics traditionally associated with the feminine (hysteria and pleasure, for example). The problem with theories which attempt to locate resistance in every micropolitical strategy, in every libidinal impulse, is that subversion is located everywhere and nowhere; the valorization of the "feminine" as a site of resistance fails to acknowledge that women's assignment to a distinctive "feminine" sphere has throughout history been a major cause of their marginalization and disempowerment. The distinctive contribution of second-wave feminism, by contrast, lies in its entry into the public domain and its challenge to general cultural consciousness; it has irrevocably problematized the category of gender, generating and disseminating new ways of thinking about gender which cannot be simply forgotten or revoked. The logic of the feminist counter-public sphere must thus be understood as ultimately *rational,* in a Habermasian sense, that is, not in terms of any appeal to a substantive idea of a transcendental disembodied reason, but in the procedural sense of engendering processes of discursive argumentation and critique which seek to contest the basis of existing norms and values by raising alternative validity claims.[14]

Defining Feminist Literature

The following analysis seeks to address some representative features of contemporary feminist writing which have emerged in the context of this feminist counter-public sphere. My use of the term "feminist literature" is descriptive rather than prescriptive and is intended to embrace the diversity of contemporary literary texts which engage sympathetically with feminist ideas, whatever their particular form. Even a definition of feminist literature which emphasizes representation and ideological content, however, offers obvious difficulties, given the pluralistic nature of feminist ideology and its diverse political and cultural manifestations. Feminism possesses no primary text, no definitive theoretical source from which it arose and from which it draws its legitimation. Its political roots lie in the struggle for equal civil and political rights for women in the eighteenth and nineteenth centuries; this pragmatic orientation is still apparent in continuing attempts to improve the social status of women, attempts which often show little interest in any systematic theoretical foundation. The 1970s and 1980s have, however, seen an emergence of a concept of liberation very different from that of the attainment of equal rights envisaged by liberal feminism, as Seyla Benhabib and Drucilla Cornell point out:

> This tradition has its origins in the anarchist, utopian-socialist, and communitarian movements of the previous century. Unlike the bourgeois democratic and workers' movements of industrial capitalism, this latter tradition has been critical of industrialism, modernization, urbanization, and economic growth. Rather than focus on the extension of universal rights to all, these movements have emphasized the need for creating qualitatively different relations between self, nature, and others.[15]

Radical feminists in particular (Susan Griffin and Mary Daly, for example) have proclaimed the necessity of fundamental transformations of scientific and technocratic society and the importance of developing alternative forms of community, foregrounding the personal and psychological dimensions of women's oppression, and often incorporating mystical and spiritual elements. Moreover, the development of feminism as a theoretical discourse and the growth of women's studies as an academic discipline in the 1970s and 1980s encouraged women to explore a range of different intellectual traditions and theoretical paradigms, drawing upon such diverse sources as Marxism, psychoanalysis, and semiotics. Feminism can in fact be understood as an example of a "postmodern" worldview which is fundamentally pluralistic rather than holistic and self-contained, embracing differing and often conflicting positions. Consequently, unless one is to attempt "the discovery of a Platonic ideal form of feminism and the exposure of rival theories as pretenders,"[16] it becomes impossible to offer anything other than the most general definition of feminism. I thus adopt Alison Jaggar's formulation, which defines as feminist all those forms of theory and practice that seek, no matter on what grounds and by what means, to end the subordination of women.

The variety of feminist positions makes it difficult to establish absolute and unambiguous criteria for determining what constitutes a feminist narrative. The publication of large numbers of texts describing women's dissatisfaction with male society is obviously related to the increasing influence of feminism as a major political and cultural movement. At the same time it is necessary to differentiate carefully when discussing the "feminist" arguments of such texts. Ann Oakley's *Taking It Like a Woman* or Verena Stefan's *Häutungen* (Shedding) are examples of autobiographical texts which can also be seen as explicit feminist manifestos written by authors active in the women's movement. Other texts which have been associated with the growth of a new "woman-centered" literature express quite a different worldview. *Wie kommt das Salz ins Meer* (How does the salt get into the sea) by Austrian writer Brigitte Schwaiger, for example, a gently mocking and ironic account of a young woman's disillusionment in a stifling middle-class marriage, shares few of the ideological assumptions of the texts mentioned above. Frequently, the narrative of female self-discovery may take the form of an inward, spiritual journey, as in Margaret Atwood's *Surfacing* or Joan Barfoot's *Gaining Ground*.

Given this diversity of ideological positions, it is difficult to draw a clear line separating the "feminist" text from any "woman-

13

centered" narrative with a female protagonist. This problem has been discussed by Rosalind Coward, who is critical of the ideology of a unifying "female experience" and argues that "it is just not possible to say that women-centred writings have any necessary relationship to feminism."[17] Although not all woman-centered texts are feminist, however, it is certainly true that most feminist literary texts have until now been centered around a female protagonist, a consequence of the key status of subjectivity to second-wave feminism, in which the notion of female experience, whatever its theoretical limitations, has been a guiding one. It is precisely because present-day feminism has emphasized those realms of experience which are traditionally considered to lie outside the "political" (that is, public) domain, that the novel, as a medium historically suited to exploring the complexities of personal relations, has been so prominent in the development of feminist culture. It thus seems to me unwarranted to exclude the more subjective and confessional forms of recent women's writing as insufficiently feminist, given that one defining feature of the women's movement has been a concern with the intimate elements of personal experience. Within the West German context, for example, the very *point* of the feminist narrative has often been to exclude broader sociopolitical questions in order to address issues of personal relations and sexual politics ignored by male left wing intellectuals. Rather than using "feminist" as an honorific term to describe only those texts which appear ideologically sound from the critic's own perspective, it is more useful to examine the full range of literary texts which are intended and read as such, as a means of investigating the distinctive features of a feminist oppositional culture. These include its more problematic aspects such as an often uncritical hypostatization of female experience, which need to be assessed in relation to the social and historical conditions governing the development of feminism as a whole.

My definition of feminist literature is thus a relatively broad one, which is intended to encompass all those texts that reveal a critical awareness of women's subordinate position and of gender as a problematic category, however this is expressed. The decision as to which texts to include under this definition will necessarily involve a degree of subjective judgment. The novels of Erica Jong, for example, which have been marketed as examples of feminist writing, do not seem to me to reveal any serious questioning of the existing basis of male-female relations or any sustained refusal of the values of a male-dominated society. It can be noted in this context that some feminist ideas which might once have been considered radical (such as the critique of the sexual double standard) have filtered down to the extent that they are now relatively familiar. Consequently, these ideas have gradually become incorporated into a great deal of material which cannot be construed as consciously feminist or oppositional in any meaningful sense.[18]

By limiting my analysis of feminist writing to the twenty-year period since the reemergence of the women's movement in the late 1960s, I do not of course wish to imply that no texts which could be construed as feminist existed before that period. The history of literature offers numerous critical depictions of the subordination of women in a society dominated by male interests. It is, however, true to say that the last two decades have seen the emergence of a large and distinctive body of women's writing concerned with feminist themes, often autobiographical, and consciously addressing a female audience. The appearance of a distinctive body of feminist writing is a result not just of more texts being written, but also of more being published, with an expanding market for "woman-centered" texts; witness for example the new feminist publishers which have provided an important outlet for women's writing, as well as the appearance of "women's literature" sections in many of the established publishing houses.

While my definition of feminist literature does not in itself exclude any particular forms or genres, my analysis focuses in particular upon the examination of autobiographical realist narrative. This is not to deny the value and importance of contemporary experimental writing by women; probably the most extensively discussed author of recent times has been Monique Wittig, while other well-known women writers using nonrealist forms include Kathy Acker, Tillie Olsen, Christa Reinig, Barbara Frischmuth, Marguerite Duras, and Claire Lispector. But the attention paid to such writers by literary theorists has often been accompanied by a seeming lack of interest in autobiographical realist writing, although an examination of the catalogues of such publishing houses as Virago or The Women's Press clearly reveals that this kind of literature constitutes the mainstay of feminist publishing. There is a need for a discussion of feminist literature which can seriously address and account for such a phenomenon. Furthermore, the analysis of popular feminist fiction raises some particularly interesting and thorny questions in revealing a number of tensions between literary theory and literary practice, between an intellectual commitment to questioning fixed positions on the one hand and forms of writing which often appear to embrace a belief in an essential truth of female experience on the other. In a sense, this tension can be regarded as an inevitable consequence of the institutionalization of feminism as an academic discipline, with feminist intellectuals engaging in increasingly sophisticated forms of theoretical argumentation and textual analysis, and often voicing explicit criticism of earlier feminist approaches to literature and culture. This criticism has some validity, in my view; but it does not mean that the more popular forms of feminist cultural activity are not important and cannot be defended. On the contrary, insofar as feminism constitutes not only an increasingly sophisticated body of theory, but also a political ideology linked to a social movement concerned with processes of change, there is a growing need for feminism to reflect upon the relationship between theory and practice. There is an implicit message underlying advanced contemporary literary theory, in particular theory influenced by poststructuralism, that the questions which earlier preoccupied feminist critics—questions of the representation of women or the gender of authorship—are now to be viewed as anachronistic and naive. It thus becomes important to show that such interests and needs can be defended, an aim which can best be achieved by situating the discussion of feminist literature within the context of a broader theorization of feminism as a social movement.

This is not to imply that realism in any sense constitutes a necessary or an inevitable medium for the communication of feminist perspectives. It may well be the case that the current predominance of realist forms will gradually become less pronounced, as some of the original precepts of feminism become more widely established and no longer require such explicit emphasis. It is equally important to acknowledge that avant-garde art already constitutes an important part of a feminist oppositional culture, as I argue in my concluding chapter. One should also note the emergence of a large and distinctive body of feminist science fiction and fantasy, a phenomenon which raises a number of interesting questions about the nature of feminist utopias.[19] Given constraints of space and time, however, I have chosen to devote attention primarily to the prevalence of autobiographical realism, whose social significance has not in my view been adequately addressed in feminist criticism. Two representative genres within feminist literature, the confession and the novel of self-discovery, are examined in detail, revealing a series of connections between their distinctive textual features and the interests of feminist ideology. The search for identity emerges as a dominant motif, exemplified in the construction of a model of gendered subjectivity combined with a self-conscious appeal to a notion of oppositional community.

Feminist Literature and Theory
in Comparative Perspective

This book aims at a comparative approach in several senses. It includes discussion of texts drawn from a variety of national contexts, including the United States, Canada, England, West Germany, and France. This selection makes it possible to analyze representative structural and thematic features of recent women's fiction which recur across national boundaries, while allowing for at least a brief consideration of some important differences among feminist texts in the context of individual cultural traditions. The analysis is not, however, extended to Eastern bloc countries to include the work of authors such as Christa Wolf, perhaps the best known of contemporary German women writers. The arguments developed in my analysis regarding the contemporary political functions of realist and avant-garde art and the sociological phenomenon of a feminist public sphere derive from a discussion of Western late capitalist societies and cannot be applied to Eastern bloc countries, where such issues as feminism and the oppositional status of literature acquire a quite specific meaning and importance, and the constraints upon literary production differ fundamentally in nature and degree. It does not seem to me that it is possible to develop a general analysis of the political significance of feminist literature which transcends such differences.

This comparative approach is echoed in the theoretical frameworks and methodological approaches which are employed. Although I discuss what I perceive to be some of the limitations of American and French approaches to feminist literary theory, my argument is clearly indebted to insights made possible by writers working within these traditions. My analysis also draws upon the arguments of English Marxist and feminist critics and social theorists (among them Michèle Barrett, Terry Eagleton, Anthony Giddens, Janet Wolff) and has been influenced by the German tradition of social and aesthetic theory (Peter Bürger, Jürgen Habermas), including important recent work in this area by feminists such as Nancy Fraser and Iris Marion Young. In my view, there is a need for feminism to develop further interdisciplinary approaches, whether in the form of more extended interaction among such different areas of feminist research as literary theory, social theory, and philosophy or in the process of engaging existing nonfeminist theoretical traditions, of which Marxism must count as one of the most important. With regard to the former issue, in spite of the interdisciplinary framework of women's studies, feminist research appears at times merely to reduplicate existing disciplinary splits, for example between an empirically based sociology or history on the one hand and a purely textualist literary theory on the other. As for the second question, the claim sustained throughout this book is that any detailed consideration of the relationship between feminism and literature immediately raises a number of questions which cannot be adequately explained in terms of a purely gender-based analysis. One of the main achievements of contemporary feminism has been to show that gender relations constitute a separate and relatively autonomous site of oppression, which cannot, for instance, be satisfactorily explained as a mere function of capitalism. But it does not follow that gender relations can be viewed in abstraction from the complex web of historically specific conditions through which they are actually manifested. Thus discussion of feminist literature immediately raises a number of problems which go beyond gender, as I have already indicated: the status and function of literature in contemporary capitalist society, divisions between "high" and "mass" culture and their implications for feminism, and indeed the historical significance of contemporary feminism itself as a social movement and a political ideology that constitutes an important part of the "crisis of modernity."

CHAPTER ONE ✍

Against Feminist Aesthetics

The question of a feminist aesthetics regularly reemerges in discussions of what either constitutes or should constitute the specificity of women's writing. By "feminist aesthetics" I mean in this instance any theoretical position which argues a necessary or privileged relationship between female gender and a particular kind of literary structure, style, or form.[1] Depending upon the theoretical standpoint of the critic, the case for such a relationship can be argued according to quite different assumptions; by claiming that women are more likely to write in a particular style because of the existence of a specifically feminine psychology, for example, or by asserting that experimental literature, whether written by women or even in some cases by men, constitutes a "feminine" mode insofar as it undermines the authority of a "masculine" symbolic discourse. I will seek to demonstrate that there exist no legitimate grounds for classifying any particular style of writing as uniquely or specifically feminine, and that it is therefore not possible to justify the classification of literary forms along gender lines or the study of women's writing as an autonomous and self-contained aesthetic body. Consequently, the question of the most appropriate strategy for a feminist writing practice cannot be determined a priori, in relation to a concept of the "feminine" text, however defined, but instead requires a theoretical approach which can address the social meanings and functions of literature in relation to women writers and readers.

Recent attempts to develop a feminist analysis of the relationship between gender and literature fall into two dominant categories. The first proposes a distinctive female consciousness or experience of reality as the legitimation for a feminist aesthetic; the second is linguistically based and antihumanist and appeals to a notion of the "feminine," understood as a disruption or transgression of a phallocentric symbolic order rather than as a characteristic of female psychology. Jane Gallop locates one reason for the difference in the opposing positions adopted by French and American feminist theories on the relationship between subjectivity and language: "Americans— like Nancy Chodorow—speak of building a 'strong core of self', whereas French—like Josette Féral—talk of the 'subversion of the subject'. . . The 'self' implies a center, a potentially autonomous individual; the 'subject' is a place in language, a signifier that is already alienated in an intersubjective network."[2] National and cultural differences have in fact significantly influenced recent developments within feminist theory, although these differences should not be oversimplified. It has been noted that the reception of French feminism in the English-speaking world has been highly selective, focusing on Hélène Cixous and other proponents of *l'écriture féminine* to the detriment of alternative positions, and creating the misleading impression that contemporary forms of French feminism derive exclusively from linguistic and psychoanalytical models.[3] It is of course also true that a significant number of English and American critics have taken up and developed the insights of French poststructuralist theory, so that the use of the terms "French" and "American" feminist theory must be taken to refer to a grounding in a particular intellectual tradition, rather than simply to the nationality of the individual critic. Nevertheless Elaine Showalter's summary continues to possess a certain if schematic validity: "English feminist criticism, essentially Marxist, stresses oppression; French feminist criticism, essentially psychoanalytic, stresses repression; American feminist criticism, essentially textual, stresses expression."[4] It is in the United States and France respectively that the main feminist approaches to writing and gender have been most extensively developed. In England much of the innovative and influential work in the area of feminist theory has occurred in the areas of film and cultural studies rather than literature. Although the influence of Lacan in particular has been significant, English feminism has on the whole been more reluctant to examine gender in isolation from other determining influences upon cultural production, most notably class. If most American criticism assumes the preeminence of the self, and French feminism relies heavily upon the theorization of language and *jouis-*

sance, then the category of ideology has been central to the work of many English feminists concerned with the analysis of structures of symbolic meaning in relation to their function in sustaining systems of oppression. The interest in cultural politics within English feminism has furthermore encouraged the development of reception-based models which theorize texts in terms of their potential political effects. Given this stress on reception, and an interest in forms of communication such as cinema and the mass media, which do not lend themselves to analysis in relation to a notion of individual authorship but rather require consideration of the ideological status and function of systems of representation circulating within society as a whole, English feminism has tended to give less weight to notions of female difference as exemplified in a privileged psychological or linguistic position.

Although numerous works of feminist criticism have emerged from West Germany in recent years, German feminism has yet, in my view, to develop a distinctive and innovative body of literary or aesthetic theory. Much of the significant recent feminist research has been content-based analysis in the areas of literary and cultural history, focusing primarily on representations of women in the tradition of German literature.[5] While the emergence of a distinctive body of feminist literature in the 1970s inspired a number of critical texts dealing with the topic of women's writing, most of these have taken a largely impressionistic, biographically based approach, emphasizing the "radical subjectivity" of recent women's literature. Gisela Ecker's collection of essays entitled *Feminist Aesthetics* clearly reveals the tendency of much German feminist criticism to ground the analysis of women's literature and art in a hypothesized feminine consciousness or mode of perception.[6] The absence of any sustained engagement with the writings of the Frankfurt School and an extensive German tradition of Marxist aesthetic theory is perhaps surprising, given the potential relevance of many of the issues raised in addressing the specific question of a feminist aesthetics. The reasons for this absence need to be sought in the particular history of the development of the women's movement in West Germany, its strong sense of alienation from the Left, and a consequent stress on forms of gender-specific subjectivity accompanied by an indifference or hostility toward theory; there exists relatively little of the kind of cross-fertilization between Marxist and feminist theory which has occurred in England in recent years.[7]

21

The dominant discourses on women and writing in recent years, then, have originated from American and French sources. In counterposing their differing positions—the one expressive and typically content-based, the other linguistically conscious and antihumanist—important aspects of contiguity should not be ignored. Similarities can be identified in the writings of French feminist theorists and American feminist critics; both stress the liberating aspects of female difference and frequently refer to a notion of the feminine which is associated with fluidity, multiplicity, openness. Nevertheless, the governing paradigms of the two discourses reveal fundamental differences: American critics speak of creative self-expression and authenticity, French theories of the subversion of phallocentric discourse; American feminism valorizes female consciousness as inherently oppositional, French feminism tends to consider the notion of the unified subject a remnant of patriarchal ideology which needs to be deconstructed. These two positions of affirmation and negativity embody in fact what Teresa de Lauretis perceives as a fundamental dialectic characteristic of feminism as a whole: "a tension towards the positivity of politics, or affirmative action in behalf of women as social subjects, on one front, and the negativity inherent in the radical critique of patriarchal, bourgeois culture on the other."[8]

The distinction is also at least in part a historically determined one. In the earliest feminist writings on literature as exemplified in the anthologies of Susan Koppelman Cornillon and Josephine Donovan,[9] female subjectivity provided the central category around which a feminist aesthetic was defined, and feminist critical response was validated on experiential rather than theoretical grounds. Showalter, writing in 1975, could comment upon the conspicuous absence of theory in a strongly empirically grounded feminist literary criticism.[10] Theoretical critique was in fact frequently perceived as exemplifying a patriarchal desire for abstraction and systematization, and linguistically conscious methods of textual analysis were rejected as embodiments of an alienating "formalism."

By contrast, current feminist criticism is defined by an increasing preoccupation with theory. Although the appeal to personal experience remains an important factor in feminist criticism, particularly in the United States and West Germany, it has ceded a great deal of ground to reading practices relying heavily upon French poststructuralist theory, specifically the work of Lacan and Derrida. The effect of this shift in paradigm on feminist theory has been significant. Feminist critics have moved increasingly toward linguistically based methods of analysis such as semiotics and deconstruction, directing their attention to textual practices which seek to subvert the coherence of language as a signifying system. Psychoanalysis has become an increasingly important analytical tool, which is used to uncover the workings of desire in the literary text. At the same time, questions of feminist content or female authorship are increasingly perceived as of marginal importance to feminist literary theory, given that the gendered subject is understood as a relational identity constructed through discourse, a product, rather than a producer, of language. Thus the emphasis has shifted toward a kind of erotics of the text, in which the multiple perspectives, plural meanings, and ironic ambiguity of experimental writing are linked to a notion of the feminine as subversion, a transgressive force linked with the realm of the mother's body that continually threatens to disrupt the single fixed meanings of an authoritarian and repressive phallocentric discourse.

In spite of these fundamental differences, however, American feminist criticism and French feminist theory are linked by the common aim of attempting to develop an explanatory framework which can go beyond the political critique of literary texts to offer a comprehensive explanation of textual signification in terms of gender. The issue, in other words, is not only that of exposing the workings of patriarchal ideology on the level of literary representation, but of establishing some kind of systematic account of the relationship between gender and form, which can provide the basis of a distinctive feminist literary or aesthetic theory. The question that follows is whether it is in fact possible to account for textual signification in such terms, or whether this approach necessarily raises problems and reveals contradictions which cannot be answered in terms of the assumptions of the model itself.

American Feminist Criticism: Achievements and Limitations

Feminist criticism originated as a primarily content-based approach to literature which catalogued the response of the female reader to the sexual stereotyping codified in literary texts. Its first achievement was thus to make readers sensitive to the question of gender as an important factor in interpretation through the political critique of representations of women in the texts of male authors. One of the most influential of these early texts was of course Kate Millett's *Sexual Politics* (1970), which was rapidly followed by numerous other critical studies of "images of women" in literature and culture. The next task for feminist criticism was to rediscover a lost tradition of women's literature; such ground-breaking texts as Showalter's *A Literature of Their Own* (1977) were able to delineate a female counter-tradition within literature, an enormous body of women's writing which had been forgotten or repressed and which revealed significant patterns of continuity in its themes and preoccupations. Summarizing the achievements of critical research in this area, Showalter wrote in 1986: "We now have a coherent, if still incomplete, narrative of female literary history, which describes the evolutionary stages of women's writing during the last 250 years from imitation through protest to self-definition, and defines and traces the connections throughout history and across national boundaries of the recurring images, themes, and plots that emerge from women's social, psychological, and aesthetic experiences in male-dominated cultures."[11] Feminist analysis of the historical reception of these forgotten women writers revealed that the most common response of a male-defined critical establishment had been to read women's texts according to its ingrained sexual prejudices, practicing the kind of "phallic criticism" documented by Mary Ellman and more recently Joanna Russ.[12] The common use of male pseudonyms in Victorian England allowed for some particularly telling examples of rapid shifts in the value attributed to the work of George Eliot or the Brontës after the true sex of their author had been revealed.[13]

The result of this analysis was to generate a new consciousness of the ways in which ostensibly literary judgments of women's writing had been influenced by the assumptions of a male-dominated culture, with a consequent attempt by feminists to recover this lost tradition and to engage in a reappraisal of the work of women writers. This project in turn raised the question of the relationship between aesthetic theory and feminist ideology as an important issue in feminist literary theory. The clear evidence of gender bias in aesthetic judgment increasingly provoked feminists to question the possibility of gender-neutral aesthetic values. Given the fact of a male-defined cultural history, did it therefore follow that all existing aesthetic judgments were reducible to gender interests? And if so, what would an alternative feminist aesthetic look like? Could autonomous criteria be developed for judging women's writing, and on what basis?

24

One response has been, as I have suggested, to attempt to ground a feminist aesthetic in women's experience; whether defined as immutable, as a result of inherent biological and psychological characteristics, or as the consequence of female socialization under patriarchy, this experience is believed to embody the legitimating source of a gynocritical theory of women's writing. It is claimed by some critics that female consciousness generates structures of aesthetic production which are quite distinctive and different from those of male authors. Judith Kegan Gardiner asserts for example: "Thus I picture female identity as typically less fixed, less unitary, and more flexible than male individuality, both in its primary core and in the entire maturational complex developed from this core. These traits have far-reaching consequences for the distinctive nature of writing by women."[14] Speaking of the "fluid" and "interior" nature of women's literature, Gardiner goes on to claim that "the woman writer uses her text, particularly one centering on a female hero, as part of a continuing process involving her own self-definition and her empathic identification with her character. Thus the text and its female hero begin as narcissistic extensions of the author."[15] Gardiner's argument suggests that the "fluid" writing style (the description is typically vague) attributed to women is more "spontaneous" than the linear and ordered texts supposedly characteristic of male authors and that women's writing reveals the unmistakable imprint of the author's sexual identity. Such denial of women's capacity for conscious invention and artistic organization implies, in Joanna Russ's words, that "what has been written is *not art* (a version of the nineteenth-century idea that women write involuntarily)."[16] Russ's comment is an indictment of the prejudices of male critics, but some feminist criticism reiterates such prejudices in its assumption that women necessarily write in a more spontaneous and intuitive manner and consequently reduces all fiction by women to a form of autobiographical self-expression. It is of course true that for quite specific historical reasons (restricted access to means of publication, for one) women have often preferred genres such as the journal, and also that contemporary texts by women often blur the distinction between autobiography and fiction (although this is a general recent literary phenomenon rather than one exclusive to women). To attempt to establish a direct link between female psychology and "fluid" and unstructured literary forms, however, leaves the critic unable to account for either the historically determined causes of changes in literary style or the large numbers of highly crafted and carefully structured texts by women authors which cannot be adequately described in these terms. It is in fact agreed by many feminist critics that it is impossible to distinguish reliably between the language and writing styles of male and female authors when judging work "blind," without knowing the sex of the author.

Nevertheless, the notion of a distinctive female sensibility continues to influence writing on the question of a feminist aesthetic; thus Julia Penelope Stanley and Susan J. Wolfe distinguish between a female "expressive" mode and a male linear and dualistic mode, referring to women writers' use of specific "organic" verbs and a "discursive, conjunctive, style."[17] They assume a direct link between the literary text and a female authorial consciousness, without considering the effects of mediating structures such as genre, narrative conventions, or literary style. While other critics such as Showalter firmly reject the notion of a uniquely female language or style, the criteria for a feminist reading of women's literature within American criticism as a whole remain largely anchored in a reflectionist model which measures the work's ability to reproduce realistically female experience. It is the authenticity of personal response that provides the legitimating instance for the search for new aesthetic forms and that provides the touchstone against which to measure any particular examples of language use. This understanding of the specificity of women's consciousness is also strongly represented in German feminism; thus Silvia Bovenschen, for example, poses the question of a feminine aesthetic in the following terms: *"How can the specifically feminine modes of perception be communicated?"*[18]

This experientially based position presupposes a distinctive female consciousness which manifests itself both as a psychological constant within women and as an identifiable recurring characteristic in women's writing. But attempts to define the specificity of female experience or imagination, such as that of Patricia Spacks, are vulnerable to criticism on the grounds of their vague and impressionistic nature: "there appears to be something that we might call a woman's point of view . . ."[19] Black women have criticized the tendency of white middle-class females to deduce a generalized notion of female experience from their own lives, and both they and Marxist feminists have challenged attempts to deduce a distinctive common denominator which unites the experiences of all women across historical, class, racial, and national boundaries.[20] It can be and has been shown that specific themes and metaphors frequently recur in women's writing within and sometimes across particular cultural traditions and that women's use of literary genres has often revealed consistent distinguishing features—the focus on internal rather than external development, for example—resulting from similarities in the social status of women across a variety of historical and cultural contexts. There has not yet been any convincing demonstration, however, of any form of unifying consciousness which can be detected across the whole range of writing by women and which can form the basis of a distinctive feminist aesthetics. There are, moreover, obvious problems with a theoretical position which enshrines existing ideologies of sexual difference through reference to the supposedly intuitive and emotional quality of female consciousness, thereby merely reaffirming rather than questioning the authority of existing gender stereotypes.

American feminist criticism thus tends to rely on an inadequately theorized reflectionist model of art, that is, a belief that women's writing necessarily mirrors their particular experience in the same way as texts by male authors reflect a patriarchal perspective, and consequently suffers the limitations of an approach which reduces literary meaning to the self-expression of a writing subject who is defined exclusively in terms of sexual difference. This kind of gynocritical position typically operates with a conception of patriarchal ideology as a homogeneous and uniformly repressive phenomenon masking an authentic female subjectivity, rather than conceding that ideology needs to be understood as a complex formation of beliefs, structures, and representations which shapes and permeates the subjective sense of self of both men and women. It consequently applies a dualistic model to the analysis of literary texts; the work of a male author is assumed to affirm unconditionally the sexual ideology it portrays, whereas the work of a woman is read as containing an implicit critique or subversion of patriarchal values. Clearly, insofar as women acquire a gendered identity by means of the very culture and ideology which they seek to challenge, feminism cannot find a legitimating source in an authentic female self untouched by such structures. As Toril Moi points out in an analysis of Gilbert and Gubar's *The Madwoman in the Attic,* which she discusses as a representative example of American feminist criticism: "Gilbert and Gubar's belief in the true female authorial voice as the essence of all texts written by women masks the problems raised by their theory of patriarchal ideology. For them, as for Kate Millett, ideology becomes

27

a monolithic unified totality that knows no contradictions; against this a miraculously intact 'femaleness' may pit its strength."[21] This lack of any developed theory of ideology leads American critics to posit the submerged but authentic voice of the woman victim as a central category of their reading of women's texts. The truth of female experience in turn constitutes the source of the oppositional function of women's literature, with little attention given to the ways in which the notion of a female reality is itself mediated by ideological and discursive systems that are neither innocent nor transparent and that a feminist critic may not wish to accept automatically.

A content-based feminist aesthetic is further unable to account adequately for the "literariness" of texts, the fact that literature signifies in complex ways by virtue of its form. While one should not fetishize the literary text as a purely self-referential artifact, it is clear that fictional works are shaped by relatively autonomous aesthetic structures which mediate the text's relationship to ideology. A reflectionist understanding of literature as authentic reproduction of authorial experience pays inadequate attention to the ways in which texts signify as literature. Michèle Barrett has commented upon the limitations of a feminist criticism which conflates textual meaning with authorial gender and results in an impoverished understanding of literary signification:

> There has been a general tendency for feminist criticism to approach male and female authors very differently. Female authors are "credited" with trying to pose the question of gender, or women's oppression, in their work, and male authors are "discredited" by means of an assumption that any sexism they portray is necessarily their own. It seems extraordinary that these tendencies, both of which in their rampant moralism deny precisely the fictional, the *literary* structure of the texts, should have taken such a hold in the field of "women and literature."[22]

Current subject-based theories of women's writing cannot in fact be said to constitute an *aesthetic,* since they fail to establish any convincing connection between the gender-specific themes which characterize at least some of women's writing and a gender-specific account of literary style and structure. Female experience is assumed to generate a unique women's writing, without consideration for the fact that literature also involves an organization of meaning as *form,* the cultural and aesthetic significance of which is necessarily shaped

28

by its relation to existing literary traditions and conventions. Any attempt to analyze women's writing as a separate aesthetic body must be able to justify its autonomous status within a broader intertextual network of genres, conventions, and literary styles before it can justify the notion of two aesthetics and two literatures; I have suggested that an experientially based model cannot provide any such account. Thus recent attempts by women to write "authentically" of their experience have typically resulted in realist and often autobiographical genres which cannot be said to reveal any uniquely feminine structural or stylistic features, although, as I show in Chapters 3 and 4, they do significantly modify existing plots to conform to the contemporary social and ideological conditions shaping women's lives as they have been affected by feminism.

American theories of feminist criticism have, moreover, had significant consequences for the kinds of texts chosen for analysis; given an understanding of language and form as transparent media through which an extratextual reality is reproduced, American feminist criticism has tended to devote its attention to the realist novel, which does not obviously foreground its own fictive and literary status, and has carried out little analysis of experimental and avant-garde texts. The limitations of a reflectionist aesthetic as the basis for a literary theory is revealed, as Moi points out, when Showalter passes a negative judgment on Virginia Woolf because the ironic, elusive quality of her writing cannot be reconciled with this prescriptive notion of women's writing as an expression of female experience. A strict adherence to such a position would preclude any serious consideration of virtually the entire corpus of innovative and formally self-conscious twentieth-century literature and art by both women and men, which has been concerned with challenging existing conventions of representation, creating new forms, and subverting the relationship between language and experience rather than affirming it.

In conclusion, then, the achievements of American feminist criticism include its valuable reintroduction of political interests into the interpretation of literary texts in opposition to the general drift toward formalism; it has served to remind critics that literature does not only refer to itself, or to the workings of metaphor or metonymy, but is deeply embedded within existing social relations, revealing the workings of patriarchal ideology through its representation of gender and male-female relations. Such feminist criticism has also been able

29

to show convincingly that certain themes and preoccupations occur in much, although by no means all, of women's writing, but it has not been able to establish any convincing proof of a uniquely or specifically feminine form of writing. Its limitations are those of all biographically based literary criticism: a tendency to reduce the complex meanings of literary texts to the single authenticating source of authorial consciousness, an inability to analyze intersubjective, intertextual conventions of signification which cannot be explained in terms of the gender of the writing subject, and a theory of literary meaning which is unable to account for literature as form and to acknowledge the aesthetic significance of self-reflexive, consciously experimental examples of modern literature and art that cannot be dealt with in experiential terms.

From the Female Self to the Feminine Text

As a result of the problems described above, an increasing interest in the political dimensions of literary forms has emerged within feminist criticism, accompanied by a consciousness that linguistic and textual structures need to be questioned at the most fundamental level. The assumptions underlying earlier theories of feminist aesthetics— literature as a form of self-expression, identification between reader and author—are discarded as relying on an inadequate understanding of literary signification as a reflection of individual experience. Utilizing recent developments in literary and linguistic theory, women have been engaged in a critique of a reflectionist aesthetics as part of a critical assessment of male-defined cultural models; the focus of feminist aesthetic and literary theory has thus shifted toward a critical negation of existing codes of representation and the search for alternative forms.

The political function of art is consequently redefined; it is not the text which reflects female experience that best serves feminist interests, but rather the work which disrupts the very structures of symbolic discourse through which patriarchal culture is constituted. The artistically radical (experimental and innovative) text is also perceived to be politically radical, in that it seeks to challenge the most fundamental assumptions of a patriarchal society as embedded in its codes of representation and structures of discourse. In the area of film studies, for example, the interest in avant-garde form has been particularly intense and has been accompanied by discussion of the ways in which a feminist cinema can disrupt narrative structures and mechanisms of identification and can problematize the very process of the construction of meaning.[23]

This notion of a "negative aesthetics," that is, an art which critically distances or undermines existing conventions of representation, is not of course unique to feminism, but has also characterized various antirealist schools of Marxist aesthetics. In the writings of Adorno, for example, one finds criticism of both explicitly didactic and politically committed literature (Brecht) and of a conception of literature as a representation of the social totality (Lukács); art in modern society must retain a critical distance from the reified social world, a distance which can only be attained through the refusal of conventional codes of meaning. "Art is the negative knowledge of the actual world."[24] It is thus only the formally difficult, autonomous work of art characterized by contradiction which can remain resistant and antagonistic to the false harmony of the all-pervasive "culture industry." A similar critique of realism, although within the context of an Althusserian theoretical framework, was articulated in English Marxist film and literary theory in the 1970s, represented most notably in the journal *Screen;* the realist narrative was perceived to encourage "illusionism" by pretending to show things "as they really are" and by organizing the various discourses of the text around the presumed authority of an "objective" and coherent narrative structure and voice, thus obscuring the production of that reality and of the reader's own sense of coherent and autonomous identity through the very discourse of the text as ideology. Instead, only the experimental, self-reflexive work which exposed the conventional and ideological nature of any construction of "the real" could provide the basis for a radical aesthetics.[25]

As an approach to textual signification, the concept of a negative aesthetics offers certain clear advantages for feminism over the experiential model sketched out above in its theorization of the ideological dimensions of aesthetic forms, allowing greater freedom for formal experimentation within literature and art. The central difficulty, however, of a formally based theory of the text is that of defining its relationship to feminism. What is the exact nature of the connection between "open," formally complex works of art and feminism? Given that large numbers of modern literary texts are concerned with challenging established modes of representation, is it possible to establish any necessary connection between formal experimentation as such and feminism, and, if so, on what grounds?

My own view is that there exists no necessary relationship between feminism and experimental form, and that a text can thus be defined as feminist only insofar as its content or the context of its reception promote such a reading. An exploration of avant-garde form can constitute an important part of an oppositional women's culture; but the fragmentation and subversion of patterns of meaning do not in themselves bear any relationship to a feminist position and will be perceived to do so only if the themes explored in the text bear some relation to feminist concerns—if, for example, the text seeks to undermine an obviously patriarchal ideological position. An experimental or avant-garde feminist text would thus be characterized by a formal openness, allowing the reader a certain freedom in negotiating a position, but always in relation to a certain set of political ideas.

An important argument within contemporary feminist theory has attempted to establish a necessary connection between the interests of feminism and fragmented, experimental forms as such. It is here that the notion of a "feminine" language or text acquires a fundamental importance. In Annette Kuhn's summary: "A feminine language, or a feminine relation to language, would challenge and subvert . . . by posing plurality over against unity, multitudes of meaning as against single, fixed meanings, diffuseness as against instrumentality. That is to say whereas Western discourse—'the masculine'—tends to limit meaning by operating a linear and instrumental syntax, a feminine language would be more open, would set up multiplicities of meaning."[26] The assumption here is that ambiguous language is to be understood as in some sense quintessentially feminine, whereas any text that argues an explicit position is characterized by an ideological closure which can be designated as masculine. It may not be immediately clear why indeterminacy and plurality should be linked with a notion of the feminine, or indeed be automatically viewed as desirable, given the importance many feminists place upon the pursuit of quite specific and determinate social goals. Moi claims that the desire to regulate meaning bears witness to a nostalgia for first causes and a suppression of difference which springs from a patriarchal Western history ruled by a notion of a "phallic self, constructed on the model of the self-contained, powerful phallus" that "banishes from itself all conflict, contradiction and ambiguity."[27] Against this is counterposed the feminine, as that complexity and indeterminacy which resists and undermines the patriarchal desire for mastery, repression, and control. Hence the formally experimental text embodies the most radical challenge to patriarchal structures, which are embodied in the very structures of symbolic language.

Feminism's development of the notion of the "subversive," experimental text thus reveals some important differences in emphasis as compared to the Marxist theories mentioned above. Primary among these is its reliance on the categories of psychoanalytical discourse. The key status of modernism in Adorno's aesthetics, for example, is ultimately grounded in the cognitive function assigned to art, the fact that it leads to knowledge, if only of a negative kind; ruptures and contradictions in the text make possible a critical understanding of the false harmony propagated by capitalist ideology which saturates contemporary culture. While this conception of experimental art as critical knowledge is by no means absent from feminist theory, another and perhaps more dominant understanding of the avant-garde text, as represented in particular in French feminism, posits the text's importance as a source of resistance in terms of erotic pleasure rather than cognitive value; the playful text is linked to female desire, to the chaotic and fragmented patterns of the unconscious or the polymorphous female body. The subversive significance of the text thus lies, primarily, not in its critical distance from the real, but in its ruptures of semantic and syntactic order, which allow the play of desire.

Writing as Subversion

Kristeva's concept of the semiotic has undoubtedly been one of the most influential of recent arguments on the relationship between desire and language. As her theories have by now been extensively explicated and elaborated by numerous critics,[28] I will confine myself to an examination of the main problems arising from any attempt to use them as a basis for a feminist literary theory. Like the Russian formalists, Kristeva centers her analysis of literature on those texts which contain "poetic language," namely, symbolist poetry and modernist prose, and is less interested in more discursive forms, such as the realist novel. The texts of such (male) writers as Artaud, Mallarmé, Joyce, and Lautréamont exemplify Kristeva's conception of the semiotic, a term she uses in an idiosyncratic sense to designate psychosexual drives which disrupt the socially constructed order of coherent meaning and communication. The ruptures in syntactical and semantic unity, the explorations of patterns of rhythms and repetition in poetic language, do not allow the reader to apprehend any coherent and unified signified; instead they are connected to instinctual drives which Kristeva sees as preceding language and as repressed through entry into the realm of social communication. She draws an analogy between the language of the avant-garde text and the incoherence of psychotic discourse or a child's babble; all disrupt the communicative capacity of language through the multiplicity and chaos of random signifiers: "This heterogeneousness to signification operates through, despite, and in excess of it and produces in poetic language 'musical' but also nonsense effects that destroy not only accepted beliefs and significations, but, in radical experiments, syntax itself . . . for example, carnivalesque discourse, Artaud, a number of texts by Mallarmé, certain Dadaist and Surrealist experiments."[29]

The semiotic and the symbolic are not, as it were, different languages; rather, the two dimensions of discourse are intertwined within the communicative act, and Kristeva is at pains to point out that linguistic theories which do not acknowledge the inevitability of the constraining, legislative, and socializing aspects of language are naive. The symbolic is necessarily present in the text's existence as social fact, for a "multiple and sometimes even uncomprehensible signified is nevertheless communicated";[30] the analogy between the language of art and the babble of the infant or psychotic should not blind us to an essential difference, to the fact that the avant-garde text organizes incoherence as literary form. The semiotic does not, therefore, exist independently of symbolic discourse as meaningful communication, but constitutes its other face, the link between language and the body, embodying the materiality of the sign as a source of pleasure. In the avant-garde text this semiotic dimension becomes more predominant, erupting in the patterns of sound and rhythm which subvert the instrumental function of language as a transmission of coherent signifieds.

The central question raised by Kristeva's writing in the present context is that of the relevance of her theories to feminism and the reasons why they have exercised such a significant influence upon feminist literary theory. If the semiotic is a shaping force in the early stages of language development in children of both sexes, and given that Kristeva's examples of literary texts which foreground this semiotic function stem from the works of the male avant-garde, in what sense is gender a functional category in her theory? Can the semiotic be understood as being in some sense distinctively feminine, and, if not, in what sense is it a useful concept in attempting to theorize the relationship between women and language?

It does not seem to me that a satisfactory answer is offered to this question. Some feminist theorists appear to suggest that there is indeed a specific connection between the semiotic and the "feminine," insofar as the former is closely associated with the mother's body before the child's entry into a male-defined symbolic order. Alice Jardine writes in her explication of Kristeva, "This space before the sign, the *semiotic,* has been and continues to be coded in our culture as feminine: the space of privileged contact with the mother's (female) body."[31] This argument seems to me unsatisfactory in that it reinscribes at the level of theoretical abstraction those gender specifications whose inevitability feminists should be calling into question; from the social given that young children are primarily cared for by the mother, it extrapolates an abstract dualism grounded in the equation of the masculine with culture and the feminine with the body and the presocial, an extrapolation with strong ideological implications. Moi disagrees with this interpretation, arguing that Kristeva's semiotic is not to be understood as in any sense "feminine"; the point instead is that as a disruptive and deconstructive force it undermines all fixed identities, including those of masculine and feminine.[32] This interpretation avoids the problem of essentialism but makes it difficult to see why this anarchic, disruptive semiotic which subverts all meanings should have any particular relevance to a feminist theory of language or literature, a connection which is established, as Moi concedes, on the basis of a rather weak homology: "As the feminine is defined as marginal under patriarchy, so the semiotic is marginal to language. This is why the two categories, along with other forms of 'dissidence', can be theorized in roughly the same way in Kristeva's work."[33]

Unlike Kristeva, Hélène Cixous posits a more direct relationship between language and desire; rejecting the Lacanian conceptualization of the feminine as that which cannot be spoken in language, she espouses the notion of a "feminine" textuality directly echoing the plural and diffuse quality of female sexuality: "This is how I would define a feminine textual body: as a *female libidinal economy,* a regime, energies, a system of spending not necessarily carved out by culture. A feminine textual body is recognized by the fact that it is always endless, without ending: there's no closure . . . There's *tactility* in the feminine text, there's touch, and this touch passes through the ear. Writing in the feminine is passing on what is cut out by the Symbolic, the voice of the mother, passing on what is most archaic."[34] As such passages suggest, Cixous gives little importance to cultural determinants of sexuality. By defining feminine textuality as a spontaneous outpouring from the female body, she manages to avoid the question of whether *l'écriture féminine* actually reveals any significant differences from existing modes of experimental writing. As Mary Jacobus comments in her survey of theories of *l'écriture féminine:* "Utopian attempts to define the specificity of women's writing—desired or hypothetical, but rarely empirically observed—either founder on the rock of essentialism (the text as body), gesture towards an avant-garde practice which turns out not to be specific to women, or, like Hélène Cixous in 'The Laugh of the Medusa,' do both."[35]

But Jacobus's own attempt to answer the question "Can there be a (politics of) women's writing?" through an application of the theories of Luce Irigaray is open to similar objections, given that Irigaray's work is also based on a celebration of the open and plural nature of female sexuality and writing. Carolyn Burke has defended Irigaray in a sympathetic article, arguing that her references to the female body constitute poetic analogies, metaphors which seek to challenge existing patriarchal myths of the phallus, and do not indicate any kind of belief in a biological essentialism.[36] Nevertheless, Irigaray's texts are also marked by a continual counterposing of "phallic" discourse against a potential "fluidity," "plurality," and "multiplicity" as the appropriate modality for an oppositional discourse, a position which offers a number of problems as a basis for a feminist theory of writing.[37] It is the nature and insufficiency of such a dichotomous opposition which I will now examine in more detail.

In spite of their obvious differences, the crucial assumption to all the theoretical positions within French feminism discussed above is that of the *gendered nature of language*. Either discourse can be disrupted only from within, or, as in the case of Cixous and other advocates of *l'écriture féminine,* women have potential access to an alternative, "feminine" language; in both cases, however, language as a structured medium of social communication is designated as inherently masculine and repressive. Recent French-influenced feminist theory speaks of the "phallocentric" or "phallogocentric" nature of discourse and has developed an entire rhetoric around the notion of the "feminine" text, which is described as open, polysemic, disruptive, hysteric, fluid, and so on. This opposition of "phallic" and "feminine" forms exemplifies a separation of the social and political sphere from the erotic and linguistic sphere, which underlies much French feminist theory. The social realm, and indeed the very fact of language as a communicative and symbolic act, is coded as repressive, and an erotically based linguistic play appears to constitute the primary form of liberating activity. Ann Rosalind Jones, discussing this cultural pessimism as exemplified in the writings of Kristeva, concludes that her view of the "blissful anarchy of pre-Oedipal mother/child fusion" is a highly idealized one, in which the psychic repression necessary for entry into the symbolic order is "equivalent to expulsion from the paradise of infantile contentment, to exile in the fallen world of language as law."[38] A similar perspective permeates much French feminism; structures of any kind, whether social or discursive, are repressive, "phallic," exemplifying a masculine desire for mastery and order, whereas the "feminine" is idealized as a realm of undifferentiated and diffuse linguistic and erotic pleasure.

A number of difficulties arise from this conception of the feminine and its association with particular forms of "radical" signifying practice as represented in the avant-garde text. It should first be noted that the celebration of feminine sexuality apparent in the writings of Cixous and other French theorists tends to assume a separation of the sexual from the social, embracing a metaphysics of desire which fails to acknowledge the historical mediation of conceptions of the body and of sexuality by culturally specific systems of signification. The celebration of "feminine" desire as plural, spontaneous, chaotic, and mysteriously "other" itself reiterates and is easily assimilated into a long-standing cultural symbolization of woman in Western society.[39]

It is equally problematic to construct a homology between sexuality and textuality by assuming that "fluid" writing styles and the disruption of syntactical and semantic structures bear any necessary relation to either women's writing or the "feminine," understood as the realm of the pre-Oedipal. Language use is always overdetermined by multiple factors, including generic constraints and the structuring of signification by historical and cultural context. Proponents of *l'écriture féminine* stress its radical and innovative features, a strategy which forms an understandable part of an attempt to reject patriarchal influences and accentuate female difference; nevertheless, it does not seem possible to mount any convincing case for a gender-specific literary language. Features of recent French feminist writing such as linguistic playfulness and nonlinear syntax are in no sense unique or specific to women but are indicative of a more general cultural shift away from analytical and discursive modes and a blurring of the distinction between literature and theory which marks a range of contemporary critical and metacritical discourses, most specifically those influenced by Lacan and Derrida; the historical roots of such forms lie with the linguistic experiments of modernism. Advocates of *l'écriture féminine* frequently fail to theorize this crucial contextual and intertextual dimension of recent women's writing. Consequently, it would appear that the gender-specific qualities of recent French feminist writing can only be sought in their particular *content,* in representations of the female body or recent explorations of mother-daughter relationships for example, rather than in any stylistic features which can be designated as uniquely feminine.

Kristeva does not of course subscribe to the theory of a unique women's language, but rather deduces her notion of a negative semiotic from the poetic language of a male avant-garde. Yet her understanding of what constitutes a radical signifying practice fails to address systematically social and ideological constraints on meaning and appears to decontextualize the text. It is noteworthy, for instance, that her examples of "revolutionary" writing are not only from male authors but from texts written fifty to a hundred years ago—works which have become part of literary history and often of an established canon. Kristeva's analysis suggests, however, that the "revolutionary" nature of a text is less a condition of its historically specific and hence limited subversive function as a negation of the dominant aesthetic of the time than an inherent feature of language which resides in the repetition of certain sounds and disruptions of syntax, which in turn relate to the rhythms of psychosexual drives. Jones comments upon this "onomatopoeic essentialism" as a surprising feature in the work of a post-Saussurean critic and asks: "For *whom* does the poet call the finality of language into question? Are grammar and memory publicly or permanently subverted by Modernist textual practice? Kristeva offers a new interpretative mode to critics of Modernism, but her focus on the psychogenesis of texts blinds her to issues of literary context and reception. This is a curiously private revolution: the poet, solitary, original and unique, and the critic/semiotician are the only participants it requires."[40]

Kristeva's argument in fact raises two issues: the role of the unconscious in the production of discourse, and the connection between the activities of this unconscious and the revolutionary potential of a literary text. It can indeed be plausibly argued that the subject's relationship to language cannot be adequately understood through exclusive attention to the latter's communicative and symbolic function, and that the pleasure in sound and rhythm which shapes early language acquisition remains influential at a fundamental level in later language use. In focusing on French modernist and avant-garde writers as the primary embodiments of this semiotic function, Kristeva shifts the argument into a broader sociocultural dimension, moving away from the issue of libidinal gratification as a factor in individual language use to the attribution of a privileged status to the avant-garde as the potentially revolutionary manifestation of this eruption of desire. Philip Lewis claims that Kristeva possesses no illusions regarding the immediate political efficacy of the modernist text, that she situates its radicalism in an exemplary, if necessarily marginal, resistance to a general homogenization and rationalization of meaning (and here there are obvious links to Adorno). Nevertheless, his own quotation from Kristeva, "the avant-garde thus assails closed ideological systems (religions), but also social structures of domination (the state),"[41] suggests a massive overestimation of the revolutionary potential of experimental form, which leaves unclear the nature of the relationship between the subversion of literary discourse and liberating transformation, whether on an individual or a social level. By situating the radical function of literature in an inherent relation to psychosexual drives, Kristeva's argument evades the question of whether the disrupting force of the semiotic does in fact constitute a permanently revolutionary field, or whether it is reintegrated into a coherent symbolic system within the cultural institutions of contemporary society, as exemplified in the emergence of academic industries centered on the exegesis and interpretation of difficult modernist texts.[42]

Accompanying this lack of interest in contextual determinants of literary signification is a separation of private and social realms which underlies much French-influenced feminist theory. Liberation is located in the realm of textual subversion, resulting in a linguistic idealism which fails to acknowledge either the ideological implications of its own stance or to ask the question as to the ultimate nature of the relationship between textual and political revolution. The open and polysemic text is assumed to be the primary concern of a feminism which defines itself in terms of a recovery of *jouissance* and a valorization of erotic drives in literature. As Elaine Marks writes: "Reading becomes the subversive act par excellence."[43] It is noteworthy in this context that the reception of psychoanalysis by French feminism has been a highly selective one, which lays strong emphasis upon the repressive and alienating aspects of entry into language and society, and deemphasizes the necessary and enabling nature of this process as a means to the construction of a stable identity and an avoidance of psychosis. Social and symbolic structures are defined as repressive forms of objectification, the embodiment of the realm of male reason and order, which disrupts the primary erotic pleasure induced by the mother's body, and there exists a prevalent idealization of madness and unreason, as exemplified in the current fascination with the figure of the hysteric. While there are obvious reasons for women's skepticism regarding the value of engagement within a male-defined political arena, a refusal of the social and political realm as repressive and "phallocentric" in favor of a withdrawal into linguistic and erotic play serves only to reaffirm existing structures and women's traditionally marginalized role. Although a feminist politics must necessarily *include* consideration of the question of women's pleasure, since the history of women's oppression is so closely tied up with the regulation of female sexuality, feminism is not *reducible* to the play of desire, nor, in particular, to the *jouissance* liberated by the literary text. The subversion of fixed meanings and the unified subject does not in itself necessarily imply anything other than anarchism or relativism and can just as well serve the interests of a reactionary irrationalism as the aims of a feminist politics. That the attention given to linguistic subversion in much French theory does in fact coincide with a hostility to political activity is apparent in statements by Cixous and other advocates of *l'écriture féminine*.[44] Jones's analysis of the work of Kristeva leads her to conclude that it reveals a similar devaluation of women as active participants in the public sphere: "Kristeva still believes that men create the world of power and representation; women create babies."[45] Kristeva's own perspective on political action appears to have become increasingly negative (and in this her trajectory can be seen as representative of a more general tendency in French intellectual life as a whole); having progressed through various political modes, concluding in Maoism, she stated in 1984: "I belong to a generation that no longer believes in the miraculous political solution . . . We try not to be political."[46]

Is Language Phallocentric?

The influence of Lacan on French feminist theory has played an important role in shaping the conceptualization of the relationship between women, language, and society discussed above. In the

Lacanian account of the child's acquisition of language, the symbolic
order is defined as the Law of the Father, thereby necessarily
excluding the feminine as that which lacks a relationship to the
phallus. It is frequently stressed that Lacanian theory locates power
not with the individual father, but with the entirety of a cultural
system based upon laws of symbolization, prohibition, and exchange;
it is also claimed that the phallus bears no relation to the penis and
instead represents the "transcendental signifier," the fundamental
object of symbolic exchange which can never be possessed. Nevertheless, such terminology blurs the distinction between the "necessary
repression" which is the precondition for existence within a linguistic
and cultural system, and the "surplus repression" of patriarchy as a
social structure based on the exploitation of women, which is
contingent and open to change. In Lacanian theory, the use of such
terms as "phallus" and "Name of the Father" to describe the
positioning of the subject within the symbolic order, terms with a
mythical resonance which endows them with the authority of
universal symbols, blocks any consideration of the specific sociohistorical determinants of sexual and familial relations. Jane Gallop
comments:

> The question of whether one can separate "phallus" from "penis"
> rejoins the question of whether one can separate psychoanalysis from
> politics. The penis is what men have and women do not; the phallus is
> the attribute of power which neither men nor women have. But as
> long as the attribute of power is a phallus which refers to and can be
> confused (in the imaginary register?) with a penis, this confusion will
> support a structure in which it seems reasonable that men have power
> and women do not. And as long as psychoanalysts maintain the
> separability of "phallus" from "penis," they can hold on to their
> "phallus" in the belief that their discourse has no relation to sexual
> inequality, no relation to politics.[47]

Lacanian theory thus tends to ontologize existing social and cultural
relations in such a way as to suggest a necessary and inherent
connection between the structures of symbolic language on the one
hand and patriarchal power on the other, and thus to rationalize
existing systems of domination by making them appear as the natural
and inevitable extensions of the constraints imposed by linguistic
structures.[48]

To point out the inadequacy of such a theorization of the relationship between gender and symbolic structures is not thereby to imply
that language constitutes a neutral and transparent instrument which

women can effortlessly appropriate for their own needs. Clearly, language as a socially determined medium of symbolic communication bears the marks of a male-defined cultural history, which in the context of Western societies has seen the development of binary conceptual models that privilege the masculine as rational and universal and have defined the feminine as its complementary or negative pole; women have consequently experienced a sense of alienation from a philosophical and cultural tradition which has consistently excluded or marginalized them.[49] For this reason, the critical analysis of existing discursive systems and conventions of representation has played an important part in recent feminist theory. To move, however, from the recognition of an androcentric bias in language use as exemplified in existing hierarchies of meaning to the assertion that social and symbolic discourse is inherently phallocentric is a highly reductive jump. Such an argument simplifies the complex nature of the interaction of feminism as a counter-ideology with a dominant patriarchal culture, a relationship necessarily defined by both dependence and critique; in attempting to avoid a voluntarism which assumes that language is a transparent instrument free of ideology, it falls into the opposite trap of a linguistic determinism, which interprets all discursive language as a reinforcement of patriarchal structures. Recent French theory has usefully reemphasized the point that discourse is not interest-free and has developed a number of analyses of the nexus of relations between language and power; but simply to *equate* language with power (that is, symbolic discourse with patriarchy) is to obliterate fundamental distinctions between the various functions and contexts of language use and to devalue subjective agency and critical intervention in such a way as to negate the very legitimacy of the writer's own theoretical position. The definition of language proposed is a circular one; symbolic discourse is phallocentric, therefore processes of communication are always and necessarily phallocentric. Whether it is men or women who speak and whatever the context and content of their language, in speaking discursively they are doomed to speak the masculine. This view thereby serves to reinscribe women in a position of speechlessness outside language, theory, and the symbolic order, denying any potential power and effectivity to female discourse.

Correspondingly, attempts to define literary forms and structures in gender-specific terms—the argument, for example, that narrative as a "goal-directed form" is in some sense a quintessentially masculine mode—are not only politically counterproductive for feminism, but appear inappropriately abstract, attempting to ground a textual theory in ideologically shaped preconceptions about gender difference, while paying little attention to the texts that women are actually reading and writing. The notion of a purely "feminine" writing is defended as a utopian moment within feminism by several commentators; *l'écriture féminine* is to be understood as a liberating form of writing which cannot as yet even be fully imagined.[50] It may well be the case that a utopian perspective constitutes a necessary inspiratory vision for feminism as an oppositional ideology. Nevertheless, this vision of an autonomous women's language and aesthetic also appears to generate intense anxiety; by claiming that women's writing must be radically *other* than anything which has gone before, feminism sets itself the hopeless task of generating a new aesthetic by means of a negation of the entirety of existing cultural and literary traditions. As a result, an accusation often leveled at women's writing by feminist critics is that it is not *different* enough, that it fails to excise all traces of male influence from its language, structures, or themes. This "anxiety of influence" is, I believe, an unavoidable consequence of positing the ideal of an autonomous women's language and aesthetic outside existing literary and linguistic systems. Rather than coding language as masculine or feminine and defining forms as gender-specific, a feminist cultural politics should be engaged in questioning the value of such categories in textual analysis and opening up the range and richness of existing cultural traditions as potentially accessible and adaptable to the specific political and aesthetic interests of women.

French feminism has continued, however, to lay exclusive emphasis upon a notion of difference, which is typically situated in relation to an avant-garde textual practice. Apart from the fact that this position relies on what I have argued is an untenable equation of the "feminine" with the avant-garde, it also offers further difficulties in that it can account for only a very limited range of texts written by women. On the one hand, both Kristeva and Cixous make statements to the effect that "it is impossible to *define* a feminine practice of writing,"[51] a claim which suggests a laudable openness to the potential of a variety of textual strategies; on the other hand, this statement appears in practice to mean that feminine writing is "that which cannot be defined," in other words the same old equation of the feminine with the negative, mysterious, unknown. Those examples of women's writing which are not formally experimental, for instance, the overwhelming use of realist genres in contemporary feminist fiction, are thus explicitly excluded from the canon of *l'écriture féminine*. Cixous observes that "most women are like this: they do someone else's—man's—writing, and in their innocence sustain it and give it voice, and end up producing writing that's in effect masculine."[52] Kristeva is also dismissive; "Women generally write in order to tell their own family story (father, mother and/or their substitutes). When a woman novelist does not reproduce a real *family* of her own, she creates an imaginary story through which she constitutes an identity: narcissism is safe, the ego becomes eclipsed after freeing itself, purging itself of reminiscences. Freud's statement 'the hysteric suffers from reminiscence' sums up the large majority of novels produced by women."[53]

The Limits of Negativity

French feminism thus suffers from an exclusive focus on and cele-bration of an avant-garde textual practice accessible only to a few as the primary locus of the feminine, and a consequent inability to offer any adequate analysis of what is perhaps *the* major body of contem-porary women's fiction, realist novels with female protagonists in which language is not foregrounded or defamiliarized. Arguing a necessary relationship between linguistic experimentation and "women's writing," French criticism can theorize meaning and identity only in terms of patriarchal mastery and repression and thus is unable to offer a more differentiated analysis, which could engage more sympathetically with the issue of identity formation as a defining feature of recent feminist literature and an important stage in the development of an oppositional politics. Instead, the celebration of an anonymous and amorphous textuality as the location of the feminine leads to the erasure of issues which previously preoccupied feminist critics, for example, women as producers of literary texts. These questions are now perceived to reflect a nostalgia for origins, for a "metaphysics of presence" which seeks to suppress the poly-semy of language by attributing fixed and unified meanings to the text in relation to an illusory concept of a determining subject. "The notion of the 'self'—so intrinsic to Anglo-American thought—becomes absurd. It is not something called the self that speaks, but language, the unconscious, the textuality of the text,"[54] writes Jardine in her summary of this position. The conclusion which inexorably follows from this deconstruction of fixed identities is indeed the undermining of all the normative grounds of feminist criticism itself, as Peggy Kamuf argues: "If feminist theory lets itself be guided by questions such as what is women's language, literature, style or experience, from where does it get its faith in the form of these questions to get at truth, if not from the same central store that supplies humanism with its faith in the universal truth of man? . . . To the extent that feminist thought assumes the limits of humanism, it may be reproducing itself as but an extension of those limits and reinventing the institutional structures that it set out to dismantle."[55]

Kamuf's argument is indicative of the limitations of deconstructive skepticism, which seeks to undermine all the claims of the women's movement as epistemological errors and is unable to offer a more differentiated account that, while acknowledging the socially constructed nature of these claims, is also able to assess their pragmatic function and political importance. On the one hand, it is obviously pointless to pursue an ideal of a quintessential female experience, understood as an unproblematic source and an ultimate legitimation for a feminist politics; in the practice of feminist literary criticism in particular, there is a need to move away from those forms of interpretation which reduce the polysemic capacity of the literary text to a direct expression of authorial gender. On the other hand, although women's interpretation of their experience does not embody some form of absolute truth, one cannot therefore conclude that this experience constitutes an invalid basis for political activity that must be dismissed as another logocentric fiction. Rather, gender constitutes a difference which manifests itself in a diversity of ideological and cultural practices and which is institutionalized in fundamental ways in the distribution of political and social power within society. Given this fact, the diversity, but also the communality of women's lives, as exemplified in their experience of marginalization and oppression in social and cultural domains, necessarily provides the primary focus in terms of which feminism as a counter-ideology must define itself. Deconstructive readings which merely draw attention to the instability of meaning, the absence of fixed identities, and the indefinite play of interpretation are unable to provide any grounds for making such political choices or guidance in the adoption of certain political and cultural strategies rather than others.

There are of course important reasons for feminism's recent preoccupation with theories of language. As I have already suggested, feminism differs fundamentally from Marxism in that many feminists do not regard material and specifically economic conditions as the primary determinants of women's oppression, and the spheres of language and literature have consequently provided important sites for political activity. The fundamental difficulty of feminism is that the position from which a critique of patriarchy is undertaken—that of female difference—does not provide an autonomous source of legitimation but is itself constituted through a patriarchal cultural tradition, which women must work within even as they question it. It is this impossibility which has inspired the application of deconstructive techniques to the questioning of meaning structures from within, analyzing the ways in which heterogeneity is discursively organized around a masculine primary term, so that the feminine is constructed as its opposite and inverse.

However, feminism as an oppositional ideology necessarily relies on the privileging of certain ethical and political values and normative assumptions. Consequently, a theoretical position which seeks to deconstruct the notion of "woman" in order to operate with a conception of "the feminine," understood as that which remains marginal to but subversive of existing discursive systems, cannot provide an adequate basis for a feminist politics or theory of literature. By favoring linguistic subversion and deconstructive readings as the most authentically oppositional practices, we make it impossible to account for the differing ways and contexts in which women may legitimately choose to use language for feminist aims in the present cultural context: to negate but also to construct, establish, and affirm, as a form of play and also as a means of developing sophisticated tools of theoretical analysis. A definition of the "feminine" as perpetual negativity and dissidence simplifies the complex relationship between feminism and existing ideological and cultural traditions and has the consequence of leading feminist theorists to dismiss all forms of discursive argumentation as inherently patriarchal without considering the fact that any form of critique, if it is not to lapse into arbitrary subjectivism, depends upon intersubjective norms and values. Negativity plays an important role within feminism in the critique of patriarchal ideology and institutions, but it cannot in itself provide the defining moment of a feminist aesthetics or politics.

While this notion of the "feminine" constitutes far too narrow a basis for a feminist politics, in another sense, it is applied far too loosely and widely, as a general synonym for any marginal and negative stance, with a consequent blurring of crucial distinctions between different forms of oppression and exclusion within society, whether on the grounds of gender, race, or class. This common equation of the feminine with the oppositional as such is exemplified in the following claim: "For the 'female aesthetic' is simply a version of that aesthetic position that can be articulated by any nonhegemonic group . . . a specialized name for those practices available to those groups—nations, sexes, subcultures, races, emergent social practices (gays?)—which wish to criticize, to differentiate from, to overturn the dominant ways of knowing and understanding with which they are saturated."[56] This kind of generalization collapses fundamental distinctions in the ideology, social position, and cultural politics of a range of oppressed groups through an appeal to an undifferentiated notion of negativity, which is in turn equated with the female or feminine. The same writers go on to conflate a female aesthetic with modernist and postmodernist art forms, a confusion symptomatic of a more general tendency to blur the distinction between what is termed linguistic marginality (the writing practices of the avant-garde) and social and cultural marginalization as exemplified in the status of women. That the two are not identical is apparent when an author such as Joyce is cited as an example of a male avant-garde artist whose work is "constructed as marginal by the symbolic order."[57] It is debatable whether Joyce's writing can in any sense be perceived as marginal, given his canonical status and that of modernism generally within official cultural and educational institutions such as universities. There exists, moreover, no direct connection between the experience of cultural alienation, which is symptomatic of modernity and exemplified in the formal experimentation of modernist writing, and the specific social and cultural oppression of women as an exploited group. It is difficult to see how the linguistic experiments of male avant-garde artists bear any direct or indirect relationship to the liberation of women, however broadly conceived.

Most important, however, the notion of the "feminine" absolutizes a particular relationship between women and culture. While attempting to go beyond biological determinism by theorizing the feminine as that which is culturally repressed in both men and women, the term encourages a continuing association between being female and being marginal and idealizes this position through a conception of linguistic play as the ultimate subversive act. This position is unable to account for the many different examples of feminist cultural production; these do indeed include experimental forms but also large numbers of texts concerned with the construction of narratives of female identity, which cannot be dismissed as

47

phallocentric merely because they seek to emphasize the referential dimension of the literary work in order to articulate an explicit political critique of patriarchal values. A formulation of the "feminine" as an attribute of *texts* excludes serious consideration of the literature actually being written by women, consideration which surely must remain of central importance to a feminist criticism concerned with the relation between discourse and power. Makward comments with reference to recent French theory, "there is still a glaring imbalance between the attention given to women's texts and that to 'great writers.' Except for George Sand, Colette, Marguerite Duras, and Simone de Beauvoir, few feminist readings of women's texts have reached print."[58]

Recontextualizing Women's Writing

I suggest that the difficulties inherent in the project of a feminist literary theory are best negotiated by acknowledging the reality of gender as a construct deeply embedded in existing ideological frameworks and social institutions which fundamentally affects men and women's perceptions and experiences, while simultaneously recognizing that the relationship between gender and the spheres of culture and literature is a highly complex one which cannot simply be reduced to that of a one-to-one correspondence. Consequently, the political meanings of women's writing cannot be theorized in an a priori fashion, by appealing to an inherent relationship between gender and a specific linguistic or literary form, but can be addressed only by relating the diverse forms of women's writing to the cultural and ideological processes shaping the effects and potential limits of literary production at historically specific contexts. In the present instance, then, the question of what can or should constitute feminist literature requires a more general consideration of the aims and goals of feminism as a set of political ideologies and cultural practices which are characterized by diversity as much as unity.

A theoretical position which relates the literary text to its conditions of production and reception does not of course assume that the diverse conditions shaping women's lives are "translated" into writing in any simple and unmediated way; obviously, formal determinants of textual meaning such as genre possess a relatively autonomous status. Thus contemporary feminist fiction, for example, cannot be said to mirror women's lives in any reliable way; rather it offers a range of "mythologies" of female identity structured around certain recurring narrative patterns which refer back to and modify already extant generic traditions in relation to changing conceptualizations of gender. In turn, the influence of feminist ideology cannot be said to bear any straightforward relationship to the material conditions of women's lives as exemplified in changes to their socioeconomic status (hence the frequently made observation that the cultural and ideological impact of feminism is far ahead of any transformation of women's lives in the political and economic realms). Consequently, feminist literary theory needs to renounce the struggle to construct a unilinear model of textual determination which moves directly from authorial gender to text in favor of a recognition of the relative autonomy of and resulting interaction and conflict between multiple structures of determination.

This recontextualization of women's writing in relation to female writers and readers is thus not a return to the notion that authorial intention delimits meaning or to the belief that there exists any necessary or absolute distinction between the writings of men and women. It is clear that a range of textual positions is available to both sexes, and that it is often impossible to construct a straightforward determining relationship between the gender of the writing subject and the distinctive formal and thematic features of a literary work. For this reason, a feminist approach to women's writing needs to proceed from a recognition of the heterogeneity of texts produced by women writers in different periods and cultures which cannot be reduced to exemplifications of a single underlying essence. Nevertheless, in the present cultural context, owing primarily to the influence of the women's movement, the question of gender has been unambiguously posed as a crucial theme in a range of women's texts, which clearly differ from the work of male authors in dealing explicitly and self-consciously with the question of female identity. Here, some of the questions which might usefully be asked include the following: what kinds of genres are characteristic of contemporary feminist fiction? What do such structures reveal about the status and influence of feminism as an oppositional ideology in relation to changing narrative representations of women's lives? What is the social function of such texts and how are they received by women readers?

It should not be necessary to point out that a consideration of the current social significance of feminist literature does not imply that its meanings can be limited to or exhausted by this social function. It is a defining characteristic of texts as such, as recorded forms of communication which outlive the original conditions of their production, that they will constantly be subject to new interpretations that neither their authors nor their original readers could have anticipated. This phenomenon is, of course, particularly evident in the case of those texts which are classified as belonging to the domain of "literature"; this term signifies, among other things, that a text is perceived to possess a cultural importance which transcends any pragmatic function and therefore to lend itself to unlimited reinterpretation.[59] Nevertheless, the social and ideological conditions of textual production play an important role in determining the limits to what the individual text can and cannot say. Moreover, if a feminist approach to literature is to link the analysis of texts to broader questions of social and cultural change, it must situate literature in relation to a theorization of social processes as they affect the status of women; the connections between feminism and literature cannot be satisfactorily established by means of a subjectivist reading of an individual literary text, however sophisticated.

An important advantage of a theoretical position which relates women's literature to a consideration of its social functions is that it provides a framework for a sympathetic yet critical analysis of contemporary feminist fiction, something which I suggest both French and American theories of women's writing have been unable to achieve. An experientially based model is theoretically inadequate in its tenet of an autonomous women's literature grounded in authentic female experience and its consequent inability to account for ideological and intertextual determinants of both subjectivity and textual meaning. French feminism, while offering a model which is more alive to the "literariness" of the text, is marred by an overestimation of the revolutionary potential of experimental form, and has consequently been unable to offer any adequate account of the predominance of realist forms in contemporary feminist literature. An alternative socially based position makes it possible to undertake a closer investigation of contemporary feminist literature in relation to its potential function as a critique of patriarchal society, without making premature judgments as to the "correct" form which a feminist literature should take. As a result, it offers the possibility of a more differentiated reading of women's writing—whether realist or avant-garde—grounded in a critical assessment of the ideological interests it articulates and the cultural needs it seeks to fulfill.

CHAPTER TWO ⋙

Subjectivity and Feminism

A consideration of the social meanings and functions of feminist literature immediately introduces the question of subjectivity as a central factor for analysis. The biographical structure which characterizes much of recent women's writing is a consequence of the central importance given to personal change within feminist politics; it is therefore important that we explain the stress on subjectivity in the contemporary context without resorting to some notion of a pregiven essential female self. I will examine some of the issues involved in theorizing the subject before going on to discuss the influence of the women's movement on current representations of female subjectivity and to sketch a basis for a more detailed analysis of some representative genres within feminist writing.

It is clearly no longer possible to justify the value of feminist literature by simply asserting that it offers an authentic representation of the female subject. Although such claims continue to appear within feminist literary criticism, they beg the fundamental question of the status and value of subjectivity as a source of cognition and a reference point for political and cultural activity, and fail to address the recent critiques of subjectivity by feminists working in poststructuralist theory, as discussed in the previous chapter. Given the current status of subjectivity as a contested concept, it becomes necessary first to establish the relevance of a notion of self to feminist theory before going on to consider the more specific question of the literary manifestations of subjectivity in contemporary women's writing.

The insufficiency of existing accounts of the subject within feminist literary theory emerges from the positions surveyed in the previous chapter, which draw upon certain presuppositions about the subject and its relationship to language without systematically addressing the theoretical and political ramifications of these assumptions in relation to a feminist account of women's writing. Thus what I have termed "American" literary criticism typically assumes an autonomous female consciousness prior to or outside patriarchal symbolic and linguistic structures. By contrast, feminist poststructuralist theory has explicitly sought to displace notions of identity and experience as categories of a supposedly discredited patriarchal tradition and has been unable to offer a theoretical framework which can account for political agency and the function of subjectivity in relation to oppositional practices.

This dichotomy within feminist theory can be seen as one example of a more general difficulty in theorizing the relationship between social and discursive structures on the one hand and a concept of agency or self on the other. John B. Thompson comments that this recurring difficulty within social theory is usually resolved by an elevation of one term over the other: "Either social structure is taken as the principal object of analysis and the agent is effectively eclipsed, as in the Marxism of Althusser, or individuals are regarded as the only constituents of the social world and their actions and reactions, their reasons, motives and beliefs, are the sole ingredients of social explanation."[1] If "linguistic" is substituted for "social," this statement can serve as a fair summary of the current state of feminist literary theory, which tends to presuppose that the intentions of the female writing subject provide an adequate basis for the elucidation of literary texts, or else defines consciousness as the product of a transsubjective semiotic field which possesses no independent or critical status. Clearly, given contemporary developments in linguistic, philosophical and social theory, it is increasingly difficult to hold onto any notion of the female subject as a privileged and autonomous source of truth. It is equally true, however, that the feminist appropriation of the work of Derrida and Lacan, frequently accompanied by a privileging of the linguistic indeterminacy liberated by the polysemic text, has given no satisfactory account of the pragmatic social functions of language use, as constituted in the diverse communicative practices of women, and has conspicuously failed to provide anchorage and justification for the aims of feminism as an oppositional social movement and sustained theoretical critique. Instead, the critique of self-consciousness as fully present to itself is

52

articulated from a standpoint which reduces subjectivity to a purely epiphenomenal construct, a reflection of structural determinants. An inadequate voluntarism is thus replaced by an equally one-sided and mechanistic determinism; individuals remain unconscious of and unable to reflect upon the discursive structures through which they are positioned as subjects.

Whereas the question of the relationship between language and the subject is of little relevance to formalist analysis, which takes as its object of study the internal structural organization of literary texts, it must of necessity remain a key issue for any theory that seeks to establish a connection between literary texts and an emancipatory politics by relating the semantic dimension of the text to potential social agents. It is particularly relevant to feminism, which has typically sought to address individual women, often isolated in the home, and which has consequently emphasized the importance of personal change and the transformation of consciousness. As Henriques and his coauthors point out:

> Against the accusations made by the traditional left that feminism was individualistic and therefore bourgeois, feminism produced a form of politics and analysis which has perhaps more than any other modern movement asserted and demonstrated the necessity of personal change. *See Meridian* This is crucial because, unlike traditional forms of resistance, it was insisted that subjective transformation was a major site of political change. Indeed it was implied that significant political change cannot be achieved without it.[2]

It is in fact probably true that most feminist critics working in poststructuralist theory would not deny the pragmatic value of some notion of the female self as necessary to feminism's political struggles in the public domain. Yet this commitment to a goal-directed "identity politics" sits uncomfortably with a privileging of the literary text as a subversive space which deconstructs truth and self-identity, resulting in tensions and contradictions which are in practice often resolved by reaffirming the radicalism of theory and disparaging a conservative feminist politics of experience grounded in a naive epistemology.[3]

Against this view, it can be argued that "radicalism" is necessarily a relative issue and that textual theories which are the provenance of a minority of feminists working in the academy need to be balanced against the politics of the women's movement as a whole, as an important and relatively influential agent of social change. This is not, it should be stressed, an argument against theoretical intervention, nor a belief that feminist intellectuals should uncritically assent to the more simplistic manifestations of feminist ideology. To problematize the more extravagant claims made for poststructuralist readings by reasserting the equal importance of more mundane levels of feminist practice should not lead to the opposite error of a populism which unconditionally privileges the realm of everyday social experience as in some sense more "authentic" or less ideologically saturated. On the contrary, the importance of feminist engagement in rigorous forms of intellectual critique needs to be recognized as an important dimension of an oppositional politics, which should not shrink from critical appraisal of tendencies within the women's movement itself. Similarly, the effectivity of feminist grass-roots practices can be used to call into question those more rigid intellectual schemata which, by the very logic of their conception of language, serve to privilege the standpoint of the deconstructive theorist as the only genuine site of resistance. If it is the case that a supposedly conservative subject-based politics has been a powerful and effective force in mobilizing large numbers of women to assess critically and change aspects of their own lives, then it is important for feminism to develop an analysis of the subject which is not theoretically inadequate, yet which is able to account for the emancipatory potential of the women's movement as a politics that has been strongly grounded in the dynamics of everyday life, rather than seeking its primary legitimation in the "subversive" writings of an elite of literary theorists and avant-garde writers.

On examining current feminist appropriations of poststructuralism, including both the texts of "French" feminism and recent American examples such as Alice Jardine's *Gynesis,* two common underlying theoretical assumptions emerge which require further discussion. First, the reliance upon a Saussurean linguistic model grounded in the categories of signifier and signified engenders a focus upon the internal structural relations within language in isolation from any investigation of the historically specific conditions of language use, as shaped by ideological processes linked to structures of power and institutions which cannot be theorized at the level of discourse alone. Second, the feminist application of poststructuralist thought is frequently underpinned by a vague periodization of culture which links contemporary textual theories to a notion of the "modern" or "postmodern" understood as a radical rupture with the conceptual frameworks of the past; it is claimed that the present era marks the death of the subject, history, representation, and other tired fictions of patriarchal bourgeois humanism, and that feminism, as a movement grounded in specificity and difference, both accelerates and benefits from this dissolution of universals. I will briefly discuss what I perceive as the limitations of both these presuppositions, which can lead to a disassociation of theory and practice insofar as they are unable to provide a basis for legitimating the political goals of the women's movement. There is a need for feminism to rethink the relationship between discourse and subjectivity in such a way as to both acknowledge the structural determinants influencing communication and simultaneously account for the validity of women's writing and speaking in the development of an oppositional feminist politics.

Subject and Structure

It is possible to reject both the notion of a self-determining ego and a theory of structural determination which defines subjectivity as an epiphenomenal product in the self-reproduction of social and discursive systems, and to opt for a dynamic model of social reproduction and human communication which allows for a more dialectical understanding of the relationship between subjectivity and social structures. Giddens's structuration theory can be usefully drawn upon at this point as a means of moving toward a more differentiated and multidimensional conception of the relationship between structure and agency, a conception which is necessary if feminism is to be able to ground its own oppositional politics. "The concept of structuration involves that of the *duality of structure,* which relates to the *fundamentally recursive character of social life, and expresses the mutual dependence of structure and agency.*"[4] On the one hand the activities of human beings must be understood as situated and constrained, although determinants of human action are multiple and often contradictory and cannot be reduced to functions of a single, over-riding explanatory cause such as gender or class. On the other hand, it is necessary to recognize the "duality of structure," the fact that "social structures are both constituted *by* human agency and yet at the same time are the very *medium* of this constitution."[5] In other words, the relationship between structure and agency is dynamic, not static;

55

human beings do not simply reproduce existing structures in the process of action and communication, but in turn modify those structures even as they are shaped by them. "Structure is both medium and outcome of the reproduction of practices";[6] structural determinants both influence and are themselves influenced by social action and interaction.

This notion of the duality of structure makes it possible to move away from a conceptual model which counterposes linguistic, cultural, and social structures, understood as purely constraining forces, against a pregiven subject. Rather, structures are only constituted through the practices of social agents, who produce these structures anew in the process of reproducing them. Giddens develops a theoretical model of social activity which allows for an analysis of unacknowledged motives and unintended consequences of individual action while rejecting functionalist positions which seek to explain human behavior in terms of its function in the self-perpetuation of social systems. "According to the theory of structuration, social systems have no purposes, reasons, or needs whatsoever, only human individuals do so. *Any explanation of social reproduction which imputes teleology to social systems must be declared invalid.*"[7] This does not of course imply that social theory can ground itself in the analysis of individual consciousness; it is clear that the concept of agency cannot be adequately defined through that of intention, but requires systematic consideration of the sphere of ideology, defined as the mobilization of structures of signification to legitimate the interests of hegemonic groups. But the various, complex, and contradictory activities of social agents cannot be subsumed under their supposed function in maintaining the continued existence of some unified and homogeneous domain such as "society," "patriarchy," or "capitalism." Such terms are analytical concepts applied to the analysis of the social world in order to elucidate aspects of its operation, not transcendental structures whose logic determines all aspects of human activity.

Giddens develops an account of subjectivity which rejects any notion of the self as pregiven or transparent to itself, while still attempting to account for the dialectical and recursive nature of social life and the possibility of social change. The critique of humanism correctly recognizes the subject as a construct whose origins have to be accounted for, and not as a self-evident given of consciousness; but we may not conclude that because subjectivity is constructed, it constitutes an illusion which merely serves to reproduce the status quo. "The fallacy is to assume that, because the subject, and self-consciousness, are constituted through a process of development . . . they are merely epiphenomena of hidden structures."[8] Human subjects are not simply constructed through social and linguistic structures, but themselves act upon and modify those structures through the reflexive monitoring of their actions. Reasons and intentions constitute one important factor in the explanation of social activity but are not therefore to be conceptualized as discrete mental events which lurk behind and cause social practices. Society neither "expresses" the intentions of human beings nor "determines" them; rather, human reflexivity is constituted and intentions actualized in various forms of social and cultural activity.

Giddens then constructs a tripartite model of the subject by distinguishing among practical consciousness, discursive consciousness, and the unconscious. His notion of practical consciousness emphasizes that human activity relies on a fund of tacit knowledge which an individual can apply skillfully and appropriately without necessarily being able to formulate such knowledge at a discursive level (the use of language is itself an obvious example). The unconscious is represented as essential to social theory, as one important motivation of human actions which remains outside the conscious self-understanding of the individual. Nevertheless, Giddens remains critical, correctly, in my view, of any attempt to reduce all forms of social life to reflections of unconscious processes, a move that "fails to allow sufficient play to autonomous social forces."[9]

Situating the unconscious within a broader theorization of structure and agency offers a more productive basis for addressing the category of the subject from the standpoint of feminism, allowing for an incorporation of the work carried out by feminists in psychoanalytical theory, while at the same time acknowledging the autonomous influence of other social and ideological processes. It is crucial for an emancipatory feminist politics to allow free space for desires which cannot be subsumed into some notion of "ideological correctness," particularly in such areas as sexual pleasure and fantasy, which cannot be unproblematically reconciled with an emphasis upon autonomy and equality. In recent years, feminist theorists have drawn upon the methodological tools of psychoanalysis as a means of moving beyond a model of ideology as false consciousness, which defines women as unwitting victims of ideological mystification. Concepts of pleasure,

57

identification, and libidinal gratification are clearly of considerable importance in explaining the continuing power of patriarchal systems of representation and women's active participation and investment in the maintenance of existing social relations. Psychoanalysis, however, while helping to account for the construction of the female subject and current manifestations of sexual difference, cannot offer any kind of theory of social transformation and is unable to account for the possibility of women acting on and changing aspects of the structures which shape them. Lacanian theory, for example, avoids the residual biological determinism evident in some appropriations of Freud but is equally reductive in its equation of symbolic language with the power of the phallus. As Wendy Hollway correctly points out, Lacan's

> inbuilt phallocentricism and universalism is incompatible with theorizing the production of subjectivity in a way which accounts not only for how the processes may occur under existing patriarchal social relations, but would also allow that things could be otherwise . . . Despite the shift of emphasis onto signification as opposed to biological differences between men and women, and the production of subjectivity in accordance with cultural laws, the phallus as the sign of difference remains, for Lacan, the "signifier of signifieds"; and, following Lévi-Strauss's emphasis, universals of culture are taken as inevitables. This produces a simple deterministic reductionism, so that any discussion of the possibilities of change has to operate outside of the terms of reference of the account itself.[10]

By contrast, theorizing a more dialectical interrelation between subject and structure avoids the twin pitfalls of determinism and voluntarism, allowing for the recognition that the female subject is necessarily constructed through a variety of structural determinants—psychological, ideological, social—without thereby simply reducing her to a passive reflection of male-defined schemata. It offers a way out of the either/or dichotomies which underpin much of feminist theory, the belief, for instance, that if feminism is not a radical negation of everything that has gone before it, it is necessarily irredeemably compromised by patriarchal ideology and masculine systems of representation. This polarization of masculine and feminine spheres, for all its satisfying polemicism, is reductive and ultimately counterproductive in leaving feminism no means of legitimating its own oppositional position and digging the ground out from under its own feet. Having rejected existing theoretical frameworks and cultural traditions as the products of patriarchal history, feminism is confronted with the problem that its own oppositional discourse relies upon concepts and arguments derived from this same tradition, which are used in order to criticize it, leading to the conclusion by some theorists that feminism is itself irredeemably phallocentric. The inadequacy of this conclusion is a result of the falsity of a premise which tends to equate all existing discursive structures with masculine repression and which fails to recognize that all forms of activity, however radical, can be realized only in relation to and within systemic constraints. This is not simply an unfortunate failure of current feminist practice, but the very condition of all forms of social activity; the feminist critique of patriarchal values cannot occur outside ideological and social structures in some privileged space, but constantly interacts with the very frameworks it challenges. The current equation of social and symbolic structures with phallocentrism and of the feminine with the marginal is unable to conceptualize adequately feminist practices, which cannot be seen as either authentically "feminine" or as a passive reflection of existing patriarchal structures, but are rather engaged in a much more complex appropriation, revision, and development of existing cultural frameworks. Gender-based dualisms which seek to divide such fundamentally intersubjective spheres as those of culture and ideology into autonomous "masculine" and "feminine" domains are unable to deal with this kind of complex dialectic.

It is equally necessary for feminist theory to acknowledge that gender is only one of the many determining influences upon subjectivity, ranging from macrostructures such as class, nationality, and race down to microstructures such as the accidents of personal history, which do not simply exist alongside gender distinctions, but actively influence and are influenced by them. To define gender as the primary explanation of all social relations, to speak of the male and female subject in abstract and ahistorical terms, is in fact ultimately counterproductive for feminism, in that such an account can offer no explanation of how existing forms of gender inequality can be changed. If, however, an active role is attributed to feminist ideology as a means of bringing about such changes, a factor is introduced which cannot be explained purely in gender terms, but which is related to a variety of social and cultural factors (in the current context, the status and function of social movements in late capitalist society) which are not limited to women, although they will of course affect men and women in different ways.

59

In other words, female identity is a necessary but not a sufficient condition for feminist consciousness, which does not arise spontaneously out of women's subordination but is shaped by a historically specific set of interrelations between socioeconomic conditions and ideological and cultural processes. Consequently, any interpretation of the female subject, insofar as it wishes to allow for the possibility of change rather than simply analyzing existing patterns of gender socialization, will need to take into account social influences which cannot be explained in terms of gender distinctions alone. Furthermore, while feminism seeks to engage with the gender-specific aspects of women's lives which have been ignored or trivialized in a patriarchal society, it must avoid hypothesizing an essence of femininity which is blind to the diversity of female subjects as shaped by heterogeneous historical and cultural influences. Structuration theory is useful in this context, first because it provides a model compatible with historically specific analyses of the multiple and varied influences upon gendered subjectivity, and second because it has the capacity to conceptualize the potential for critical activity on the part of female subjects within given constraints, who are potentially capable of modifying aspects of existing structures in the process of reproducing them. It appears, in this context, that certain dominant social attitudes relating to female sexuality or women in the workforce have proved relatively easier to challenge than more deep-seated and institutionalized structural inequalities affecting women's lives in late capitalism, which, it is argued, have in fact intensified in recent years with the increasing feminization of poverty.[11]

The conceptualization of the duality of structure, applied to the specific interests of a feminist analysis of language and culture, thus allows for a more differentiated understanding of structure as not only constraining but *enabling,* a precondition for the possibility of meaningful choices, which is necessarily implicated in even the most radical processes of change. As Giddens argues, *"structure thus is not to be conceptualised as a barrier to action, but as essentially involved in its production."*[12] This point is worth stressing in the context of texts such as Jardine's *Gynesis,* which, drawing heavily on the work of Derrida and Lacan, defines symbolic and discursive structures as patriarchal and repressive and speaks of a "subversive" cultural space outside such constraints that is codified as "feminine." Although it is both necessary and inevitable that oppressed social groups draw attention to the rigidity of dominant discourses which exclude or marginalize them, the attempt to argue the possibility of a domain outside the constraints of symbolic signification necessarily results in self-defeating self-contradiction. Social and discursive practices are meaningful only as specific choices among given possibilities, which in turn exist in relation to past events, which provide the conditions for their initiation; there is no discursive position which is not multiply determined and implicated within ideology. Consequently, women are forced to confront the question of the relative value of one discursive strategy over another in a given context and cannot escape the constraints of symbolic meaning as such by taking refuge in a metaphysic of the "feminine."

Structuration theory, by acknowledging the potential for self-reflexivity and critique on the part of social actors, also provides a theoretical basis from which a movement such as feminism can justify its oppositional politics. Giddens comments upon the tendency of structuralist theories, most prominently in the case of Althusser, to discount individuals' reasons for their actions, in order to discover the "real" meaning of which they remain ignorant. The political implications of this are potentially suspect, he argues: "If actors are regarded as cultural dopes or mere 'bearers of a mode of production', with no worthwhile understanding of their surroundings or the circumstances of their action, the way is immediately laid open for the supposition that their own views can be disregarded."[13] A similar danger is implicit in the feminist position which defines language as inherently phallocentric; in Giddens's terminology the practical and discursive understanding which women possess of the meaning and conditions of their own actions is discredited by being reduced to the unconscious reinforcement of a patriarchal system of representation, a process from which only the critic's own mode of discursive argumentation remains miraculously intact.

The very purpose of a critical theory such as feminism is to uncover concealed determinants and consequences of actions and to examine critically the seemingly natural and self-evident truths of everyday life; clearly the conscious intentions of individuals do not in themselves constitute an adequate explanatory category for the theoretical analysis of society. At the same time, it is both elitist and reductive to suggest that only certain highly specialized intellectual reading and writing practices can pierce the veil of ideological mystification, an implicit consequence of both the Althusserian distinction between science and ideology, which locates all critical thought outside the practices of everyday life, and of the deconstructionist emphasis on textual analysis as a privileged form of subversion, both of which have had a powerful influence on feminist theory. Such a position ignores the historically specific, complex, and contradictory nature of human subjects and the varying degrees of dissent, resistance, and potential for change which exist in particular social contexts.

Feminism and Language

Deborah Cameron, in a forceful critique of forms of linguistic determinism, argues that feminist theory has been led astray by the belief that language is "man-made," regardless of whether this notion is articulated within a humanist framework as a state of female alienation within language or else in psychoanalytical terms, with reference to women's negative entry into the symbolic order. The nature of the relationship between gender and language is determined not by the repressive nature of language as such, but by structures of power, exemplified in institutional frameworks which serve to legitimate and to privilege certain forms of discourse traditionally reserved for men (public speaking, academic writing, literature). The nature and degree of female exclusion within existing discursive practices is thus not invariable, resulting from abstract psychosexual antagonisms, but contingent, revealing significant differences according to cultural and historical context. "The negative relation of women not to 'language' or 'meaning' but to various discourses is a variable and piecemeal affair."[14] The generalized assertion that women are automatically excluded or absent from a repressive, male language ignores both the flexible, innovative, and creative capacities of language itself and particular instances of the richness and complexity of women's language use—Cameron cites the example of "women's talk" as practiced in all female groups.

The textual strategies advocated by such theorists as Kristeva and Irigaray, Cameron argues, reveal a fundamental prejudice against spoken communication as a site for opposition and resistance. Similarly, deconstruction presupposes a solitary reader free to engage in a process of rigorous critique of a written text, with all the investment in intellectual training and free time which this involves. I do not mean to imply a devaluation of intellectual work as a form of political practice, but to indicate the limitations of a feminist theory of language which defines its politics exclusively in such terms. This privileging of writing over speech is closely linked to the deeply ingrained conviction in contemporary theory (undoubtedly shaped by Barthes's influential discussion of myth as ideology in *Mythologies*) that a skeptical and self-reflexive discourse is politically and morally superior to one which presents itself as "natural" and inevitable. Clearly, such a demystificatory and self-critical stance is much more easily sustained in certain forms of reading and writing in the academy than in the communicative practices of everyday life, which necessarily rely much more heavily on norms and beliefs that are taken for granted.

Recent feminist theory reveals the clear influence of such assumptions, exemplified in Irigaray's hypostatization of indeterminacy and hostility to definition and Kristeva's often quoted statement: "A feminist practice can only be negative, at odds with what already exists so that we may say 'that's not it' and 'that's still not it.' In 'woman' I see something that cannot be represented, something that is not said, something above and beyond nomenclatures and ideologies."[15] The appeal of such a theoretical position is self-evident; by remaining negative and eschewing definitions, feminism hopes to retain its oppositional purity, uncontaminated by the will to power which it detects in the discursive positions of others. What is ignored, however, is that the fetishization of *jouissance* and linguistic indeterminacy can itself easily become reified as a new ideology of the text. Ideology needs to be seen as a potential *function* of all forms of cultural activity, not as an inherent *property* of particular kinds of discourse. If ideology is understood as the cultural legitimation of the interests of dominant groups, then it becomes clear that the ideological status of texts can be ascertained only by examining their functions in relation to existing constellations of social and political power, and not by attributing an inherent value to particular linguistic forms. The opposition of open and subversive linguistic forms and closed reactionary ones reveals itself in this context as oversimple; heterogeneity, the play of figurative language and the notion of fundamental linguistic indecidability can potentially serve ideological ends just as easily as unity, coherence, "logocentrism," and the authority of tradition, as recent critiques of American deconstruction have amply demonstrated.[16]

To put it another way, the political status of a particular discourse cannot simply be read off from the epistemological claims which it seeks to make; a skeptical, relativistic, or ambiguous discourse is not necessarily more radical than one which claims the authority of certain conviction. Oscar Kenshur has criticized this elision of epistemology and politics in recent deconstructive theory which assumes that a discourse which makes unambiguous truth claims automatically carries reactionary political connotations. On the contrary, it can just as plausibly be argued that skepticism and relativism are more easily afforded by ruling elites, while oppositional or revolutionary groups have often sought to validate difficult political struggles by insisting upon privileged access to truth. "For a group that lacks the power that it thinks it deserves, all sorts of knowledge claims can be ideologically useful."[17] Particular uses and definitions of language, however rigid, cannot be designated as oppressive in themselves but will only become so if social groups possess the power to enforce those definitions at the expense of others.

Abstract generalizations about the politics of language thus need to be replaced by a more carefully differentiated analysis which assesses the social functions of particular communicative forms in relation to existing power structures. Furthermore, a feminist approach to language must theorize the various gender-related determinants which shape and constrain processes of social communication, while simultaneously recognizing that gendered subjects cannot be reduced to passive reflections of monolithic systems of domination, since they retain a capacity for varying degrees of critical reflection upon or resistance to their environment. It would be misguided to assume, for example, that women's choices before the advent of feminism were always the result of an uncritical acceptance of an all-pervasive patriarchal ideology rather than motivated by a pragmatism faced with few viable social alternatives. As Giddens notes, there is a tendency to conceptualize ideology as an all-pervasive and unified phenomenon and to underestimate the degree of critical understanding of and opposition to dominant ideologies which exists within subordinate groups. At the same time, however, any theory of the duality of structure is necessarily highly abstract and will require further and much more specific differentiation. Obviously the interaction between structural constraints and the capacity for agency will vary enormously, not only according to historical and cultural contexts but also according to the subject's positioning in terms of such variables as gender, class, race, age, and so on, so that the question of the precise relationship between structural determination and the potential capacity for oppositional or critical activity will need to be specifically located in analysis.

Feminist critics thus need to be wary of either over- or underestimating the nature and degree of female agency, a goal best attained not by abstract and ultimately irresolvable discussions about what constitutes an authentically "feminine" language, but by situating historically specific analysis of particular communicative practices in relation to changing constellations of power and the range of options available to women. For example, the reemergence of feminism as one of the most influential oppositional movements of the last two decades has significantly extended the ideological and social choices available to many women, whose lives still continue to be shaped both by continuing and deeply ingrained gender power hierarchies and by a variety of other material constraints and ideological influences within late capitalist society, structures which feminism cannot in itself adequately explain or transcend (of which class and race are only the most obvious).

The recognition that individuals are not "spoken" by an abstract, preexisting linguistic system, but that language is rather a social practice which is contextually determined and open to varying degrees of modification and change makes possible a more differentiated understanding of discourse which is potentially more productive from the standpoint of a feminist politics. The significance of particular communicative practices needs to be located in the contexts of their use, in the functions they serve for particular social groups at specific historical conjunctures. In this context Giddens turns to Wittgenstein for a theory of social communication: while both Wittgenstein and Derrida reject the notion that meaning is inherent in language, for Wittgenstein this very question is revealed as misplaced, the consequence of an idealistic quest for certainty which seeks a relationship of correspondence between words and things and which is consequently disappointed. Rather, meaning is necessarily derived from use; language constitutes a form of social interaction which presupposes publicly shared intersubjective meanings. The sense of terms is to be located in their functions, as exemplified in their actualization within forms of life. "Language is intrinsically involved with *that which has to be done;* the constitution of language as 'meaningful' is inseparable from the constitution of forms of social life as continuing practices."[18]

To situate language in relation to social practices and forms of life is not necessarily to sanction *existing* practices or to imply that the conventions of communicative interaction constitute some ultimate and unchallengeable reality.[19] Feminist critics are acutely aware that the most mundane and commonsensical of activities are often the most ideologically saturated. One must recognize, however, the limits of a deconstructive skepticism; while meaning is not inherent in words, neither is it ever in practice infinitely plural (not even in the deconstructive reading, itself a clearly circumscribed language game), but is constructed in relation to norms and conventions of communication applied in socially and historically specific contexts. Similarly, language is continually modified through use, as existing meanings are contested, revised, and reformulated, acquiring a new significance in different contexts; there exists a dialectical relationship between language and life worlds.

This assertion that meaning is produced through use offers a potentially more fruitful theoretical framework for feminist analysis in revealing language use as plural, fragmented, heterogeneous, composed of a variety of overlapping but often very different communicative strategies with varying functions which cannot be organized into any unified linguistic system. Such a position makes it possible to move away from the counterproductive (because abstract and one-dimensional) "prisonhouse of language" model, which has influenced much feminist theory. Language is to be understood as a form of social activity which is both rule-governed and open, which does not simply determine consciousness but can also be employed to contest existing world views and to develop alternative positions. A theoretical model which is able to situate language in relation to social life by foregrounding its semantic and pragmatic functions allows a more differentiated analysis of women's communicative practices by moving away from the abstract dichotomy of "masculine" versus "feminine" speech. One alternative currently being explored is a critical reading of the benefits and limitations of the Habermasian model of communicative interaction in relation to the specific interests of feminist theory.[20]

The End of Reason, the Death of the Subject?

To argue for the importance of a social theory which can interrelate an account of structure and agency is not in itself to address the historically specific question of the changing cultural perceptions and representations of the subject which emerge within particular social contexts. The two issues are obviously related insofar as a determinist position, which denies any independent or critical status to agency

66

per se, will consider the question of the changing self-understanding of social groups as irrelevant to any explanation of the functioning of society. At the same time, however, a theory which allows for human agency within given structural constraints does not necessarily entail an uncritical acceptance of all elements of prevailing ideologies of subjectivity, although it may recognize that such ideologies can constitute a powerful mobilizing force in the self-definition of oppositional groups. At this stage, then, my general argument that any theory of social and discursive interaction must allow a certain minimum of critical reflexivity on the part of human agents needs to be applied to a consideration of the current importance of subjectivity in feminist politics and culture—a profoundly ambivalent cultural phenomenon which has played a defining role in the construction of an oppositional women's movement yet which also bears witness to the more problematic aspects of the contemporary pursuit of self-identity.

Although the self-conscious affirmation of subjectivity is the product of the development of bourgeois society, it does not necessarily follow that its present function can be adequately explained through reference to such origins. Thus Andreas Huyssen writes:

> Doesn't poststructuralism, where it simply denies the subject altogether, jettison the chance of challenging the *ideology of the subject* (as male, white, and middle class) by developing alternative and different notions of subjectivity? . . . To raise the question of subjectivity at all no longer carries the stigma of being caught in the trap of bourgeois or petit-bourgeois ideology; the discourse of subjectivity has been cut loose from its moorings in bourgeois individualism.[21]

The emergence of individualism within bourgeois society is obviously a necessary precondition for the development of contemporary feminist ideology. Carole Pateman discusses the complex interconnections between feminism and liberalism, arguing that neither ideology "is conceivable without some conception of individuals as free and equal beings, emancipated from the ascribed, hierarchical bonds of traditional society."[22] She goes on to suggest, however, that feminist theory offers a radical critique of the dichotomy between public and private which is inherent in bourgeois liberalism, a critique that has wide-ranging political implications. Thus the importance of subjectivity in the women's movement is counterbalanced by an important dimension of communal solidarity absent from the liberal

tradition of atomic individualism. Feminism is defined by a fundamental tension and interaction between individual and collective
identity. Nancy Fraser writes of a "discourse ethic of solidarity" as a
specific feature emerging from the development of feminism and
other contemporary social movements, arguing that this concept
entails an understanding of human beings not as abstract and isolated
entities, but as "members of collectivities or social groups with
specific cultures, histories, social practices, values, habits, forms of
life, vocabularies of self-interpretation and narrative traditions."[23]

As these comments make clear, the meaning and function of
subjectivity in the context of feminist culture and politics is a complex
one which needs to be differentiated more precisely in terms of both
its similarities to and differences from the tradition of male bourgeois
subjectivity. While feminist theory challenges the masculine bias of
dominant concepts of the subject, an appeal to female self constitutes
an important defining element of the politics of the women's
movement. The articulation of disjunctures between received ideology and social experience, the assertion of political rights to autonomy and a degree of self-determination, provides an important means
by which subordinate groups define and react against their oppression. To expose critically the inadequacies of the rationalistic and
self-sufficient individualism of liberal political theory is not thereby
to argue that subjectivity should be abandoned as a category of
oppositional political thought, nor does the decentering of the subject
in contemporary theory mean that discourses which appeal to an
experience of self are therefore anachronistic. Subjectivity remains an
ineradicable element of modern social experience, bringing with it
attendant needs—for autonomy, but also for intimacy—which must
be addressed in the context of an emancipatory politics.

The recent pronouncements of the death of the subject, which have
appeared in the writings of Foucault, Barthes, and numerous other
theorists, are symptomatic of a general "legitimation crisis," which is
perceived to characterize contemporary culture and to manifest itself
in the eclipse in authority of such concepts as truth, rationality, and
the human subject as reference points and objective legitimations for
human action. If Western history is seen as tracing the gradual
emancipation of the rational subject from external constraints, then
the current era, it is argued, contains the most sustained challenge to
the Cartesian *cogito,* to rational self-consciousness as fully present to
itself. The epistemological authority of subjectivity is undermined by

a variety of intellectual disciplines that define subjectivity as a mere nodal point of various determining structural relations—social, psychoanalytical, linguistic—which are inaccessible to conscious thought. This decentering of the subject is seen to challenge the entire legacy of Western humanism, constituted by the belief that the individual embodies the source of knowledge and meaning, and it is in turn exemplified in a crisis of metanarratives, of legitimating frameworks which can provide an objective foundation for human activities.

Some theorists have suggested that this disintegration of values is intrinsically gendered. Jardine, for example, arguing that "the demise of the Subject, of the Dialectic and of Truth has left modernity with a *void* that it is vaguely aware must be spoken differently and strangely,"[24] goes on to state that "this new space, new place is tenaciously feminine,"[25] that modernity is characterized by the dissolution of such concepts as rationality, ethics, and truth, which are the products of a purely masculine cultural history. A similar claim is made by Josette Féral, who, speaking of the current crisis in "capitalist, monotheistic, patrilinear society," suggests that the interests of women are fundamentally interlinked with this crisis, and refers to "the feminine structure defined . . . as absence of structure."[26] Such statements are representative of a more general opposition of "masculine" symbolic systems and a "feminine" structurelessness typifying certain trends within feminist poststructuralist thought, which assume that the disintegration of reason and of symbolic coherence is a liberating cultural phenomenon emblematic of modernity, a phenomenon that is to be unconditionally affirmed as favorable to the interests of women.

The relationship between such categories as subjectivity and truth on the one hand and gender politics on the other cannot, however, be understood in terms of simple opposition. The evident malaise of such enlightenment narratives as the emancipation of Man does not therefore mean that the legitimation crisis is as absolute and allembracing as some theorists would claim, or that intersubjective systems of meaning and emancipatory narratives have ceased to exist. Neither does it follow that a dissolution of all frameworks of legitimation and the triumph of relativism can be seen as beneficial to oppositional political movements. There have been a number of recent critiques of the problematic political implications of the radical contextualism espoused by Lyotard or Rorty which need not be reiterated here.[27] I merely wish to suggest that feminist theory cannot proceed by assuming that the demise of subjectivity, truth, and reason are events to be hoped for and uncritically acclaimed; on the contrary, an espousal of linguistic free play and a rejection of critical reason can have strongly conservative political consequences by encouraging a relativism which lacks any evaluative, critical, or oppositional edge. Thus it is becoming increasingly apparent that theories of postmodernity as they are currently formulated are not necessarily appropriate for engaging with the specific positioning of women in late capitalist society, and that feminism provides a vantage point from which to argue the prematurity of some of the more glib and sweeping diagnoses of contemporary culture. For women, questions of subjectivity, truth, and identity may be not outmoded fictions but concepts which still possess an important strategic relevance.[28]

Rather than dismissing subjectivity and reason *en bloc,* then, it is more useful to look at the precise ways in which feminism has been instrumental in challenging the universal subject of philosophical and political theory by exposing its patriarchal presuppositions. Iris Marion Young writes: "Recent feminist analyses of modern political theory and practice increasingly argue that ideals of liberalism and contract theory, such as formal equality and universal rationality, are deeply marred by masculine biases about what it means to be human and the nature of society."[29] The idea of a disinterested, impartial, and universal reason is revealed as an ideological construct which, in believing that it can transcend all specific perspectives, merely reproduces the logic of the same and seeks to eradicate difference. Feminism is predicated upon the perception that women's interests and needs differ in fundamental ways from those of men, and that these conflicting interests cannot be addressed within the category of a universal subject. The recognition of distinct and often opposed gender interests does not, however, imply a turn to relativism; on the contrary, feminism makes a *general* claim for the recognition of the *specificity* of female interests. While demonstrating the gender bias of existing theories, feminism does not thereby advocate a pluralism which grants patriarchal and feminist positions equal value as rival forms of interpretation rooted in the difference of male and female experience. Rather, it asserts the unambiguous reality of women's oppression and is engaged in a variety of modes of critical argumentation which seek to convince others—whether other women or

70

men—of the legitimacy of its critique of patriarchal society. As a result, feminism cannot be easily reconciled with a postmodern relativism which argues the impossibility of adjudicating between different language games.[30]

In other words, feminism does not so much negate reason as engage in more diversified forms of discursive argumentation and critique which can take into account previously repressed aspects of personal and social life—emotion, desire, the body, personal relations—and which can remain receptive to the specificity of female experience and the need for cultural and group identity. Although feminism is understandably preoccupied with the politics of difference, it is also evident that the stress on particularity cannot resolve all the social problems facing women and that many of the issues involved in addressing problems of the self-reproduction of society involve both men and women and cannot be reduced to gender questions alone. As Boris Frankel writes:

> It is one thing to reject technical rationality, male heterosexual definitions of what is "good" and "desirable", undifferentiated notions of social and moral Progress, and other negative legacies of the Enlightenment. It is quite another thing to believe that, once women, gays and environmentalists have defined their values and priorities, all questions of rationality, equality, democracy in the public, as well as interpersonal private spheres, disappear. There seems to be a tendency to believe that . . . all these women, gays, Greens, etc. are not living in the same society, not encountering similar problems to do with war, economic power, public administration, religion, education, poverty, legal rights and other overlapping and interconnecting public issues. The answers may be different, but any "post-modern" or post-industrial society will also have to resolve issues of the public application of reason, as well as solve the issues of how plural identities are to be reconciled with public identities and rights.[31]

Feminism as a Social Movement

The emergence of subjectivity as a fundamental category of feminist discourse must be understood in relation to the development of the women's movement as a whole. Whereas the first wave of feminist activity was primarily concerned with the extension of male rights and privileges to women, as exemplified in the struggle for universal suffrage, the second wave of feminism which emerged in the late

71

1960s and early 1970s took as its starting point the particularity of women's social and cultural experience. Along with other oppositional social movements such as those representing blacks or gays, feminism has challenged the abstract universality of political theories such as liberalism and Marxism, stressing the inability of existing political models to deal with the varied constitution of human subjects and the oppressive consequences of the suppression of difference. The 1970s saw the emergence of more differentiated notions of political activity which challenged previously clear-cut distinctions between public and private, personal and political spheres, and which took as a central theme not only economic exploitation but also other forms of culturally based alienation and deprivation. Young summarizes this shift:

> The new social movements of the 1960's, 70's and 80's . . . have begun to create an image of a more differentiated public that directly confronts the allegedly impartial and universalist state. Movements of racially oppressed groups . . . tend to reject the assimilationist ideal and assert the right to nurture and celebrate in public their distinctive cultures and forms of life . . . The women's movement too has claimed to develop and foster a distinctively women's culture and that both women's specific bodily needs and women's situation in male dominated society require attending in public to special needs and unique contributions of women. Movements of the disabled, the aged, and gay and lesbian liberation, all have produced an image of public life in which persons stand forth in their difference, and make public claims to have specific needs met.[32]

Thus it is significant that a central focus of feminist theory has been a critical exposure of the political implications of the separation of public and private spheres. It has been argued that the "theoretical and practical exclusion of women from the universalist public is no mere accident or aberration";[33] rather, the emergence of a public sphere is itself intimately related to women's containment within the private domestic realm. This guarantees the unity and cohesion of the rational discursive public and contains desires and emotional needs within the realm of the family, which provides an emotional refuge for the alienated male worker while simultaneously constituting the site of women's subordination and exploitation. The slogan that "the personal is the political" serves to emphasize ·that the supposedly "personal" problems which have particularly affected women—rape, abortion, child care, the sexual division of labor—are in fact political issues which involve fundamental questions of power, underpinning the most deeply rooted aspects of social organization. Equally important, however, the feminist critique has sought to expose the personal dimensions of the political, to examine the ways in which the supposedly impartial sphere of rational public discourse has itself depended upon an exclusion and objectification of a female other which is associated with the realm of the body and which inspires deep-seated anxieties and corresponding defense mechanisms.

It is in this context that the category of the subject occupies a central position in the feminist project; not in terms of an appeal to an essential female self, but in the recognition that women's positioning within existing social, familial, and ideological structures differs fundamentally from that of men in distinct although often varied ways, and that the emancipation of women requires an examination of the nature and implications of such differences. While Kathy Ferguson claims that "a theory of liberation must address the problem of achieving self-knowledge that is not colored by the definition of self which the dominant party prefers and is willing to enforce,"[34] it must be recognized that this goal can never be realized in an absolute sense, given that oppositional discourses are necessarily influenced by the cultural norms against which they define themselves. This acknowledgment of the conditional and contingent nature of knowledge does not invalidate the importance of an oppositional politics as a process of critical self-reflection which can test the assumptions of prevailing ideologies against the specificity of women's changing interests and needs.

Although discourses of female subjectivity are not in themselves new, the self-conscious self-recognition of women as a subordinated group within society is a consequence of the development of feminist ideology, as a framework which organizes the various life experiences of women in a meaningful political pattern and makes it possible for women to reflect critically upon gender as a category which has become problematic. The fact that feminism constitutes an example of a subject-based political movement does not mean that it offers an unfiltered account of female subjectivity. There is no archetypal female subject which provides an ultimate grounding for feminist knowledge; rather, feminist discourse itself constructs a necessarily streamlined conception of subjectivity which can address the politics of gender as relevant to its particular strategic concerns. As a complex, changing, and multiply determined body of thought,

73

feminism continues to reveal its debt to a variety of political and cultural traditions even as it is instrumental in setting up new paradigms and cannot therefore be defined as a unified, homogeneous, and autonomous "worldview." As a political ideology, moreover, feminism cannot be understood as disinterested knowledge, but is located in relation to changing value systems, shifting balances of power, and the struggles of oppositional groups.

The influence of feminist ideology needs to be situated in the context of a resurgence of cultural and ideological conflicts in the last two decades, exemplified most clearly in the student and civil rights movements of the sixties and the growth of the women's movement in the seventies. Forms of radical opposition in the Western world in the last twenty years have not arisen primarily from the most economically deprived sectors of society, but have emerged from groups who perceive their interests to be in direct conflict with prevailing cultural values and whose political significance cannot be adequately explained in terms of a traditional class-based model. This is not to deny the fundamental importance of economic and class interests in determining social development, nor to assert that oppositional ideologies such as feminism render other levels of political and economic analysis redundant. It has become apparent, however, that there exists a multiplicity of arenas of oppression within social and personal life; movements such as feminism have made visible forms of discrimination and inequality which cannot be understood or dealt with solely in economic terms. It is no longer possible to assign the working class the status of a privileged historical subject or to assume that the emancipation of the proletariat would bring all forms of exploitation to an end. Forms of oppression, and consequently of opposition, can occur on a variety of levels; contemporary society is characterized by a structural complexity, an interaction of intersecting and often conflicting ideological positions, whose significance and effects cannot be reduced to an affirmative function in the self-reproduction of capitalism.

This diversity makes it impossible to isolate a "pure" feminist position; rather, the various feminist positions are themselves shaped by a range of determinants, from the intertextual influences of such political discourses as socialism, liberalism, and anarchism to the multiple ideological affiliations of female subjects, whose political allegiances are necessarily also shaped by such factors as class, race, and sexuality. The articulation of subjectivity in feminist culture and politics thus bears witness to a complex network of resonances. On the most general level one might wish to state that a common denominator of feminist positions is a recognition of the interconnection (although not necessarily identity) of private and public, personal and political, subjective and objective domains. As an example of a "postmaterialist" movement concerned not only with economic deprivation, but also with the meaning and value of different forms of life, feminism touches upon a whole range of different cultural, personal, and sexual issues. Political ideology is frequently related to all aspects of self and is expressed in everyday life through appearance, speech, and modes of personal interaction, as is evident in the emergence of distinctive "alternative" life styles.

The recognition of subjectivity as a central category of feminist politics and culture does not imply its unconditional affirmation; any criticism needs to proceed from a specific analysis of the historical manifestations of subjectivity rather than from an abstract condemnation of it. Feminism does not simply negate but is itself shaped by the broader domain of late capitalist society; Giddens's notion of structuration allows one to see that as an emancipatory ideology, feminism necessarily remains both outside and inside, both oppositional and system immanent, offering a critique of patriarchy while itself continuing to be influenced by existing ideologies and conceptual frameworks. As I will show in more detail in discussing specific texts, the quest for self in feminist literature must be read as a critical response to women's sense of their cultural marginalization, a response that cannot of itself resolve all existing social contradictions. The ambiguous status of subjectivity in contemporary women's writing will become apparent, for instance, the possibility that the very pursuit of authenticity can become a self-defeating process. Some of the more obviously problematic elements of the feminist ideology of the subject are briefly indicated below.

Essentialism and Apoliticism

Feminism can, for example, be held at least partly responsible for the present resurgence of idealist notions of masculinity and femininity in the domain of cultural politics, as exemplified in the assignment of an innate value to women's bodies and the claim that women possess a privileged affinity to nature and to peace. Similar arguments have also been proposed by some male theorists who claim that the develop-

75

ment of a "feminine" consciousness is the only means of saving society from masculine rationality and aggression.[35] Aspects of feminism tie in here with widespread manifestations of cultural pessimism in contemporary Western societies, as expressed in the current reactions against industrialism and technology and the increased prevalence of ecological and back to nature movements. Mary Daly, Susan Griffin, and other "cultural feminists" espouse a dualistic vision which counterposes a conception of a holistic, harmonious, and organic "femininity" against an alienated, rationalist, and aggressive masculinity. These dichotomies constitute a significant dimension within feminist ideology, which in turn finds its expression in numerous fictional texts, in which the heroine discovers her true "feminine" self beyond male-defined social roles, a subjectivity frequently described in strongly neo-Romantic terms as a form of mystical, intuitive empathy with nature.

This element within feminism is open to criticism for several reasons. First, its reiteration of existing ideologies of gender which differs only in its privileging of the feminine pole serves to reinforce gender distinctions, to narrow women's options rather than expand them; women are to remain determined by the stereotypes from which they have long struggled to liberate themselves. The celebration of woman as nature, maternity, mutuality, emotion, the body, has strongly conservative implications. Consequently, this position is unable to offer any explanation of the means by which the women's movement can hope to achieve a general social and political transformation; instead, feminism remains a mystical secret knowledge residing in the inner worlds of women, a position which brings with it all the attendant dangers of quietism.[36]

Second, this position is inadequate in its uncritical celebration of the pole of experience which it defines as "feminine" and the inability to mediate between or indeed to problematize the oppositions which it sets up. Although an important aspect of the feminist critique lies in the questioning of the goals of technology and progress, the nostalgic longing for an idealized past does not offer a solution to existing social problems. The criticism of modernity can become a naive antimodernism, in which the wholesale rejection of rationality undermines the basis of feminism's own critique of injustice and exploitation. Similarly, although the value of intimacy and emotion in psychological development needs to be affirmed, this affirmation should not occur at the expense of a dismissal of the value of

autonomy and independence as in some sense quintessentially masculine. To affirm uncritically the moral and emotional superiority of
the feminine is to remain entrapped within an inherently limited
model of dualistic thought.

Another important function of contemporary movements such as
feminism has been to redirect attention to personal and everyday
experiences of alienation and oppression. Traditional notions of
politics are redefined so as to acknowledge the permeation of power
relations into the most mundane social practices. Since political
struggle can occur on a variety of levels, it is no longer limited to
activity within the broader public sphere directly concerned with the
transformation of state institutions. This focus on the subject in the
context of an increased interest in various forms of grass-roots
political activity embodies a critical response to the proliferation of
increasingly impersonal and bureaucratic social institutions, not
excluding many of the traditional left organizations, whose hierarchical and often authoritarian modes of operation have frequently
been accompanied by a profound indifference to such issues as sexual
politics. The displacement of political action into a variety of social
practices which touch on all aspects of everyday life can, however,
also engender indifference toward broader political questions, a
dismissal of systematic theoretical critique and a belief that introspection in itself embodies a form of radical activity. The increasing
prevalence of a therapeutic consciousness is one indication of this shift
of emphasis from social to individual transformation. While the value
of therapy as a means of helping individuals to cope more adequately
with their everyday lives should not be dismissed, the focus on
self-development can become an exclusive preoccupation which
replaces rather than complements further forms of critical and
political activity. In this context the stress on personal growth and
meaningful life experience can be seen to fit comfortably into the
doctrine of self-improvement and the marketing of lifestyles within
contemporary consumer society, and can remain oblivious to the
ways in which individual life experience is itself determined in
relation to structural inequalities and systemic social constraints.[37]

Nevertheless, with the reservations indicated above, the conscious
assertion of a separate identity is still clearly an important priority for
women, given that their subordinate position has traditionally manifested itself in an acquiescence to male demands and an internalization
of a cultural tradition which defines the feminine as trivial and

77

inferior. Furthermore, even the most subjective feminist writing, as I hope to show, appeals to a notion of communal identity which differs significantly from the literature of bourgeois individualism, combining an examination of individual experience with a dimension of solidarity and group identity through an acknowledgment of a shared experience of subordination. In this context it is important that the theoretical "vanguard" of the women's movement does not confuse its own interests with those of other women. For female intellectuals who underwent consciousness raising fifteen years ago, the process of self-discovery described in the feminist novel now appears passé. For women with little other access to feminist ideas, however, its significance may continue to be very different. Stanley Aronowitz suggests that intellectuals trained in reflexivity and articulate self-analysis can undervalue the novelty of self-expression for members of subordinate groups, for whom it is not a tired literary convention, but a powerful political discovery.[38] The assertion that the self needs to be decentered is of little value to women who have never *had* a self; a recurring theme of feminist literature is the difficulty many women still experience in defining an independent identity beyond that shaped by the needs and desires of those around them. It is precisely for this reason that the autobiographical novel continues to remain a major literary form for oppressed groups, as a medium for confronting problems of self and of cultural identity which fulfills important social needs.

Realism in Feminist Fiction

The crucial status of subjectivity within the women's movement is echoed in the current popularity of autobiographical woman-centered narratives. The value of such texts as a medium for working through contradictions in women's lives and as a source of powerful symbolic fictions of female identity is not dependent, I have suggested, on the location of such writing "outside" existing discursive and ideological frameworks. Rather, the literary text needs to be seen as one important site for the struggle over meaning through the formulation of narratives which articulate women's changing concerns and self-perceptions. Writing should be grasped in this context as a social practice which *creates* meaning rather than merely communicating it; feminist literature does not reveal an already given female identity, but is itself involved in the construction of this self as a cultural reality. In this context Jochen Schulte-Sasse notes

78

the necessity of discussing literary texts as representative texts, as models of human behavior, and as participants in the constant struggle for interpretive power within society. If anything, an overemphasis on epistemological questions prevents us from seeing that the literary media and the public spheres of cultural production are to be highly prized socially because they make it possible for individuals to work through their material experiences and understand them as "consciously" as they can.[39]

Thus while it is no longer possible to accept the epistemological claims of a naive realism and to believe that a text can transmit an unmediated representation of the real, this does not negate the strategic importance of feminist writing as a medium of self-exploration and social criticism. Given that all discursive positions are constructed, and that there is no privileged space beyond ideology, the question which confronts women is that of the relative value of particular discursive and textual forms in relation to their changing needs and interests. The use of realist forms in feminist fiction in this context denotes a concentration upon the semantic function of writing rather than its formal and self-reflexive component. Because many women writers of the last twenty years have been concerned with addressing urgent political issues and rewriting the story of women's lives, they have frequently chosen to employ realist forms which do not foreground the literary and conventional dimensions of the text, but encourage a functional and content-based reading.

Of course, the popularity of feminist realism suggests that the success of specific literary forms cannot be analyzed in isolation from such material determinants as the economics of publishing. Feminism, by its very prominence, has become a catch phrase which can be used as a marketing tool to increase sales of books to a largely female reading public. It is thus feasible to make a case for the claim that publishers have promoted autobiographical realist women's novels with feminist themes which encourage identification and are relatively accessible to a large audience, and to concede that the current predominance of realist genres does not in itself necessarily provide an accurate reflection of the variety of texts currently being produced by feminist writers.

The commercialization of feminist writing in mass publishing, significant as it is, does not provide an adequate explanation for the prevalence of realist forms in feminist fiction, a trend intimately related to the centrality of the notion of personal change to the politics of feminism, and to the consequent interest in literature as a medium

79

for working through contradictions in existing definitions of femininity and dealing with ambivalent and conflicting experiences. Clearly, autobiographical feminist writing fulfills important cultural needs. Yet the interest shown by feminist critics in experimental writers such as Monique Wittig has often been accompanied by a seeming lack of interest in the sociological question of the reasons for this dominant status of realism within contemporary women's writing.

Before proceeding further, however, the use of the term 'realism' in the present context needs to be more precisely defined. The realism of contemporary feminist writing is in important ways very different from that of the nineteenth-century European and American novel. The general usage of the term "realism" to designate any text which is not obviously experimental in form and language has tended to blur the distinction between different kinds of realism and is in turn often accompanied by a misreading of realist aesthetics; Lukács is set up as the straw man of a theory of realist art as transparent reflection, which the critic has no difficulty in refuting. This kind of wholesale and undifferentiated dismissal of realism is unfortunate; it obscures the difference between the various forms and social functions of realism at particular historical moments and is unable to explain the continuing importance of realist fiction in the present day, not only in commercial mass publishing, but also as an important medium for articulating the interests of oppositional sectors within society.

The emergence of the term "realism" in the France of the 1840s as a term applied to the nineteenth-century novel bears witness to the belief in an objectively present social reality independent of mind, a reality which it was considered the duty of the artist to represent as faithfully as possible. In the words of Edmond Duranty, realism is "the exact, complete, sincere reproduction of the social milieu and the epoch in which one lives."[40] Of course not all writers of nineteenth-century novels which are now labeled as realist would have either accepted the term or agreed with such a definition, and it would be unwise to assume that they remained unaware that they were constructing a fictional world which could at best be seen as analogous to reality rather than a reflection of it. It is nevertheless possible to identify certain recurring representative features of the nineteenth-century novel, whether English, French, German, or Russian, which embody a more general cultural confidence in the reproducibility of an objectively present world. A defining element is that of narrative omniscience; whether seemingly absent as in Flaubert, or partisan as in the work of Balzac, the narrator of the nineteenth-century realist novel sets out to survey an entire social world and to give authoritative information and insight into characters and events. A correlative of this breadth of perspective is a concern with the dynamics and complexities of the relationship between the individual and society within a political and socioeconomic context. The historical dimension of narrative becomes of supreme importance, both in recording the changing destinies of individuals no longer bound by a rigid social order, and in depicting the political and social forces transforming society as a whole. Finally, the nineteenth-century novel is marked by a fascination with the solid materiality of the social world, containing detailed and elaborate taxonomies of the various objects and artifacts through which an increasingly urbanized and industrialized society asserts its power over nature.

The nineteenth-century realist novel can thus be described in the most general terms as revealing an attentiveness to the depiction of a social reality which is not relativized as the product of a subjective consciousness. It is precisely this confidence in an external and knowable world which dwindles with the relativization of knowledge and the crisis of confidence in science and language which marks the entry into the twentieth century. One aesthetic response to this crisis of meaning is the modernist subversion of the relationship between subject and object (Woolf, Musil), the observing self fragmenting into a collection of unstable elements and language forms. As Judith Ryan notes, "perception looses itself by degrees from its personal anchoring and becomes increasingly disembodied . . . subjectivity is dissolved, and 'world' and 'self' are reduced to a loosely associated bundle of elements."[41] Another and equally significant reaction is the retreat into the self; an existential concept of the subject as sole guarantor of meaning leads to a pursuit of authenticity through self-analysis. "The urge to be sincere," writes Henri Peyre, "is one of the most significant cultural phenomena of our age."[42] The dominant status of autobiography and autobiographical writing in the twentieth century attests to this concern with questions of personal identity and the struggle to locate a stable internal sense of self.

It is in the 1970s, after the more overtly politicized culture of the 1960s, that the problem of self-identity reemerges as a major cultural preoccupation within Western society. The enormous body of auto-

81

biographical writing published in the last fifteen years reveals a concern with selfhood as a critical response to, but also undoubtedly as a refuge from, the perceived anonymity of mass society. Largely because of the influence of feminism, women's writing has been one of the most important recent forums for self-analysis and autobiographical narrative. Insofar as this search for identity is often articulated through texts which attempt the "close rendering of ordinary experience,"[43] and which tend to avoid irony, self-reflexivity, and other markers of self-consciously literary discourse, many examples of feminist writing can be described as embracing a form of realism. It is, however, a "subjective" autobiographical realism which possesses few of the features of the nineteenth-century novel. The omniscient narrator is typically replaced by a personalized narrator whose perspective is either identical with or sympathetic to that of the protagonist; there is a consequent shrinking of focus from the general survey of the social world to the feelings and responses of the experiencing subject. The stress is on internal rather than external self, upon the exploration of conflict and ambivalences in relation to the problematic of self-identity. Even if the social world is depicted in detail, as in the American feminist realist novel, it is always subordinated to the central biographical theme of the heroine's development. This "subjective" form of realism, centered upon the experiencing consciousness, can thus incorporate the depiction of dreams, fantasies, flights of the imagination as part of its conception of the real, and often contains strongly neo-Romantic elements.

Subjectivity and Genre

To define this subjectivity more precisely, we must look more closely at the formal properties of contemporary fictions of female identity, which are shaped not only by ideological influences, but also by the relatively autonomous conventions of literary production. The category of genre is relevant here as the organizational framework which mediates between text and context; the text becomes meaningful only insofar as it is read in relation to existing expectations governing the reception of forms of textual communication. Thus the function of generic conventions, as Jonathan Culler points out, "is essentially to establish a contract between writer and reader so as to make certain relevant expectations operative and thus to permit both compliance with and deviation from accepted modes of intelligibility."[44] Genre, in other words, provides the cultural matrix against which the significance of the individual text can be measured. What kinds of genres are appearing in feminist writing and what do they reveal about the symbolic organization and narrativization of contemporary female experience? How are these generic forms related in more general terms to the status of feminism as an oppositional movement within society?

By choosing in Chapters 3 and 4 to analyze two representative genres in more detail, I seek to elucidate more clearly the social significance of feminist literature. There exists, I suggest, a dual focus within feminism which is exemplified in a tension and productive interaction between the categories of the personal and political; this dialectic is in turn exemplified in feminist writing, which can be seen as pointing simultaneously in two directions. On the one hand it is autobiographical, exploring women's changing perceptions of self; on the other, this examination of subjectivity acquires a representative significance through the superimposition of a transsubjective pattern of meaning, a narrative of emancipation derived from the political ideology of feminism.

These two moments are most clearly realized in two specific genres in contemporary women's writing. The confessional text seeks to distill an unmediated subjectivity, an authentic expression of authorial self which circumvents as far as possible the constraints of narrative organization and of literary structure. Here it is the moment of autobiographical self-revelation as such which is dominant and which inspires a sense of face-to-face intimacy between female author and reader. By contrast, the fully developed feminist realist novel traces a clear developmental plot in which the heroine moves from a state of alienation to a discovery of female identity through a process of separation from male-defined values; biographical narrative is clearly shaped according to the demands of a politically inspired teleology based on an emancipation narrative. These two genres, which I categorize under the headings "confession" and "novel of self-discovery," exemplify points on a continuum rather than mutually exclusive categories, since an individual text may partake of several genres (Stefan's *Häutungen,* for example, is discussed under both headings). Thus all the texts analyzed contain at least an implicit autobiographical element, insofar as the fact that they are texts written by women about female protagonists is relevant to their reception as feminist literature. Similarly, they all to some degree

83

superimpose a broader politically inspired pattern of meaning onto the representation of subjective experience, whether this is objectified in the text in the form of a narrative of self-emancipation, or simply affirmed by the narrating consciousness which comes to realize that the feminist interpretation of gender provides the hermeneutic key to decoding the meaning of individual life histories.

These generic categories of the confession and the novel of self-discovery provide a means to illuminating two key features of feminist literature—its autobiographical function and its construction of narrative—and to elucidating their meaningfulness in relation to the broader question of the influence of the women's movement on women's writing. As such, they are interpretative grids which are applied to a body of heterogeneous material in order to bring to light representative features, rather than internal structures already embedded within the text. If the two main approaches in contemporary genre criticism are the hermeneutic and the structuralist, which ask the questions "what does it mean?" and "how does it work?" respectively, my main concern lies in the answer to the former question.[45] Given that realist feminist writing does not comprise unique genres, but rather appropriates and reworks existing literary structures to create distinctive woman-centered narratives, only an approach which links formal and thematic analysis to a theorization of frameworks of reception can remain sensitive to the historical specificity of feminist literature as a cultural product.

This choice of analytical perspective is itself related to the blurring of conventional genre categories, which makes it increasingly difficult to classify contemporary writing according to the unique and distinctive formal features of particular kinds of text. This has of course been a problem for traditional genre classification since the emergence of the novel, which has been seen as the "end of genre,"[46] if genre is understood as a set of formal rules which unambiguously distinguishes a particular textual type. The novel constitutes the first posttraditional genre, a "chameleon" form characterized by a seemingly infinite formal and thematic flexibility. This dissolution of traditional generic categories continues into the present as the boundaries between autobiography and fiction, the novel and the short story, the diary and the autobiography, become increasingly difficult to demarcate in much of contemporary writing. While it is still of course possible to attempt to classify women's writing according to precise formal criteria (diary, autobiography, autobiographical novel,

the novel as genre

diary novel, *monologue intérieure,* and so on), classification tends to result in an unwieldy methodological apparatus of subcategories which is of little help in elucidating the question of the social functions of this literature in relation to its particular audiences.

It is for this reason that my discussion of genre attempts to seize upon those representative features of feminist writing which are particularly relevant to the interaction and tension between the personal and the political within the women's movement as a whole. Thus, under the rubric of "confession," I discuss those texts which aspire to the unmediated self-exposure of the authorial self as a potentially liberating process, whatever the particular variations in formal structure (autobiography, diary, and so on) which characterize the particular text. The category of "novel of self-discovery," by contrast, is used to designate all those recent texts by women writers which trace a clear narrative of female emancipation through separation from a male-defined context, although individual exemplifications of this general pattern reveal important and interesting narrative and structural differences. My categories are clearly recognizable as modifications of existing genres—the autobiography, the *Bildungsroman*—whose distinctive properties will require more specific elucidation. Raymond Williams notes that the proliferation of textual types within modern society and the consequent limitations of traditional genre classification necessitates the application of diverse and heterogeneous criteria such as form, subject matter, and nature of intended readership in the attempt to distinguish meaningfully between groups of texts.[47] All three criteria are relevant here in defining the similarities and differences between contemporary feminist writing and the tradition of bourgeois realist literature. If, as Fredric Jameson argues, "genres are essentially literary *institutions,* or social contracts between a writer and a specific public, whose function it is to specify the proper use of a particular cultural artifact,"[48] then the basis of this contractual relationship must be sought not simply in the formal properties of the text, but also in the condition governing its reception, and the particular subject matter which it seeks to address.

CHAPTER THREE ✑

On Confession

Autobiography has played a central role in contemporary women's writing, raising a number of questions regarding the value and limitations of this trend toward literary self-disclosure. Is the act of confession a liberating step for women, which uncovers the political dimensions of personal experience, confronts the contradictions of existing gender roles, and inspires an important sense of female identification and solidarity? Or does this kind of writing merely reveal what Christopher Lasch calls "the banality of pseudo self-awareness,"[1] a narcissistic soul-searching that uncritically reiterates the "jargon of authenticity" and the ideology of subjectivity-as-truth which feminism should be calling into question?

Autobiography as a literary genre has received a great deal of critical attention in recent years, with a proliferation of studies from a variety of theoretical perspectives. Among these are feminist analyses which have convincingly shown that theories of autobiography typically reveal a male bias. The normative criteria of objectivity and distance used to evaluate autobiography in the writings of such critics as Wayne Shumaker and Karl Weintraub are of little relevance in discussing the tradition of women's autobiography, which typically focuses upon the details of domestic and personal life and is fragmented, episodic, and repetitive, lacking the unifying linear structure imposed upon a life by the pursuit of a public career. Cynthia Pomerlau observes, "the traditional view of women is antithetical to the crucial motive of autobiography—a desire to synthesize, to see one's life as an organic whole, to look back for a pattern."[2] Clearly women whose social status was largely determined by a shift from a father's to a husband's tutelage were unlikely to perceive their lives in terms of a meaningful and self-directed progression toward an ultimate goal. It is argued that this lack of control by women over the direction of their lives, resulting from their confinement to the private sphere, is responsible for the predominance of the episodic journal structure rather than the synthesizing narrative in women's autobiographies. Estelle Jelinek writes: "Surveying quite a number of bibliographies from various countries and periods, one is struck by the number of women writing diaries, journals, and notebooks, in contrast to the many more men writing autobiographies proper. From earliest times, these discontinuous forms have been important to women because they are analogous to the fragmented, interrupted, and formless nature of their lives."[3]

It is also necessary, however, to consider historically determined cultural changes as they interact with and affect such gender distinctions. The division between sequential, public autobiographies by men and subjective, disjointed autobiographies by women has become far less clear-cut in the twentieth century, which has seen an increasing subjectivization of literary texts arising from a breakdown of generic norms. Many of the criteria derived from the analysis of autobiography up to the nineteenth century are patently inadequate to deal with the variety of modern autobiographical writing by both men and women. It is for this reason that the genre has received so much theoretical attention in recent years. Modern autobiographies are often fragmented and highly subjective, and the boundaries between fiction and autobiography become difficult to demarcate. Autobiography, as William Spengemann notes, is increasingly viewed as part of the sphere of literature rather than as a subcategory of historical biography, as was previously the case.[4]

In examining the influence of feminism on women's autobiography, I focus upon the confession, a distinctive subgenre of autobiography which has become prominent in recent years, and whose importance in the context of feminism is clearly related to the exemplary model of consciousness-raising. The term "confession" has occasionally acquired slightly dismissive overtones in recent years. No such connotation is intended here; I use "confession" simply to specify a type of autobiographical writing which signals its intention to foreground the most personal and intimate details of the author's life. Francis Hart writes: " 'Confession' is personal history that seeks to communicate or express the essential nature, the truth, of the self."[5] Like consciousness-raising, the confessional text makes public that which has been private, typically claiming to avoid filtering mechanisms of objectivity and detachment in its pursuit of the truth of subjective experience. Examples of recent women's writing which can be regarded as conforming to this description include the following: in the United States, Alice Koller, *An Unknown Woman* (1982), Audre Lorde, *The Cancer Journals* (1980), Kate Millett, *Flying* (1974) and *Sita* (1977); in West Germany, Svende Merian, *Der Tod des Märchenprinzen* (The death of the fairytale prince) (1980), Judith Offenbach, *Sonja* (1980), Verena Stefan, *Häutungen* (Shedding) (1975), Karin Struck, *Klassenliebe* (Class love) (1973) and *Kindheits Ende* (Childhood's end) (1982); in France, Marie Cardinal, *The Words to Say It* (1975); in the Netherlands, Anja Meulenbelt, *The Shame Is Over* (1980); and in England, Ann Oakley, *Taking It Like a Woman* (1984).[6]

Although a number of differences exist among these texts both formally and ideologically, they share an explicit rhetorical fore-grounding of the relationship between a female author and a female reader and an emphasis upon the referential and denotative dimension of textual communication rather than its formal specificity. These features distinguish them from more consciously stylized and "literary" examples of twentieth-century women's autobiography by such writers as Simone de Beauvoir, Janet Frame, Lillian Hellman, Mary McCarthy, and Nathalie Sarraute. The questioning of self is frequently inspired by a personal crisis which acts as a catalyst: cancer (Lorde), crippling neurosis (Cardinal), the death or departure of a lover (Millett, Offenbach). Whereas Jelinek argues that "neither women nor men are likely to explore or to reveal painful and intimate memories in their autobiographies,"[7] this is clearly *not* the case in feminist confessional literature, which explicitly seeks to disclose the most intimate and often traumatic details of the author's life and to elucidate their broader implications. I am less interested in a detailed thematic interpretation of individual examples of this recent feminist autobiographical writing than in a consideration of the logic of confessional discourse as such in relation to its recent appropriation by the women's movement, mapping out the ambivalent status of this pursuit of self-identity. The question which arises is whether this confessional writing is an indispensable aspect of a process of critical self-understanding which constitutes part of feminism's emancipatory project, or whether, as Richard Sennett suggests, the current fascination with intimacy and self-discovery engenders an ever more frantic pursuit for a kernel of authentic self which continually eludes one's grasp: "Expression is made contingent upon authentic feeling, but one is always plunged into the narcissistic problem of never being able to crystallize what is authentic in one's feelings."[8] In this sense, the confession poses in exemplary fashion the problem of the relationship between personal experience and political goals within feminism as a whole.

Autobiography: Problems of Definition

What are the defining features of autobiography which allow it to be distinguished from related genres? Early critical surveys such as Roy Pascal's *Design and Truth in Autobiography* could posit a normative model of autobiography as a cohesive, chronological, and retrospective account of the author's life centered around a unifying vision of self-identity, a definition which was able to account for the canonical texts such as Rousseau's *Confessions* or Goethe's *Poetry and Truth,* which were Pascal's main concerns.[9] But this definition has proved patently inadequate for dealing with the formal and thematic diversity of modern autobiography. Many of the conventional "rules" which once governed readers' expectations of the genre are now regularly broken; autobiography can be the form chosen for a writer's first work, for example, and is often written serially in several volumes, rather than in a single text which encapsulates the entire direction and meaning of an author's life.

Increasingly, theorists of autobiography have moved away from prescriptive definitions to an examination of the more fundamental problems involved in establishing a satisfactory distinction between autobiography and fiction. Thus Elizabeth Bruss, in her discussion of the genre, argues that "there is no intrinsically autobiographical form"[10] and warns against attempts to define autobiography according to inflexible stylistic or compositional criteria which are unable to encompass the processes of historical development and change. The process of definition, however, cannot be dispensed with insofar as it is necessary to clarify the underlying expectations which govern our reading of autobiography and make it possible to recognize elements of continuity as well as change in autobiographical writing. According to Bruss, we can best achieve this clarification by understanding autobiography as a speech act which makes certain claims rather than as a structure governed by unique formal rules. We may generalize these claims as follows. First, the author is assumed to be both creator and subject matter of the literary text (the autobiography presupposes "that some shared identity bind author, narrator and character together").[11] Second, a claim is made for the truth-value of what the autobiography reports, however difficult it may in fact be to ascertain this truth-value in practice. Third, the autobiographer purports to believe what she or he asserts.[12] The possibility that one or more of these rules may be broken in practice does not negate the fact that such expectations define the matrix against which the individual autobiography is interpreted and assessed. More specific and detailed distinctions among types of autobiography in terms of form and function cannot be adequately made by examining them as isolated textual entities. Instead, Bruss argues, we must direct our attention to the sociohistorical contexts in which they emerge in relation to changing patterns within literature and culture as a whole.

The question arises as to how this "autobiographical act" is signaled to the reader, how she or he realizes that a text is intended as autobiography and not as fiction. Obviously, the knowledge of parallels between the life of the author and the protagonist does not in itself constitute sufficient grounds. Many texts contain such autobiographical elements, but the assimilation of real life material into the literary work does not carry any obligation to truthfulness on the part of the author. The autobiography, by contrast, makes claims to historical veracity as the account of part or all of the life of a real individual written by that individual. That this claim can be undermined by exposing the distortions inherent in the writing process or problematizing the very notion of what constitutes "truth" does not negate the fact that the intention of honest self-depiction is a determining feature of the "autobiographical contract" which is familiar to every reader.

It is in this context that Philippe Lejeune's notion of an autobiographical contract has been an influential one. Lejeune's own definition of autobiography is relatively circumscribed: "a retrospective prose narrative produced by a real person concerning his own existence, focusing on his individual life, in particular on the development of his personality."[13] In practice, Lejeune concedes, a certain flexibility is required in applying this definition. But one element is indispensable if a text is to be classified as autobiography; the identity (rather than mere factual resemblance) of author and narrator/ protagonist. This identity constitutes the foundation of the autobiographical contract and can, according to Lejeune, be signaled to the reader in a number of ways: through a title or introduction which unambiguously identifies a text as autobiography, or, more commonly, through identity of names. By giving the narrator/

protagonist of a text the same name as herself, an author indicates that a work is intended as autobiography; otherwise, however strong the parallels between a work and an author's life, the pact is not evoked, and the work asks to be judged according to the criteria of fiction rather than those of verifiable truth. The dividing line between autobiography and fiction is thus distinct and final, Lejeune argues, determined in the last instance by the identity or difference of the author's and narrator/protagonist's names, resulting in the application of different interpretative paradigms by the reader: "Autobiography . . . does not admit of degrees: it is a matter of all or nothing."[14]

Lejeune's stress on the contractual nature of autobiography makes it clear that a satisfactory definition of the genre cannot be grounded in terms of either form or content alone, but requires an investigation of the cultural conventions governing processes of interpretation. But his highly schematic model does not allow for consideration of the complex and historically variable range of conditions governing textual reception. Lejeune's statement that autobiography is a question of all or nothing is excessively rigid and unable to deal with variations in actual reading practices. If the flourishing of individualism and the emergence of a clear separation between the realms of "fact" and "fiction" in bourgeois society are necessary preconditions for the development of modern autobiography, then the modification or reformulation of such concepts in the context of changing cultural and ideological frameworks may well affect reading practices, and the kind of generic distinctions which readers actually make. The legalistic terminology of pacts and contracts can be misleading in this context in implying an unambiguous agreement as to the conditions governing the act of reading, whereas in practice the interpretation of texts is determined by a complex range of textual and contextual factors, of which gender, as Nancy Miller has argued in her critique of Lejeune, may well be one of the most important.[15] These in turn can be investigated only by moving away from abstract classifications to an examination of the distinctive features of particular autobiographies in conjunction with the ideologies shaping processes of production and reception in specific interpretative communities.

Individual and Communal Identity in Feminist Confession

This general discussion of the limitations of a purely formal definition of autobiography paves the way for my contention that the feminist confession leads, if not to a rejection, then to a modification of the traditional aims and functions of autobiography, the significance of which can only be grasped by situating these works in a sociohistorical context. Thus feminist confession often contains ambiguous or contradictory signals which problematize rather than confirm the distinction between autobiography and fiction. For example, the proper name deemed so significant by Lejeune is sometimes deliberately avoided, or else its importance minimized. In some cases, as in Lorde, Millett, Koller, Meulenbelt, Oakley, Merian, and Offenbach, the confessional texts do explicitly assert the identity of author and narrator/protagonist through identity of name.[16] By contrast, Verena Stefan's *Häutungen* is a feminist confessional work which has been generally received as an autobiographical (that is, truthful) account of the author's experiences (the subtitle of the text includes the words "autobiographical sketches"), yet the heroine remains unnamed until the end of the text, where she is referred to briefly as Cloe. Similarly, the protagonist of Cardinal's *The Words to Say It* is left nameless; in what is presumably a self-reflexive statement, the narrator writes of her intention to write a novel about "the healing of a woman as like me as if she were my own sister,"[17] yet the preface and afterword by Bruno Bettelheim invite the reader to consider the text as an essentially truthful account of Cardinal's own analysis. And how is the reader to respond to Oakley's *Taking It Like a Woman,* which is clearly designated as autobiography and thus raises the truth-claims inherent in the "autobiographical contract," yet which states in its introduction, "some of the characters in this book are real and some aren't"?[18]

The ambiguous signals sent out by examples of the feminist confession, the reader's frequent uncertainty as to whether a text is to be classified as autobiography or fiction, becomes particularly apparent in the work of an author such as Karin Struck, one of the most well-known women writers to have become associated with the confessional genre in West Germany in the 1970s. *Kindheits Ende* identifies the narrator/protagonist as writer Karin Struck, while the earlier text *Klassenliebe* is more ambiguous in that it identifies the narrator only as Karin. Struck has also written two very similar works, *Die Mutter* (The mother) and *Lieben* (Loving), whose heroines are called Nora and Lotte respectively. Apart from the change of name and other slight alterations in factual details, these works are very similar to Struck's explicitly autobiographical texts, both formally and thematically, and it has in fact been suggested by various critics that Struck's work exemplifies one single continuing autobiographical text.[19] In this context, it is questionable whether the majority of Struck's readers will make rigid distinctions between one text and another as involving different "contracts" and the application of different interpretative paradigms.

More examples of this seemingly ambiguous positioning of much feminist writing between autobiography and fiction could easily be found. Recent years have seen the publication of large numbers of feminist texts which are written in an unrelativized first-person perspective, are strongly confessional, and encourage reader identification. This alone does not unambiguously mark the text as autobiography (as Lejeune points out, such features can be imitated by the novel), but they occur within a context of *reception* which encourages an interpretation of the text as the expression, in essence, of the views and experiences of the writing subject. Thus the women's movement has been influential in "personalizing" the literary text by emphasizing its autobiographical dimension. Feminist literature is often marketed in such a way as to foreground the persona of the author through the inclusion of photographs and biographical details which link the text to the life and act as a guarantee of its authenticity. Evelyne Keitel, discussing the reception of feminist confessional literature in West Germany, suggests that it is typically read as a truthful account of the author's experiences which is used as a springboard by readers from which to examine and compare their own experiences. The text is read less for its own sake, as a literary construct, than for its content in relation to its similarities and differences to the reader's own life. Reception, in other words, is strongly functional and often collective; Keitel refers to the use of such texts as Merian's *Der Tod des Märchenprinzen* as a basis for group discussions by women on the subject of their own sexual experiences.[20]

What, then, are the reasons for this blurring of the distinction between autobiography and fiction in feminist literature? Feminist confession exemplifies the intersection between the autobiographical imperative to communicate the truth of unique individuality, and the feminist concern with the representative and intersubjective elements of women's experience. In other words, the shift toward a conception of communal identity which has emerged with new social movements such as feminism brings with it a modification of the notion of individualism as it is exemplified in the male bourgeois autobiography. It is for this reason that Oakley feels free to invent some of the characters in her autobiography, for, as the publisher's blurb states: "In this honest, somewhat painful and absorbing account of her life . . . every woman will find some reflection of her own personality and feelings."[21] The obligation to honest self-depiction which constitutes part of the autobiographical contract is here mitigated by the feminist recognition that it is the representative aspects of the author's experience rather than her unique individuality which are important, allowing for the inclusion of fictive but representative episodes distilled from the lives of other women. The fact that the authors discussed write autobiographies explicitly and self-consciously *as women* is of central importance as an indication of the shifting conceptions of cultural identity which are in turn echoed in the changing forms and functions of autobiography.

Keitel has addressed this question in an analysis of the function of contemporary forms of autobiography and autobiographical writing in relation to the self-definition of oppositional subcultures. She points to the emergence of distinctive literary "counter-public spheres" in the 1970s and 1980s, centered on the specific interests and experiences of groups such as women or gays, and reclaiming for literary discourse a representative and mimetic function which has been rendered increasingly problematic since modernism. Much of this literature is primarily concerned not with negation but rather with the affirmation of oppositional values and experiences, serving to identify communal norms which are perceived to bind together members of oppressed groups. In their emphasis on the authenticity of the writing subject and the attempt to generate a process of identification between reader and author, these literary forms can be seen as reiterating certain aspects of the narrative tradition of the eighteenth century, Keitel argues.[22] The autobiographical writing inspired by the women's movement differs, however, from the traditional autobiography of bourgeois individualism, which presents itself as the record of an unusual but exemplary life. Precisely because of this uniqueness, the eighteenth-century autobiography claims a universal significance. Feminist confession, by contrast, is less concerned with unique individuality or notions of essential humanity than with delineating the specific problems and experiences which bind women together. It thus tends to emphasize the ordinary events of a protagonist's life, their typicality in relation to a notion of communal identity. "The legitimation for reporting these experiences lies precisely in their correspondence to other life histories, and all individual traits appear blurred or disguised, in order to emphasize their general validity and applicability."[23]

On the one hand, the autobiographical status of the text is important in guaranteeing its truthfulness as the depiction of the life, and more important, the inner feelings of a particular individual. On the other, it is the *representative* aspects of experience, rather than those that mark the protagonist/narrator as unique, which are emphasized in relation to a notion of a communal female identity. It is for this reason that feminist confession is sometimes deliberately ambiguous in its use of proper names, seeking to minimize the specificity of its content as the depiction of the life of a single individual and to emphasize its exemplary status, while still retaining the claim to historical truthfulness and authenticity which form part of the autobiographical contract. As Oakley writes in *Taking It Like a Woman,* "it would be arrogant to suppose I'm unique; I'm not."[24]

Keitel suggests that this kind of autobiographical writing, precisely because of its combination of "authenticity" and representativeness, has played an important role in the self-definition of social movements in the 1970s and 1980s, serving as an identifying point of reference in much the same way as political theory (the work of Marcuse, for example) was a rallying point for the New Left in the 1960s. By writing autobiographical narratives centered on personal experience, authors avoid "theoretical abstraction"; there exists within contemporary social movements, feminism included, an ambivalence toward theory which extends from a legitimate critique of the kind of arid leftist theorizing which remains oblivious to personal relationships and their exploitative aspects, to an uncritical celebration of "feeling" and a problematic anti-intellectualism. Confessional writing, then, proceeds from the subjective experience of problems and contradictions as encountered in the realm of everyday life. At the same time, however, feminist confession selects out those aspects of experience which are perceived to possess a representative significance in relation to the audience of women it wishes to reach. Through the discussion of, and abstraction from, individual experience in relation to a general problematic of sexual politics, feminist confession thus appropriates some of the functions of political discourse. It is instrumental in the delineation of a group identity through the establishment of norms, formulates elements of a more general feminist critique, and concretizes aspects of the aims and interests of the women's movement: "The lyrical self articulated in these texts always perceives itself as part of a collective, whose experiences constitute its norms and on behalf of whose members it speaks."[25]

The Forms of Confession

Structurally, it is possible to make a rough division of feminist confession into two main groups. The first can be defined as conforming more or less closely to the journal form, that is, an open-ended structure written in the present tense, in which the author records the details of daily events as they occur. The second, to be discussed below, offers a retrospective and thus more clearly synthetic account of part or all of the author's life history from the standpoint of the writing present. Struck's *Klassenliebe* and *Kindheits Ende* adhere to the journal model most closely: both are diaries, containing a series of regular individual entries identified by dates, in which the author notes down her daily experiences as she struggles with problems of self-identity in relation to issues of gender and class. *Sonja,* an account of Offenbach's relationship with a handicapped woman which ends in the latter's suicide, contains a similar day-by-day account of the author's thoughts and feelings, although a greater part of the text is devoted to an exploration of past events, as she struggles to come to terms with an overwhelming sense of guilt. Lorde's *Cancer Journals* are more heterogeneous in form; journal entries which deal with Lorde's experiences before and after a mastectomy are juxtaposed with essays and speeches discussing the politics of cancer. Merian's *Der Tod des Märchenprinzen* offers a detailed account of an unsuccessful sexual relationship and the author's growing disillusionment with the ideology of romantic love, while Millett's *Sita* follows a similar structure in recording the final painful stages of a dying love affair. And *Flying,* by the same author, is perhaps closer in form to the stream of consciousness than the traditional journal, interweaving a variety of time levels in a detailed account of Millett's chaotic private and public life following the publication of *Sexual Politics.*

Suzanne Juhasz has discussed "dailiness" as the structuring principle of many women's lives, resulting from their traditional concern with repetitive domestic work and the task of maintaining and repairing emotional relationships. It is for this reason, she suggests, that the diary has been an important form for women, and has also been adopted by feminist writers wishing to explore critically female experience: "The diary provides the sense of factualness (of the

96

documentary, of non-fiction), the sense of the personal, the sense of process, the sense of dailiness, the sense of immersion rather than conclusion or analysis or patterning."[26] Feminist authors using the journal form discuss their reasons for doing so with varying degrees of sophistication. The guiding concern is usually the desire for inclusiveness, the belief that it is only by setting down every detail of experience as it happens that the author can hope to bridge the gap between life and the text. "It should be described as an experiment in charting and recording a relationship," writes Kate Millett of *Sita,* "Day to day. No one's ever done that. Surely not of two women."[27] Considering the possibility of turning this experience into fiction, she rejects the option, "not wanting to. Wanting to just go on and on writing it as it happens, keeping a record of time and experience, perception—however imperfect."[28] A similar refusal of aesthetic criteria as antithetical to the author's aims of honesty and inclusiveness is articulated in Offenbach's *Sonja:* "But why don't I want to filter things out? Because I'm concerned with the truth, not some 'higher' truth, but our, Sonja's and my truth. I'm also not concerned with taste and aesthetics and morality but with authenticity. Considering what's happened to us and because of us, aesthetic considerations as well as 'filtering' are ruled out."[29] And in *Flying* Millett writes about her own text, "this is not literature."[30]

The confessional diary thus often shores up its claims to authenticity and truthfulness by consciously distinguishing itself from the category of literature. Aesthetic criteria are rejected as irrelevant; a conscious artistic structure is in fact suspect insofar as it implies distance and control rather than an unmediated baring of the soul. Struck writes, "I think of the word 'fiction' and immediately see in front of me a frosted plane of glass, behind which a child is lying that can't be touched or visited. Fiction *is* remoteness, distance, separation."[31] The more obviously "literary" the text—the more clearly it signals its fictional status through such textual features as irony, parody, and self-reflexivity, extended use of symbolic and "poetic" language, or elaborated narrative structures—the less likely the reader is to respond to the text as the authentic self-expression of an authorial subject. It is for this reason that feminist confession often imitates such personal, nonliterary forms as the diary or the letter in the attempt to regulate the potential open-endedness of the literary text. It attempts, in other words, to achieve the reverse of the defamiliarization which Russian formalism identified as the key function of literature, in order to inspire a process of involvement and identification by persuading readers that they are reading an intimate communication addressed to them personally by the author.

On a structural level the diary is episodic and fragmented, depicting events as they occur rather than attempting to select and organize in terms of any unifying vision. The time span covered by the diary ranges from several months to several years and is usually centered on a particular crisis point in the author's life. Often, this is depicted in meticulous and even obsessive detail, the reader sharing every moment of Kate Millett's passion for Sita and Svende Merian's infatuation with Arno. The text appears directly immersed in the author's lived experience; repetitions, contradictions, gaps, and loose ends, which might be viewed as aesthetic flaws in a conventional literary text, here function as indications of the work's authentic status, its concern to communicate the intensity of feeling rather than to strive for aesthetic effects. Perspectives can shift dramatically as new factors are introduced, issues are noted with no knowledge of what their ultimate significance will be. The text can break off abruptly as external events intervene, or contain gaps when the author's life takes priority over the writing of a text. Through this kind of structure, the confession seeks to emphasize its status as reflecting and contingent on lived experience, rather than as a self-contained literary artifact. The author shares with her audience an uncertainty as to the final outcome of the text, which is determined by external factors rather than the logic of aesthetic form. "The perspective of the diarist is immersion, not distance," writes Juhasz. "The diary is finished when the pages run out, not when some denouement and conclusion are reached."[32]

The second main type of confessional text employs a structure based on retrospective narration and is less obviously concerned with inclusiveness and the depiction of every detail of daily events. Koller's *An Unknown Woman* and Cardinal's *The Words to Say It* can be described as conforming to the model of the psychoanalytical case history, except that here the history is written by the patient herself. In both texts a crippling anxiety and sense of impotence provides the catalyst for a confrontation with the past, an attempt to gain an understanding of one's personal history which can lead to an increased capacity for self-determination. Stefan's *Häutungen* offers a retrospective account of the author's life which spans the years between adolescence and adulthood and focuses upon her experiences of sexuality and the search for a female eroticism. And Meulenbelt's *The Shame Is Over* and Oakley's *Taking It Like a Woman* are the most public and comprehensive of the confessions discussed, conforming most closely to the traditional autobiography in dealing retrospectively with the author's life from childhood to the present.

The need for an exhaustive rendering of every detail of experience is less overriding in these texts. With the benefit of hindsight, it becomes possible to focus on those moments which have been revealed as turning points in the development of a life history. Such moments are typically defined in terms of personal relations: the loss of a lover, the experience of childbirth, the death of a parent. The depiction of the author's life frequently coincides with the narrative of a conversion to feminism, but an obviously teleological structure is usually avoided. The texts of Oakley, Meulenbelt, and Stefan break up the chronology of female development through the inclusion of poetry, dreams, essayistic discussions, or commentaries from the perspective of the author in the writing present. In spite of a seemingly more cohesive form, these examples of retrospective feminist confession tend to minimize synthesis and linearity in favor of montage. Oakley's autobiography, for example, juxtaposes episodes of factual narrative with such essayistic discussions as "The War between Love and the Family" and a highly lyrical, fictionalized account of an extramarital affair, "a paradigm of all the contradictions to which modern woman is exposed."[33] Similarly, Stefan's *Häutungen* interweaves an account of the author's increasing dissatisfaction with heterosexual relationships with episodes of lyrical description, polemic, and poetry.

In general, then, the feminist confession seeks to reduce the patterning and organization of experience which characterizes historical narrative; its structure is episodic and fragmented, not chronological and linear. The organizing principle of the text is provided by the associations of the experiencing subject. While foregrounding the consciousness of this writing self, however, the feminist confession simultaneously encodes an audience. It self-consciously addresses a community of female readers rather than an undifferentiated general public. This sense of communality is accentuated through a tone of intimacy, shared allusions, and unexplained references with which the reader is assumed to be familiar. The implied reader of the feminist confession is the sympathetic female confidante and is often explicitly encoded in the text through appeals, questions, and direct address. The importance of the reader's role is directly related to the belief that she will understand and share the author's position. "Women will understand me," writes Svende Merian after discussing her sexual problems.[34] When Lorde writes, "we share a commitment to language and to the power of language, and to the reclaiming of that language which has been made to work against us,"[35] the "we" of the text unambiguously refers to the community of women to which the text is addressed.

This attempt to evoke the illusion of face-to-face intimacy between author and reader in turn influences the style of the feminist confession. Frequently, an attempt is made to simulate the patterns of speech, in the belief that the spoken word is closer to the essence of subjectivity than the artificial and deceptive quality of the written text. Offenbach, in striving for honesty, acquires a tape-recorder and begins to dictate her text directly onto tape: "If I simply think out loud all the thoughts I have about Sonja while I'm lying in bed and speak into a tape-recorder, recklessly, without worrying about formulations, choice of words, etc., then perhaps a really authentic document could come about."[36] In general, the feminist confession tends to avoid self-consciously literary language; in an obvious paradox, it strives for the appearance of spontaneity through a simple and conversational style. At times, the text may reveal a greater degree of aesthetic self-consciousness; *Flying,* for example, employs a disjointed, deliberately ungrammatical form of writing which attempts to express the jumble of emotional and sensual experiences accompanying the tumult of Millett's personal life. Similarly, *Häutungen* self-consciously attempts to create new forms of language which can convey the author's sense of the qualitatively different nature of female eroticism. Yet even the more experimental forms of feminist confession continually refer back to the perceptions of the female subject as their source and authority; there is a conspicuous lack of interest in irony, indeterminacy, and linguistic play. Thus Millett, for example, implies that the purpose of her text is to aid the discovery of an underlying buried self, moving her closer to "recovering my being."[37] Feminist confession continually refers to the question of *truth* as its ultimate legitimation. "I must make my life clear and transparent," states Struck, "Writing as a calling of myself into being."[38]

The Eighteenth-Century Precedent

The formal features of feminist confession are thus closely related to the social function which it is intended to serve, encouraging a particular form of interaction between text and audience. They typically include an unrelativized first-person narrative perspective, a thematic concentration upon feelings and personal relationships, the frequent reliance upon an informal and nonliterary style which establishes a relationship of intimacy between author and reader, and a tendency to deemphasize the aesthetic and fictive dimension of the text in order to give the appearance of authentic self-expression.

These features are of course already in evidence in much of the literature of the eighteenth century; the enormous production of first-person narratives during the period bore witness to an intense interest in questions of personal feeling and the experiences of the ordinary individual. Women were extensively implicated in these outpourings of subjectivity, as both producers and objects of literary discourse. The position of women became in one sense paradigmatic of the changes occurring in society as a whole; Eagleton refers to the "deep-seated 'feminization' of values throughout the eighteenth century which is closely allied with the emergence of the bourgeoisie."[39] The emergence of a distinctive private sphere to which a section of the female population was for the first time confined meant that women came to function as authorities in the domain of sentimentality and romantic love, a domain which increasingly preoccupied the public imagination. Of course, this was a double-edged phenomenon, which celebrated "feminine" values only to reinforce the powerlessness of women: "The feminization of discourse prolongs the fetishizing of women at the same time as it lends them a more authoritative voice."[40]

The exploration of subjectivity in the eighteenth century is also a fundamentally *public* affair, bearing little similarity to the solitary self-scrutiny of the alienated artist in later periods. It presupposes an audience of sympathetic readers, a public community which will empathize and identify with the individual's articulation of feeling. Habermas describes this in the following terms: "Psychological interest emerges from the outset in the dual relationship to the self and to the other; self-observation enters into a partly curious, partly sympathetic relationship with the emotional stirrings of the other self. The diary becomes a letter addressed to the sender; the first-person narrative a monologue addressed to unknown receivers; both experiments, as it were, in a subjectivity discovered in the private relationships of the family nucleus."[41] Discussing the epistolary fiction of the eighteenth century, Ruth Perry suggests that the distinction between fact and fiction was often blurred for the average reader, and that "the conviction prevailed that letters were the spontaneous renderings of a person's innermost thoughts."[42] The confessional mode of the diary and letter which shaped much of the writing of the period facilitated this appearance of authenticity; the language employed was often relatively simple and unadorned, simulating as far as possible the patterns of everyday speech. This form of intimate address, coupled with an attention to realist detail, was able to inspire strong identification in the reading public, as evidenced by the contemporary reception of such texts as *Pamela* and *Clarissa*. A comparison can be made between this kind of reader response and that invited by the feminist confession; the experience of involvement and identification disdained as a "naive" reading by much of modern literary criticism regains importance, exemplifying the text's integration into the everyday life of its readers and its success in confronting the personal and political problems which affect them.

It is possible to argue, then, that contemporary feminism has inspired a new preoccupation with the problematic of subjectivity which first emerges in the eighteenth century, resulting in a renewed attention to the psychological dimension of literature in the context of gender politics. The cultural and ideological frameworks within which this occurs are of course in many ways very different; "femininity" is no longer a self-evident notion, but an ideology to be interrogated from a perspective informed by feminist critiques. Nevertheless, the attempt to use autobiographical writing as a means to self-knowledge embroils the author in a variety of problems and contradictions, some of which are already apparent in the eighteenth-century context. Thus Schleiermacher, for example, is already aware of one of the paradoxes of autobiography, namely, that the process of critical self-scrutiny can be counterproductive by destroying the spontaneity of self it intends to uncover: "Inner life disappears as a consequence of this treatment. It is the most deplorable form of self-destruction."[43] Twentieth-century critics are able to challenge more explicitly many of the assumptions underlying the project of self-knowledge through literary self-expression. A deconstructive reading, for example, can easily undermine confession's attempt to emulate speech rather than writing, its struggle to control the open-ended play of language through constant reference to an illusory ideal of a determining subject. And from a Foucauldian perspective, confession as a supposed liberation from censorship and repression through the unburdening of the self is itself revealed as a mode of production of normative definitions of subjectivity through the imperative to continual self-examination: "The obligation to confess is now relayed through so many different points, is so deeply ingrained in us, that we no longer perceive it as the effect of a power that constrains us; on the contrary, it seems to us that truth, lodged in our most secret nature, 'demands' only to surface; that if it fails to do so, this is because a constraint holds it in place, the violence of a power weighs it down, and it can finally be articulated only at the price of a kind of liberation."[44] The adoption of the confessional mode by contemporary feminism thus raises a number of questions regarding the emancipatory value of writing about the self, which can be elucidated by tracing the historically determined shift in the meaning and function of confession.

The Dialectic of Confession

Autobiography in the modern sense, as a literary genre predicated upon the possibility and legitimacy of self-knowledge, first emerges as a distinctive form in the eighteenth century. Rousseau's *Confessions* is usually held up as the first example of autobiography as a celebration of unique individualism, and thus fundamentally different from earlier texts, such as the confessions of Saint Augustine or the life of Saint Teresa, in which self-analysis is valued not for its own sake but as a means of exposing the fallibility of humanity and affirming the ultimate authority of a divine knowledge beyond the individual's grasp.[45] Protestantism's emphasis on the importance of the individual struggle for salvation prepared the way for the self-consciousness necessary for autobiography proper; the flourishing of Pietism in Germany and Puritanism in England in the seventeenth century encouraged an active interest in self-scrutiny and spiritual introspection, often in the form of diaries in which every detail of daily thoughts and actions was recorded and examined for its moral and spiritual meaning.

Autobiography, then, develops out of the genre of the religious confession; there is a gradual shift from a form of self-analysis which seeks out sin and transgression in the context of adherence to a religious orthodoxy to an exploration of intimacy, emotion, self-understanding as aspects of a nascent bourgeois subjectivity. The one English word "confession" is ambiguous in that it covers this shift in

103

meaning and function which is expressed in German by three different words: *Beichte, Geständnis, Bekenntnis.* Confession as *Beichte* or *Geständnis* refers to an institutionalized form of confession to religious or legal authority through the acceptance of individual culpability for transgression and the enactment of penance: "Confession is part of a moral-legal syndrome of practices and beliefs which include certain key concepts (the conscience, the self, interior guilt, sin)."[46] As such, as Mike Hepworth and Bryan Turner note, confession can be seen to operate as a mechanism of social control, a reaffirmation of social order and the status quo through acknowledgment of individual deviance. Yet confession acquires a more positive meaning in the development of bourgeois society; as the enforcement of confession through religious law increasingly gives way to voluntary affirmations of faith and of the self, so the confession comes increasingly to symbolize a private assertion of freedom which may challenge rather than simply conform to existing social norms. Literary confession since the eighteenth century is primarily concerned not with the admission of guilt and the appeal to a higher authority, but rather with the affirmation and exploration of free subjectivity. Yet this attempted emancipation of the self can expose a self-defeating dialectic in which the history of confession as *Beichte,* as subjection to external authority, returns in new form. For the "authentic self" is itself very much a social product, and the attempt to assert its privileged autonomy can merely underline its profound dependence upon the cultural and ideological systems through which it is constituted. The more frantic the search for an inner self, for a kernel of meaning untouched by a society rejected as oppressive and alienating, the more clearly subjectivity is revealed to be permeated by and dependent upon those very symbolic constraints from which it seeks to liberate itself. In other words, the act of confession can potentially exacerbate rather than alleviate problems of self-identity, engendering a dialectic in which the production of ever more writing as a means to defining a center of meaning merely serves to underscore the alienation of the subject even as it seeks to overcome it.

If feminist confession is considered in this light, the interpenetration of the subjective with the social and ideological domains emerges at a number of levels. Most obviously, the social constitution of the inner self manifests itself in the ambivalent self-image of women writers, which reveals the powerful psychological mechanisms by which gender ideologies are internalized. It is clear that autobiographical writing by oppressed groups will be particularly prone to conflicts and tensions. On the one hand, the depiction of one's life and experiences as a woman, a black person, a homosexual, can be a potentially liberating process insofar as it expresses a public self-acceptance and a celebration of difference. Oakley, while writing, "I want to surpass my femininity,"[47] and offering a critical account of the negative aspects of female socialization, nevertheless reaffirms in her autobiography the value and importance of many aspects of women's lives. Lorde uses her self-image as a black lesbian feminist as a source of strength in the face of cancer, wishing to see herself as "a fighter resisting rather than as a passive victim suffering."[48]

On the other hand, the internalized cultural values which define specific identities as marginal, inferior, or deviant can come to the surface in feelings of anxiety and guilt. Regina Blackburn, analyzing a number of autobiographies by black women writers, shows that black identity generates ambivalent feelings, that it can be a source of pride but just as easily give rise to a sense of shame and self-hatred.[49] This phenomenon of a strongly negative self-image can be a particular problem for women, whose socialization typically endows them with feelings of inadequacy. Discussing the autobiographies of well-known and publicly successful women, Patricia Meyer Spacks comments upon their self-deprecatory stance: "They use autobiography, paradoxically, partly as a mode of self-denial."[50]

This negative pattern in which attempted self-affirmation reverts back into anxiety and self-castigation is a recurring one in at least some examples of feminist confession. Millett, for one, is contemptuous of her own emotional responses, speaking of "debility, weakness, loss. All the hateful, the despicable traits. Dependence most of all, a paralyzing, humiliating dependence."[51] German authors Struck and Offenbach are particularly prone to self-accusation. "It's almost embarrassing, how often I use the word 'guilt' in these notes,"[52] admits Offenbach, who refers to the particular problems caused by "homosexual self-hatred."[53] Feminism appears ironically to accentuate guilt rather than resolve it by providing an ideal of autonomy which the author is unable to emulate. Thus Struck savagely condemns her own "slimy dependency."[54] The central metaphor of *Kindheits Ende* is the author's perception of herself as a child, and her consequent self-castigation for her own immaturity. Both she and Offenbach continually censure their own behavior, defining themselves as obsessive and neurotic. Any insight gained through the act of confession does not appear to be translated into action, but merely generates increased feelings of guilt in the author at the extent of her own failings: "Then I think, how sick and tired I am of it; it's always the same reproduction of the same person who suffers, but who never draws conclusions for action from this suffering. I should stop suffering some time, I think, then there'd be something new to talk about."[55] Of course, the very point of the feminist confession is to confront the more unpalatable aspects of female experience as general problems, not to present idealized images of women as positive role models. Nevertheless, such passages are an indication that the project of self-disclosure as a means to self-emancipation may be more fraught with difficulties than it first appears.

The Critique of Narcissism

These difficulties in turn expose a broader and more general problematic at the very heart of confession: the belief that self-examination and self-disclosure can provide a source of truth and meaning in a society whose public values and institutions no longer possess any such authority. This conviction is of course a defining feature of bourgeois subjectivity; the development of capitalism brings with it individual emancipation from the authority of tradition, but only at the cost of alienation from a social environment which can no longer provide unquestioningly accepted values and systems of belief. Hence the preoccupation with the self and the personal sphere in bourgeois culture, exemplified in the rise of the novel as a literary form ideally suited to the exploration of individual psychology; the public interest in sentiment and romantic love masks the increasingly commercial basis of social interaction, thus serving an ideological function, but can also be seen to articulate a form of opposition to the regulation of social life by economic interests.[56]

Western societies since the 1970s have witnessed an even greater preoccupation with the self, exemplified in the boom in various forms of therapy, the enormous increase in confessional writing, and the conviction, grounded in prevailing Romantic ideologies of the subject, that there exists a "good" inner self, beneath the layers of oppressive social conditioning, which needs only to be liberated. The regressive rather than emancipatory implications of this withdrawal into subjectivity have been argued by several writers, most notably

Christopher Lasch and Richard Sennett, who use the term "narcissism" to designate the current preoccupation with personal identity which marks most Western societies and is perhaps most clearly manifested in the United States. There exists, it is argued, a contemporary tendency to confuse or to merge public and private selves, and consequently to reduce the complex operations of social and political institutions to questions of personal feeling and individual motive. The therapeutic sensibility reigns supreme: politics is increasingly viewed in purely individualistic terms and reduced to simplistic ideologies of self-awareness and self-expression. Not only is such a cultural phenomenon dangerously naive in reducing complex social, economic, and political structures to a personal and psychological level, but it can be oppressive rather than liberating in engendering what Sennett calls "destructive *Gemeinschaft*." The pursuit of intimacy, community, and mutual self-disclosure leads to an attempt to break down all barriers between individuals, failing to recognize the importance of play, ritual, and distance in social interaction. All aspects of individual behavior take on a deeper significance in relation to the inner self they are assumed to express, burdening individuals with the imperative to prove continually their authenticity. Hence the emphasis upon personal self-validation through the exchange of confessions. Self-expression is increasingly viewed as the highest good and as its own justification, and Sennett comments upon the self-defeating logic of this compulsion to authenticate the self through continually speaking of it: "The more a person concentrates upon feeling genuinely, rather than on the objective content of what is felt, the more subjectivity becomes an end in itself, the less expressive he can be. Under conditions of self-absorption the momentary disclosures of self become amorphous."[57]

A number of criticisms have been made of the general diagnosis of contemporary culture in the writings of Sennett and Lasch, most obviously in relation to their androcentric assumptions. Lasch's nostalgia for the traditional bourgeois patriarchal family as a supposedly necessary basis for the development of a strong superego reveals a conspicuous absence of recognition of the oppression of women as a defining element of this family structure. Similarly, the "fall of public man" is revealed as exactly that, the disappearance of a form of public life enjoyed by a select male bourgeoisie from which women were almost completely excluded. Sennett in particular has a tendency to idealize the autonomous, rational and psychically repressed bourgeois individual, and he undervalues the importance of intimacy and emotion in human interaction. Both writers fail to consider the potentially liberating effects of self-discovery for groups such as women whose needs have traditionally been repressed. For all its problems, self-examination as an impetus to personal change continues to play a central, if not the only, part within the politics of the women's movement. It thus seems necessary to reaffirm the point that whether subjectivity is perceived as radical politics or self-indulgent narcissism is at least partly dependent upon the standpoint from which it is being judged and the context in which it occurs.[58]

Nevertheless, the critique of narcissism is helpful insofar as it correctly identifies the potentially self-defeating logic of a striving for authenticity which seeks to deny all mediating social and symbolic structures by uncovering a kernel of pure self-identity. The unconditional demand for intimacy, confronted with the intolerable reality of alienation and lack, reverts back into anxiety and self-hatred. The goal of the confession is to strip away the superficial layers of convention and to expose an authentic core of self, of meaning as fully present to itself. Yet the more frantically this true subjectivity is pursued, the more elusive it appears; the greater the desire for intimacy and spontaneity, the more clearly the act of writing is revealed as the most alienated of activities. Feminist confession is by no means exempt from this dialectic of intimacy and alienation, which constitutes a defining feature of subjectivity as such. Indeed, because of women's socialization toward intimacy, and because ideologies of "feminine" sincerity and spontaneity continue to mark at least some examples of contemporary women's writing, feminist confession often reveals particularly clearly the contradictions between the desire for total intimacy and union, which seeks to erase all boundaries between desire and its object, and the act of writing as a continuing deferral of any such identity.

Intimacy and Alienation

The longing for intimacy emerges as a defining feature of the feminist confession at two interconnected levels: in the actual representation of the author's own personal relationships and in the relationship between author and reader established by the text. On the level of content, the feminist confession often reflects the difficulties many women experience in defining an independent identity, and their

108

overwhelming yearning for intimacy. Offenbach, describing her tendency to fall obsessively in love with almost total strangers, writes, "an independent self hardly exists any longer."[59] Oakley, discussing the desire experienced by many women for total unity with a partner, comments, "the integrity of self is gone. Like wax, one's borders melt and run away."[60] She goes on to argue that women's excessive investment in personal relations and their reliance upon validation through others is a keystone of their oppression which needs to be critically confronted: "The problem is feeling too much . . . Let me analyse it, because it is a female problem, and therefore not mine alone . . . As a woman, in the first place, my emotions rule my life."[61] While offering a critique of "masculine" defenses against emotion, vulnerability, and dependency, Oakley points out that the socialization of women offers an equally clear manifestation of the crippling effects of existing gender roles. She discusses the oppressive and even destructive effects of the desire some women experience to merge totally with a partner; this yearning for intimacy and fusion is unable to tolerate distance and otherness, and is thus experienced by the partner as a disturbing threat to his or her autonomy. Similarly, Koller's *An Unknown Woman,* which describes how the author moves to an isolated island in order to examine and assess the assumptions by which her previous life has been guided, takes as its central theme her lack of sense of self, her narcissistic reliance upon others as a means to self-validation; "I have turned other people into mirrors for me. I look at other people in order to see myself."[62]

This pattern of an overwhelming desire for fusion which is followed by rejection, the problem of "feeling too much," emerges clearly in many examples of feminist confession. *Sita, Sonja, Der Tod des Märchenprinzen* all reiterate a similar pattern, an attempt to engulf the partner in a symbiotic union, to erase all boundaries between self and other, which is experienced by the partner as a threat and leads to rejection. The texts of Karin Struck reveal particularly clearly the negative consequences of this lack of self-identity, as the author laments her own passivity and willingness to mold herself according to the desires of each lover: "I can't separate myself from others. Where is my 'skin boundary'? . . . I let everything get too close to me."[63] In one episode after another Struck's pursuit of total union and intimacy as a means to self-validation engenders resistance or withdrawal by a partner. In turn, as Lasch points out in his discussion of narcissism, "love rejected turns back to the self as hatred";[64] feelings of aggression are introjected, resulting in repeated instances of self-accusation and guilt as the author condemns herself for her failings.

In one sense, then, the feminist confession documents the failure of intimacy. Yet clearly the production of the text itself functions as an attempted compensation for this failure, generating in the relationship between reader and author the erotic mutuality which cannot otherwise be realized. Writing, seemingly the most isolated of activities, becomes the means to the creation of an ideal intimacy. As Offenbach notes of her own text, the confession is a cry for love, allowing the author to express powerful emotional feelings to an unknown reader without fear of rejection. The writing self is profoundly dependent upon the reader for validation, specifically the projected community of female readers who will understand, sympathize, and identify with the author's emotions and experiences.

As a consequence, the boundaries between text and life can become blurred, and writing becomes both a medium of, and a substitute for, personal relations. Offenbach, for instance, describes in *Sonja* how she reads another confessional autobiography and falls obsessively in love with its author; although an actual meeting ends in disaster, a similar and more successful relationship begins in the same way, with Offenbach falling in love with a woman after reading her autobiography. Sensitive to criticism that such behavior might be considered odd, she writes: "Isn't that after all a way of getting to know another person really very closely, perhaps a lot better than if you simply meet and have a talk?"[65]

This evaluation of writing as more authentic, more real than the superficialities of everyday communication, is another topos already well established in the eighteenth century. Perry discusses an eighteenth-century epistolary novel whose hero falls in love with the heroine of another epistolary novel which he is himself reading. His friends try to persuade him to give up this imaginary love, and to find a more appropriate one, but "he insists that this new woman that they have found for him must write something, for he cannot commit himself to love unless his literary sensibility is first moved."[66] This blurring of the distinction between literature and reality is remarkably similar to the confusion between text and life which occurs in *Sonja*. Having completed part of the *Sonja* manuscript, Offenbach shows it to a female friend who falls in love with her after having read the text which Offenbach has written. This friend in turn responds by producing her own ninety-page declaration of love, this event and Offenbach's response to it being incorporated into the text of *Sonja*. This unceasing generation of texts as a catalyst for and consequence of emotional relationships is further exemplified in Offenbach's fantasy about one of the authors she falls in love with: "Once we've both come to know and maybe to love one another independently of each other, we should both write a kind of diary about it, together yet independently of each other, and then combine this into a new book; daily representation and counter-representation. Her book, my book and this third book would then form a kind of trilogy."[67] This merging of and interaction between text and life is present in an intensified form in *Sonja*, where the ceaseless generation of confessional texts which are passed on and read by others plays an important role in the creation of personal relationships. Yet the feminist confession as such, by its foregrounding of the relationship between author and reader, its intimate tone, and its frequent appeals to the reader's complicity, can be seen as an attempt to attain the "mutuality" which cannot be realized in the author's life. The ideal community of female readers provides a counterpoint to the inadequacy of actual relationships; the text, decried one moment as an irredeemably alienated and compromised medium, appears in the next as the most intimate mode of communication, exposing the essence of the self in a way which is impossible in the superficial exchanges of everyday life.

Even when the confession appears most concerned with expressing emotions toward others, however, it constantly refers back to the writing self; the act of self-disclosure embodies the attempt to construct the independent sense of self which the author often feels she lacks. The objectification of the inchoateness of experience in the form of the written text endows this experience with a distinct form and material contours, and thus appears to confirm its reality. The narcissistic dimension inherent in the autobiographical project has been compared to the Lacanian notion of the mirror stage in childhood development; in both cases, "self-alienation is integral to the process whereby a unitary self is constituted."[68] Enacting a similar mechanism of identity constitution through alienation, the autobiography reflects back to the author in objectified form a self-image which purports to be the most intimate expression of personal identity.

The ambivalence of autobiography as both the ultimate truth of the author's life and as a mere simulacrum which can never fully encapsulate the reality of which it speaks is clearly apparent in the contemporary fascination with confession. It is as if the written text has acquired the function of guaranteeing the author's identity: "I write, therefore I am." The substantiality of the written text becomes the confirmation of the objective reality of the author's existence; hence the anxiety, apparent in the hundreds of pages of *Flying* and the endless production of confessional texts by Struck, *lest something be left out,* and the validity of the text, and hence the life, be called into question. Struck writes of her "anxiety, that the book isn't intense enough, isn't thick enough, doesn't contain enough words."[69] The solid materiality of the text becomes the ontological guarantee of the author's existence. Spacks discovers a similar pattern in eighteenth-century autobiographical writing, suggesting that individual identity is saved from pure subjectivity by "converting human beings into objects: quite literally: pages with words on them: illusions of consistent substantiality."[70]

Feminist confession thus seeks to affirm a female experience which has often been repressed and rendered invisible by speaking about it, by writing it into existence. The act of writing promises power and control, endowing subjective experience with authority and meaning. Millett writes: "My notebook . . . has become my friend, solace, obsession. I will live in it, in the ability to record experience which makes me more than its victim . . . Magical transformation of pain into substance, meaning, something of my own."[71] Yet this status of the text as the validation for a life is double-edged; the more emphatically it defines its function as the communication of the real, the more clearly the unbridgeable gap between word and referent is exposed. Thus Millett immediately contradicts her earlier statement: "The notebook assumes its real aspect, an untidy scribble without meaning or body or direction. The cheapest illusion."[72] Feminist confession swerves between the affirmation of the truth of its own discourse and the recognition of the text's insufficient status, the lack of identity of the text and the life. The consciousness of this discrepancy can generate ever more writing in the attempt to fill the gap, an extravagant piling up of protestations of feeling as a means of intensifying the reality of the text. The confessions of Offenbach and Struck in particular are full of repeated references to love, guilt, pain, anxiety, hatred, as if the constant reiteration of such words will bring the text closer to its goal of transparent self-disclosure. Yet the more words that are generated by the confessional text, the more clearly it reveals itself as infinitely extendable, an endless chain of signifiers that can never encapsulate the fullness of meaning which the author seeks and which would put an end to writing itself.

This lack of identity between the text and the life, experience and its representation, is of course a central problem of autobiography, and, in a broader sense, of literature itself. "Writing perpetually stands in for a reality it can never encompass."[73] Moreover, not only does the life call into question the authority of the text, but the text begins to undermine the reality of the life. Although the confession is chosen to convey immediacy and spontaneity, the very process of recording intrudes upon that which is being recorded and changes it. "If you record a day of your life, does the decision to do so change the shape of that day? . . . Do you change the balance, distort the truth?" asks Millett.[74] Life itself is revealed as literary material awaiting processing by the author, who begins to experience her own life self-consciously as a text. The more strenuously the author pursues immediacy as a means to disclosing the truth of her life, the more clearly the confessional work reveals itself to be caught up in contradictions and paradoxes which undermine any such project.

On the one hand, then, feminist confession expresses the longing for, and belief in, the value of intimacy, as part of its critique of an instrumental and rationalized public world. The process of self-discovery through the exploration of inner feelings may help to fulfill important needs for women who have often suppressed their own desires in accordance with an ethic of duty and self-sacrifice. On the other hand, the desire for self-validation through confession can engender the self-defeating dialectic described by Sennett and Lasch. The yearning for total intimacy, immediacy, and fullness of meaning serves only to underscore the reality of uncertainty and lack, so that attempted self-affirmation *(Bekenntnis)* can easily revert into anxious self-castigation *(Beichte)*. The process of introspection, of the analysis and evaluation of motive, can intensify feelings of guilt rather than resolve them; the compulsion to disclose oneself as fully as possible leads to a search for ever more telling details, the continual interrogation of one's own motives, in the search for the impossible ideal of absolute honesty. In this context Sennett is correct to reaffirm the connection between the modern stress on authenticity and its Puritan precedents. "In both, 'What am I feeling?' becomes an obsession. In both, showing to others the checks and impulses of oneself feeling is a way of showing that one does have a worthy self."[75]

The strong Protestant element in the feminist preoccupation with subjectivity as truth in turn explains why the feminist confession appears to be a relatively rare phenomenon within the Catholic and rhetorically conscious French tradition, whereas both the United States and West Germany have seen the development of a vast body of confessional literature in the last fifteen years. In a discussion of the poetry of Adrienne Rich, Wendy Martin traces a number of connections between American Puritanism and contemporary American radical feminism. In both instances a rhetoric of pioneering militancy articulates a radical rejection of the old world and a search for regeneration and reformation, for a new and perfect society grounded in the truth of subjective conviction: "The Puritan heart prepared to receive God's grace has its parallel in the feminist raised consciousness that extirpates male-identified values."[76] Similarly, the influence of Protestantism and an extant tradition of contemplative German inwardness is clearly apparent in many of the texts of West German feminism. Struck refers explicitly to Protestant influences, whereas Offenbach writes, "always my fanaticism for truth, a kind of legacy from my moral mother."[77] In the texts of Struck and Offenbach the continuing concern with "absolute honesty" results in an endless self-scrutiny, a search for a pure female self which will guarantee redemption, and the inevitable failure of such a project expresses itself in the form of guilt and self-accusation.

The Politics of Confession

The writer of the feminist confession can thus be described as walking a fine line between self-affirmation and self-preoccupation, between critical insight and obsessive self-castigation. It becomes clear that the act of confession cannot uncover a miraculously intact female subject, that there exists no innocent place outside the symbolic order. The "self" which women find will continue to be marked by contradictions, schisms, and tensions, some relating to the more general problematic of subjectivity, others to the specific conditions of marginalization and powerlessness that have shaped much of female experience. By the same token, however, feminist confession may also cater to specific needs arising from its social function in the context of women's recent cultural and political struggles. While it

114

cannot attain the goal of total intimacy and authenticity aspired to by some of its practitioners, it can nevertheless serve to articulate some of the specific problems experienced by women both communally and individually and play a role in the process of identity formation and cultural critique.

Feminist confession, I have suggested, is marked by a tension between a focus upon subjectivity and a construction of identity which is communal rather than individualistic. It thus becomes necessary to differentiate feminist confessional discourse from the more general fascination with "self-awareness" in modern society. "Narcissism" after all acquires a more or less collective political dimension in the production and reception of feminist literature. Edwin Schur suggests that feminist consciousness-raising needs to be separated from the mass of contemporary therapy, self-help, and awareness programs for this reason.[78] While stressing the personal and psychological dimensions of experience, feminism links these to an acknowledgment of the *institutionalized* nature of sexual oppression and thus differs significantly from the individualism of forms of "awareness therapy" and its belief that all problems can be resolved by "getting in touch with one's feelings." The recognition that women's problems are not private but communal is perhaps the most fundamental message underlying feminist confession. "My attempt to emancipate myself as an individual had to fail," asserts Meulenbelt,[79] and Merian writes: "Other women have been through the same as me. I'm not at all alone with my problems."[80] Consequently, whereas the contemporary concern with subjectivity may be viewed from a male perspective as a degeneration of the public realm into an unseemly obsession with private affairs, its implications from the standpoint of women's history are precisely the opposite. Given that women's lives have until now been largely defined by their location within the private sphere, this realm necessarily constitutes the starting point for critical reflection. At the same time, the open discussion of such experiences and of their broader implications exemplifies a shift of the problematic of "femininity" from the private into the public domain.

It must further be noted that, echoes and parallels notwithstanding, there are fundamental differences between eighteenth-century representations of female subjectivity and contemporary feminist confession. Most obviously, the latter is not concerned with narrating plots of seduction and marriage, but rather addresses the problem of realizing female autonomy in a male-dominated society. Whereas the rise of the novel occurs contemporaneously with the emergence of the ideology of romantic love and the idealization of marriage, which provides the basis for most of its narratives, the feminist confession proceeds from the recognition of the redundancy of this model and its oppressive implications for women. Consequently, the previously self-evident nature of male-female relationships is raised to the level of conscious critique: women's psychological, social, and economic subordination; the problem of defining female sexuality outside the stereotypes of virgin and whore promulgated by patriarchal ideology; the implications for women of the separation of private and public spheres.

Of course, the degree of overt politicization in feminist confession differs significantly. Some authors, such as Stefan, Merian, Meulenbelt, and Oakley, analyze their experiences from an unambiguous ideological perspective; other texts, like Koller's *An Unknown Woman,* are primarily concerned with the problem of self-determination and only hint at its broader political implications. Often confession is less concerned with making an explicit political point than in "telling all," with the cathartic release which accompanies speaking about that which has been kept hidden and silent. The strength of confession as a genre lies in its ability to communicate the conflicting and contradictory aspects of subjectivity, the strength of desire, the tensions between ideological convictions and personal feelings. It can be said to expose the complex psychological mechanisms by which women "collude" in their own oppression, but it also reveals the realm of personal relations as fraught with ambivalence and anxiety, intimately interwoven with patterns of domination and subordination, desire and rejection, which cannot be easily transcended.

The context of reception must also be considered in evaluating the social significance of feminist confession; an audience sympathetic to feminist ideas allows even the most negative self-depiction of women to be viewed as an exemplary model which can be used to investigate aspects of women's oppression. The existence of a feminist readership provides the context for a politicized interpretation. Of course this is not a *necessary* reading. Like any other contemporary text cast out into an anonymous mass reading public, consisting of diverse groups governed by varied and conflicting values and affiliations, feminist confession has no control over the readings to which it will be subjected. As critical responses indicate, it can inspire disgust, irritation, or voyeuristic curiosity in the reader rather than solidarity and sympathy. Obviously, the position of implied reader constructed by the feminist confession is not one that any real reader is compelled to take up. Nevertheless, contemporary responses to, and sales of, feminist confession indicate the existence of a significant reading public which is receptive to its professed aims and concerns, and it is in the context of this, presumably mainly female, readership that its social meaning needs to be situated.

The political value of self-scrutiny and self-disclosure is explicitly asserted by almost all of the women writers using the confessional form, who often feel the need to defend themselves against the accusation of self-indulgent navel-gazing. As Oakley states, "Such a drive to self-knowledge is more than the dilatory self-interested pastime of the so-called liberated woman . . . It is a protest against the dehumanisation of society made by women on behalf of everyone, because it is women who find themselves most discomforted by the gap between who they are and what they are supposed to be."[81] Oakley's text is the most explicitly political of the autobiographies examined; the author uses her personal experience as a basis for analyzing such gender-based issues as the politics of housework and the treatment of women by the medical profession. There is however a general supposition underlying feminist confession that the process of self-examination is necessary, even obligatory, for women, a politically significant act in relation to a projected community of female readers who share a consciousness of the silence which has been imposed upon women over the centuries. This theme is rendered explicit in *The Cancer Journals;* Lorde claims that she is addressing all "other women of all ages, colors, and sexual identities who recognize that imposed silence about any area of our lives is a tool for separation and powerlessness."[82] Lorde's text exemplifies the continuing importance of confessional writing as long as privatized areas of shame, fear, and guilt continue to exist in women's lives. The author confronts the issue of breast cancer on both personal and social levels, exploring the emotions experienced before and after surgery, but also examining the politics of the American medical establishment and the trivialization of breast cancer as a cosmetic rather than a health problem.

Other examples of feminist confession devote themselves primarily to the depiction of sexual and emotional relationships; Stefan's *Häutungen* and Merian's *Der Tod des Märchenprinzen* offer two of the most explicit critiques of the distorted balance of power in hetero-sexual relations and the inability of many men to view women other than in relation to their own sexual and emotional needs. Millett's texts focus in particular upon women's sense of the unity of private and public selves and their reluctance to keep these spheres separate as men have traditionally done. Both Millett's *Sita* and Offenbach's *Sonja* depict the detailed recording of a lesbian relationship as a political act, a means of breaking the silence which has traditionally denied the existence of relations between women. And Cardinal's *The Words to Say It* provides a model of self-analysis as a means to critical awareness and rebellion; as presented here, psychoanalysis is not an indoctrination into normality but rather provides a means of overcoming the crippling fear, obedience, and self-loathing internal-ized by a dutiful daughter during a repressive upbringing within an upper middle class French family, as she reaches a new sense of autonomy which makes possible political awareness and activity.

A feminist critique of the political aims, themes, and techniques of feminist confession has been articulated by Sigrid Weigel. Whereas more consciously stylized, fragmented, and "literary" forms of writing can serve the function of estranging and calling into question gender identity, Weigel argues, feminist confession generates the illusion of a "natural" female self and is both aesthetically and politically naive, confirming the existing prejudices of readers rather than challenging them. Weigel suggests that feminist confession typically results in cathartic self-reproach rather than critical self-analysis and is essentially harmless, "without any transformative social impact."[83] In turn, the prevalence of feminist confessional writing risks encouraging a pejorative dismissal of "women's litera-ture" by the reading public as a whole as typically lachrymose and self-indulgent.

Weigel's critique has a certain validity, particularly in relation to German feminist literature, which forms the basis of her analysis and which has become strongly identified with the confessional genre. Whereas *Häutungen* was instrumental in challenging existing reader expectations and breaking the silence about women's experience of sexuality, it has been followed by a flood of confessional texts in a similar vein, which often appear to confirm rather than challenge the prejudices of female readers, reiterating gender stereotypes and often indulging in little more than self-pity and self-justification. Merian's *Der Tod des Märchenprinzen,* for example, reveals a remarkably

118

blinkered moral self-righteousness in its representation of femininity as victimhood, espousing a dogmatic conviction regarding the absolute authority of female subjective experience. As a counterexample, however, one can cite *The Cancer Journals*, which offers acute insights into the anguish and the politics of cancer while avoiding self-pity and simplistic judgments. Similarly, *An Unknown Woman* and *The Words to Say It* exemplify the potential value of confession as a process of critical reflection upon the construction of female subjectivity, illuminating the deeply ingrained passivity, dependency, and anxiety to please which frequently shape the female psyche, while revealing the potentially liberating effects of recognizing and calling into question such psychological mechanisms. Cardinal writes, "Day after day since my birth, I had been made up: my gestures, my attitudes, my vocabulary. My needs were repressed, my desires, my impetus, they had been dammed up, painted over, disguised and imprisoned."[84]

As a result, it becomes difficult to pronounce any one final judgment upon feminist confession as a genre, either to celebrate it as radically subversive or simply to reject it as self-indulgent and naive. It is certainly true, as Weigel argues, that feminist confession can at times reproduce images of women uncomfortably close to the stereotypes feminist theorists are attempting to challenge: a belief in the moral superiority of female expressiveness, an assumption that women's language is more "authentic" than that of men. Against this, however, it can also be noted that the dividing line between a repressive stereotype and an empowering symbol of cultural identity is often a very narrow one. The creation and affirmation of symbolic identities constitutes a recurring need on the part of marginalized social groups, fulfilling a desire for self-validation in the face of the hostility of a dominant culture.

This ambivalence is well discussed by Jeffrey Weeks in his analysis of "identity politics," which centers primarily upon gay rights, but has a more general relevance to questions raised here. The focus on sexuality as a defining element of cultural identity is a relatively recent historical phenomenon, as has often been shown; lesbianism and male homosexuality have increasingly come to define a whole range of cultural and political affiliations rather than simply to denote a preference for a particular form of sexual relationship. Consequently, as Weeks points out, it is misleading to conceptualize homosexual identity as a fundamental core of being which has been repressed throughout history and now awaits liberation; rather, the very notion

119

of "homosexual identity" is a contingent construct, the consequence of the emergence of new and historically determined discourses on human sexuality. The same is true of feminism, which in its present manifestations relies heavily upon twentieth-century conceptual frameworks, for example sociological role theory, in its construction of an oppositional female identity and its critique of patriarchal culture. Clearly we cannot simply project these notions backward into history by means of a teleological model which depicts women of the past as passive victims of patriarchy, unconsciously anticipating their own future liberation. The discursive representation of female identity in present-day feminism needs to be recognized as itself a product of modern thought, not a transhistorical essence. As Weeks puts it, "Identity is not a destiny but a choice . . . identities are not expression of secret essences. They are self-creations, but they are creations on ground not freely chosen but laid out by history."[85]

This recognition of the historically determined nature of identity politics can lead to it being viewed from a Foucauldian perspective as a form of prescriptive authority, a production of subjectivity which seeks to stabilize ambiguity by continually speaking of the self. Yet Weeks is correct to indicate the limitations of this view. While the claim that feminism, or gay rights, can help us to uncover our "true selves" is misleading insofar as it ignores the socially constructed nature of all identities, it nevertheless serves to articulate a genuinely experienced sense of difference which cannot simply be explained in functionalist terms as the product of a regulatory discourse. Oppositional identities are often asserted only painfully and with difficulty and serve to articulate experiences of alienation, exclusion, and suffering in people's lives. The fact that they are socially constructed does not mean that they are any less "real," or that their political function can be reduced to one of complicity with ruling ideologies. Discussing the quest for identity as an important ideal for the sexually marginalized, Weeks writes: "Categorisations and self-categorisations, that is the process of identity formation, may control, restrict and inhibit but simultaneously they provide 'comfort, security and assuredness'. And the precondition in turn for this has been a sense of wider ties, of what we can best call sexual communities. It is in social relations that individual feelings become meaningful, and 'identity' possible."[86]

As Weeks emphasizes, the significance of identity politics can only be adequately assessed by examining the needs it fulfills for particular social groups at a given historical moment. Feminist confession is not

120

a self-generating discourse to be judged in abstraction from existing social conditions; it exemplifies a simultaneous interrogation and affirmation of gendered subjectivity in the context of notions of communal identity generated by new social movements. Feminist literature addresses a potential "we" and challenges contemporary perceptions of the alienated anonymity of the individual in mass society by means of an appeal to a notion of oppositional community based upon the shared bond of gender linking author and reader. It may appear easy to expose the naiveté of such an attempt to reclaim literature for the purposes of intersubjective communication in a society in which texts are regarded as commodities to be regulated by the impersonal demands of the market, and where subjectivity is itself increasingly depicted as a mere effect of technologized communication networks, of fetishized images of pseudoindividuality manufactured and circulated by the mass media. Yet any such sweeping vision of one-dimensionality constitutes a gross oversimplification, ignoring the complex and contradictory nature of contemporary social relations as expressed in the current reemergence of forms of resistance and dissent embodied in autonomous social movements. Feminist literature *has* been an instrumental force in the creation of a feminist "counter-public sphere," an oppositional discursive space within contemporary society defined in terms of a notion of gender identity perceived to unite all participants. Confessional writing has been central to this sphere, as it has played out an anxious, often uneasy struggle to discover a female self, a struggle which is by no means free of contradiction but which constitutes a necessary moment in the self-definition of an oppositional community.

CHAPTER FOUR

Meridian

The Novel of Self-Discovery:
Integration and Quest

Perhaps the genre which is most clearly identified with contemporary feminist writing is the narrative of female self-discovery, in which access to self-knowledge is seen to require an explicit refusal of the heterosexual romance plot, the framework which has traditionally defined the meaning and direction of women's lives. Thematizing gender as the central problem for women attempting to reconcile individual and social demands, the contemporary narrative of female development exemplifies an appropriation and reworking of established literary genres such as the *Bildungsroman*. An investigation of the distinctive features of the feminist novel of self-discovery in turn reveals a number of illuminating parallels between the structure of recent fictions of female identity and narratives of emancipation shaping feminist ideology itself.

Examples of texts which conform to the self-discovery plot and which will be referred to in this chapter include the following: Margaret Atwood, *Surfacing* (1972); Joan Barfoot, *Gaining Ground* (1978); Grace Bartram, *Peeling* (1986); Marilyn French, *The Women's Room* (1977); Doris Lessing, *The Summer before the Dark* (1973); Paule Marshall, *Praisesong for the Widow* (1983); Marge Piercy, *Small Changes* (1972) and *Fly away Home* (1984); Margot Schroeder, *Der Schlachter empfiehlt noch immer Herz* (The butcher still recommends heart) (1976); Brigitte Schwaiger, *Wie kommt das Salz ins Meer* (How does the salt get into the sea) (1977); Verena Stefan, *Häutungen* (1975); Alice Walker, *Meridian* (1976) and *The Color Purple* (1983); Fay Weldon, *Praxis* (1978).

Although such examples of the feminist self-discovery novel have become familiar to large numbers of readers, there have been

122

relatively few attempts to address systematically the broader social implications of the genre in relation to the influence of feminism on women's narratives. One of the few exceptions is Abel, Hirsch, and Langland's collection of essays, *The Voyage In,* which takes as its theme the specific features of female development as they have been depicted in the literature of both past and present. The introduction offers a useful discussion of the influence of gender upon genre, and the psychological and social forces which have affected the nature of plots for women. As the editors point out, "while male protagonists struggle to find a hospitable context in which to realize their aspirations, female protagonists must frequently struggle to voice any aspirations whatsoever . . . Even the broadest definitions of the *Bildungsroman* presuppose a range of social options available only to men."[1] But the contributors' emphasis on individual psychology at the expense of any sustained analysis of ideological and discursive frameworks results in the already noted tendency toward abstract and ahistorical models of gender difference. Recent feminist theories of gender acquisition—Chodorow, Gilligan, Dinnerstein—are drawn upon as the basis for general models of female development in literature, which are used to explain texts ranging from Greek tragedy to modern black American writing. The fundamental differences in family structures, ideologies of childrearing, and models of gender identity which have existed throughout history are put to one side in the attempt to extrapolate a universal model from theories which can at best help to explain gender acquisition in specific social strata of present-day Western societies. Moreover, the argument that the passivity, withdrawal, and inward development which have often marked women's plots are directly attributable to women's distinctive psychic identity and continuing attachment to the pre-Oedipal phase, their "fluid and permeable" ego boundaries, which cause them to spurn social autonomy and separation, strikes me as problematic.[2] Such a claim runs the risk of minimizing the magnitude of the social, economic, and ideological barriers which have obstructed women's self-realization in the public world—and of idealizing such exclusion rather than acknowledging its crippling consequences—and is furthermore unable to account for a significant and relatively sudden shift in fictions of female development in recent years.

The history of women's narratives cannot be understood by referring to an abstract ideal of "feminine" consciousness, but can only be addressed by considering the complex interplay between the social and material conditions affecting women's lives and the relatively autonomous influence of dominant cultural representations of gender, which do not simply constitute "external" determinants but are embedded at the deepest level of psychosexual identity. It is in narrative that the governing ideological conceptions of male and female roles are fleshed out, the configurations of plot mapping out the potential contours of women's lives as they can be imagined at a given historical moment. As ideologies of female identity have undergone significant changes, so too has the nature of women's plots. Thus the last twenty years have seen the emergence of a distinctive new narrative structure for women, tracing a process of *separation* as the essential precondition for any path to self-knowledge. Although the extent and implications of this separation vary according to the individual text, the novel of self-discovery proceeds from the recognition of women's estrangement within a male-defined environment but also articulates the possibility of at least a partial individual liberation from existing ideological and social constraints toward a degree of self-determination.

Thus, while feminist readings have often tended to stress the underlying continuity of women's writing, attempting to establish archetypal patterns of female experience,[3] the contemporary narrative of female self-discovery offers obvious differences to earlier representations of women's lives. Nancy Miller, for example, argues that the female-centered plot of the eighteenth century is characterized by a choice of two plots: the "euphoric" in which the heroine "moves in her negotiation with the world of men and money from 'nothing' to all," and the "dysphoric," which ends with the "heroine's death in the flower of her youth."[4] In other words, the fate awaiting the heroine of the bourgeois novel is already established with exemplary clarity at its very inception: the choice is Pamela or Clarissa, the heroine who is "happily rewarded in marriage or elevated into redemptive death."[5]

The limitations of this schema become more sharply focused in nineteenth-century fiction, in which the only choices available to a female protagonist are frequently revealed as negative ones: a stifling and repressive marriage or a form of withdrawal into inwardness which frequently concludes in self-destruction. Woman emerges as a central problem for the nineteenth-century novel, a subject to which it ceaselessly returns; the fate of the "problematic heroine" for whom adultery offers the only imaginable outlet for transgressive impulses (Emma Bovary, Anna Karenina) becomes emblematic of the contradictions and tensions by which bourgeois society is riven.[6] The narrative of education or apprenticeship, in which the hero's quest for identity requires a critical engagement with social values and norms, is for the most part unavailable to the nineteenth-century heroine, whose trajectory remains limited to the journey from the parental to the marital home and whose destiny remains permanently linked to that of her male companion. Even in those texts which are able to envisage a limited degree of female self-development, such as *Jane Eyre,* this autonomy is ultimately subordinated to the demands of the marriage plot, and the necessity for the heroine's integration into the familial and domestic spheres, with the consequent emergence of an ironic tension between the heroine's acquisition of independence and self-knowledge, and the at times obviously formulaic closure demanded by the social narrative.[7]

Equally frequently, the heroine's struggle against existing constraints necessitates her symbolic or literal destruction as the price to be paid for the attempted transgression of social and sexual mores. Marianne Hirsch analyzes a range of eighteenth- and nineteenth-century novels with female protagonists and concludes:

> An alternative tradition of *female* novels of development . . . poses serious questions about the possibility of female *Bildung* in the nineteenth-century novel . . . A comparative study of this typically female pattern of growth demonstrates gender to be even more fundamental than national tradition in determining generic conventions . . . Faced with the break between psychological needs and social imperatives, literary convention finds only one possible resolution: the heroine's death.[8]

Of course, the literary representation of the circumscribed nature of women's existence does not necessarily imply its affirmation, and whether intended or not, the death of the heroine often functions as a potent critique of the contradictions inherent in women's social roles.[9]

This kind of dichotomy, of either marriage or death, is transcended in the contemporary self-discovery narrative: it is an essentially *optimistic* genre, bearing witness to women's self-identification as an oppressed group, and hence as a potential challenge to existing social values. This is not to suggest that an absolute cutoff can be established between an extant tradition of women's writing and contemporary feminist literature; on the contrary, as Rachel Blau Du Plessis has shown in *Writing beyond the Ending,* the concerns of contemporary second-wave feminism are prefigured in a number of twentieth-century literary texts in which women writers strive increasingly insistently to escape the confines of the heterosexual romance plot. Any such modification or transformation of recent women's narratives is obviously indebted to wide-ranging changes in the legal, economic, and social status of women which have rendered the situation of single, independent women a somewhat less anomalous one. At the same time, no direct correlation can be assumed to exist between fiction and social reality; the current spate of novels about women leaving their male partners obviously cannot be interpreted as an accurate reflection of actual changes taking place in familial and social structures. Nevertheless, such stories are profoundly revealing at the level of the "social imaginary," the symbolic frameworks of representation through which cultural meanings are produced and disseminated. The importance of a symbolic act of separation as a defining feature of feminist fiction suggests that certain notions which were previously unthinkable—women's right to a social identity not determined by their sexual and maternal roles, for example—have become embedded within the discursive frameworks of contemporary culture, functioning as an important and influential source of new narratives which attempt to confront and work through in story form some of the contradictions of gender identity uncovered by feminist ideology.

Emancipation Narratives in Feminist Literature and Ideology

The contemporary narrative of female self-discovery thus cannot be understood as the liberation of a "true" women's writing from the straitjacket of a patriarchal system of representation, but is itself an ideological site, an active process of meaning production. If the genre both shapes and is shaped by changing conceptions of female identity emerging from the women's movement, and if feminist ideology, as I have suggested, is plural and heterogeneous rather than comprising a monolithic worldview, then it is to be expected that narratives of female self-discovery will reveal significant differences in their preoccupations and emphases.

In selecting some of the most representative of these concerns for more detailed analysis, I make a rough division of self-discovery narratives into two groups. The first kind of text, which can be designated as a feminist *Bildungsroman*, is characterized by a historical and linear structure; female self-discovery and emancipation is de-

Two Groups of Self-Discovery novels:

1.) Bildungsroman

picted as a process of moving outward into the public realm of social engagement and activity, however problematic and fraught with difficulties this proves to be. This form of narrative is particularly strongly represented in the realist feminist fiction which has recently emerged in the United States. The second depicts self-discovery as a process of awakening to an already given mythic identity or inner self and frequently occurs in nature or in a generalized symbolic realm from which the contingent social world has been excluded. These two types of narrative can be compared to two dominant moments with feminism itself. One tendency within the women's movement, most notably represented by liberal and socialist feminism, embraces a narrative model of history as progress, emphasizing the activist and participatory dimension of politics and the necessity of engagement in the public sphere. By contrast, feminism also includes a strong strain of romantic individualism, which is critical of ideologies of modernity and progress and which typically situates truth and meaning in an edenic past rather than in the future. Most clearly exemplified in certain forms of radical feminism, this kind of politics places a particularly strong emphasis upon creating qualitatively different relationships between the self and nature and between the self and other individuals as a means of overcoming the alienated nature of modern thought and experience.

It may be objected that such a comparison is reductive in theorizing the literary text as a mere reflection of particular ideological positions. However, to undertake a comparison of emancipation narratives underlying women's writing and feminist ideology is not to attempt to collapse the differences between literature and politics, but rather to bring to light the common cultural assumptions and frames of reference on which both rely. Narrative constitutes one of the most deeply embedded and culturally significant forms of the symbolic production of meaning, and recent theorists have demonstrated the ubiquitous nature of the narrative impulse, its manifest or latent presence across a range of textual forms, whether "fictional" or "factual."[10] Both feminist literature and feminist politics organize discursive meaning around the projected liberation of an individual or collective female subject, generating a number of narrative models of emancipation grounded in different conceptions of history and truth. The evidence of underlying affinities between the structures and themes of contemporary women's writing and particular forms of feminist ideology does not necessarily imply that the ideology in question can in all cases be imputed to the author of the literary text as a consciously held political position. Rather, literary and political domains interact with each other and with the broader cultural sphere, often reflecting general trends within society—such as the current resurgence of Romanticism—whose significance and influence is not limited to the women's movement alone.

My broad division of feminist narratives into two groups derives from the degree of emphasis given to either the inward transformation of consciousness or to active self-realization within the individual text, but it should be stressed that this division does not constitute an opposition or signify that these two models of female self-discovery are to be viewed as mutually exclusive. A celebration of subjectivity, spirituality, and myth does not necessarily imply a lack of commitment to social and political change. The women's movement has played an important part in undermining oppositions between Romanticism and realism and has challenged Marxism's largely uncritical identification with forces of rationality and progress, which has failed to address adequately issues of subjectivity and symbolic identity. The same is true for other contemporary social movements, from ecological groups which argue the need for a fundamental transformation in the relationship between humanity and nature, to black communities for whom the reclamation of a collective, ancestral spiritual tradition has played an empowering role in the construction of an oppositional identity. Consequently, distinctions between "progressive," forward-looking movements and "reactionary," backward-looking ones no longer appear quite so clear-cut, as the narrative of history-as-progress loses much of its authority, and the unconditional affirmation of modernity reveals its own ideological underpinnings. Feminism and feminist fiction point outward and forward, into social activity and political emancipation, but also backward and inward, into myth, spirituality, and the transformation of subjective consciousness.

The Self-Discovery Narrative

Although the resolutions of feminist narratives reveal significant differences, they share a common starting point, typically beginning at the stage when the traditional plot of women's lives breaks off, with the attainment of a male sexual partner. The status of marriage as the goal and endpoint of female development is called into question by the emergence of a new plot which seeks to expose the insufficiences of the old. The defining feature of the feminist text is a recognition and rejection of the ideological basis of the traditional script of heterosexual romance characterized by female passivity, dependence, and subordination, and an attempt to develop an alternative narrative and symbolic framework within which female identity can be located.

The beginning of the text thus typically introduces a negative model, an image of female alienation which the text will strive to overcome. While the restrictive nature of women's social roles is often exemplified in the emblematic figure of the housewife whose entire horizon is circumscribed by the daily drudgery of catering to her family's domestic and emotional needs *(The Summer before the Dark, Wie kommt das Salz ins Meer, The Women's Room)*, the same asymmetry of power in male-female relations can be found in ostensibly "progressive" circles, where male radicals reveal themselves to be equally blind to their own sexism and to women's interests and needs *(Häutungen, Meridian)*. The sexual division of labor manifests itself in women's responsibility for the task of emotional nurturance and in prevailing assumptions that the female protagonist will invariably place the needs and desires of a male partner before her own. Women's confinement to the private sphere denies them the potential for public activity and independent self-fulfillment, while locking them into a relationship of psychological or economic dependence upon a lover who is unable to acknowledge women other than in relation to his own emotional and sexual interests.

The internalization of this view of female identity as supplementary to and supportive of a male figure by women themselves is registered as the most disturbing indication of the deep-seated influence of patriarchal ideology; the protagonist is unable to see herself except in relation to the needs and desires of others. Doris Lessing writes of her protagonist, "she knew now . . . that all her life she had been held upright by an invisible fluid, the notice of other people."[11] Verena Stefan comments on her own development: "A man's recognition was still decisive for me in confirming my existence as a particular person distinguishable from others."[12] This sense of female identity as a lack, a problematic absence, offers no basis from which to challenge existing ideologies of gender as they are manifested at the level of commonsense assumptions and everyday practices. The protagonist of *Gaining Ground* experiences only a "restlessness, an uneasiness, a spell of ennui, nothing more."[13] A sense of estrangement and unreality is expressed in recurring metaphors in which the protagonist perceives herself to be dreaming or describes herself as functioning like a puppet or an automaton: "There were months filled with that kind of emptiness, the motionlessness of a mannequin in a fairy tale who only comes alive when real people appear."[14] Schwaiger's young protagonist in *Wie kommt das Salz ins Meer* records the day of her wedding with the detached gaze of an uninvolved outsider; the heroine of *Surfacing* experiences the world from a remote distance through a pane of glass: "I watch the side windows as though it's a TV screen."[15]

This sense of remoteness from a preformed destiny which the protagonist feels helpless to alter is typically described as a splitting of inner and outer self, the heroine experiencing a powerful estrangement from the external appearance by which her social status as a woman in a patriarchal culture is largely determined. In *Praisesong for the Widow* Avey Johnson fails to recognize her own reflection and observes her own image with the indifference of a stranger; mirrors are depicted in *Surfacing* as a sinister trap which ensnare women's souls. Lessing's heroine considers this aspect of women's lives: "Had she really spent so many years of her life . . . in front of a looking glass? Just like all women. Years spent asleep, or tranced."[16] Another recurring metaphor which encapsulates the female subject's sense of alienation is the conviction that men and women speak different languages, that the qualitatively different nature of female experience remains alien and resistant to the discursive forms of a male-defined culture; the protagonist of *Surfacing* writes: "It was the language again, I couldn't use it because it wasn't mine."[17]

The key transformation of the text takes the protagonist from this stage of alienation, of sense of lack, to a conscious affirmation of gendered identity. It is here that the contemporary self-discovery narrative moves beyond earlier texts depicting the suffering and ultimate destruction of the literary heroine. Instead one finds the consistent application of a new narrative model, in which the otherness of the female protagonist does not result in her subsequent death or defeat but provides the impetus for a sustained refusal of patriarchal values. Rather than offering a negative critique of society by depicting the destruction of a female victim, the contemporary writer describes a form of opposition through the resistance and survival of the heroine. The ideological and social constraints which have traditionally defined women's plots in relation to erotic and familial ties are systematically called into question through a new narrative structure that embodies a radical rupture with the old. "Something radical had broken, and I could not get back to the old way."[18]

The possibility of this new women's plot is seen to depend upon a psychological transformation of the heroine, a shift in perspective which can occur abruptly, in the form of a sudden illumination which Carol Christ describes as similar to religious conversion,[19] or gradually, through a steady accumulation of insights into the structures of power governing relationships between men and women. The inward recognition and rejection of the ideological basis of existing gender roles is expressed externally in the narrative through the act of leaving a husband or lover, the protagonist often choosing to live alone or with other women. Sometimes, the shift in physical space is as symbolically important as any changes in personal relationships; the heroine moves outward, from the oppressive environment of the city to the empty spaces of the wilderness *(Gaining Ground, Surfacing)*, or inward to a secluded and sheltering room *(Häutungen)*. In all cases some form of at least temporary separation from traditional heterosexual relations deeply ingrained with patterns of subordination and domination is a necessary precondition for any gains in self-knowledge. The symbiosis of the couple is portrayed as inimical to and destructive of the heroine's struggle for identity. "A void. A blank. An impression of a vacuum moved by outside sources," writes one protagonist of her past married self.[20] Mira in *The Women's Room*, formulating the thoughts "I want" and "I am," realizes that "these were two statements she had never felt permitted to utter, or even to think."[21]

This emphasis upon autonomy as women's most pressing need means that sexuality rarely plays a dominant role in the self-discovery process; love relationships do not, as in the traditional *Bildungsroman*, contribute significantly to the protagonist's education. Erotic passion, by its very intensity, can sabotage the protagonist's struggle to strengthen an often precarious sense of independent identity. Lesbian relationships offer an important exception to this rule; but their significance in the text is usually determined by their narrative function in furthering the protagonist's intellectual and emotional self-understanding. Knowledge, rather than desire, is emphasized as the key to relationships between women; the other woman provides a mirror in which the protagonist discovers herself, finding her own female identity reflected: "We are doubles; when I encounter her, at the same time I encounter a part of myself."[22]

Given the rejection of the model of the heterosexual couple as a means to self-definition, the protagonist must establish alternative symbolic configurations which can provide a locus of meaning. Two motifs recur persistently in the feminist narrative: nature and the (usually all female) community. Nature is often viewed as an extension of some kind of "feminine" principle; the violation of the natural world is perceived to reflect the oppression of women, the refusal of the values of an industrialized and urbanized modernity simultaneously functions as a search for a lost female self, a return to origins. Similarly, the model of the female community offers an alternative form of intimacy grounded in gender identification. Both nature and community are perceived to complement and extend the protagonist's sense of self rather than to threaten it by absolute otherness, and thus to provide a framework within which a gendered identity can be meaningfully located.

What this self-knowledge signifies in the context of the feminist novel, the question of how gender is articulated at the level of imaginative representation, cannot be answered without a more detailed analysis of the distinctive features of the two main types of self-discovery narrative. In general, however, it can be noted that the focus upon gender as the primary marker of a subjectivity which is conceived as a source of opposition to a patriarchal society can result in a somewhat schematic distinction between the false roles imposed upon the heroine and the true self which comes to light during the course of the narrative. On the one hand, this kind of dichotomization of true and false identities serves the function of articulating resistance to dominant ideological schemata by legitimating the experience of otherness at the level of the individual subject. On the other hand, the assertion of subjective freedom can serve to obscure rather than illuminate the complex nexus of social, ideological, and psychological relations through which gender is constructed. It is as if the affirmation of female identity is felt to require at least a temporary bracketing of the multiple determinants of subjectivity that might threaten the claim to authenticity through which the narrative seeks to legitimate itself. In turn, this foregrounding of a relatively unproblematic conception of character serves to encourage processes of empathy and identification with the protagonist as a key feature of the reading process.

Consequently, the feminist self-discovery narrative tends to focus upon the process of psychological transformation rather than upon a detailed exploration of its social implications. In this sense, the resolution of the feminist narrative also functions as a beginning; the heroine's new self-knowledge creates a basis for future negotiation between the subject and society, the outcome of which is projected beyond the bounds of the text. In postulating marriage or death as the necessary conclusion of the women's text, the eighteenth-century novel confronts the question of the social possibilities available to women and answers it with an emphatic finality. The contemporary feminist novel does not usually supply any such closure, and the question of the ultimate social consequences of individual transformation is left open. The possibility of such a deferral, the fact that the protagonist is at least temporarily free to explore questions of gender identity in a space beyond immediate social constraints, is itself suggestive as an indication of the relative autonomy of ideological change in the context of a society which can no longer be conceived in terms of a monolithic and uniform structure that demands conformity or destruction of the individual. The current reality of ideological pluralism is exemplified in diverse oppositional discourses, such as feminism, which legitimate resistance and the affirmation of otherness within and against the prevailing social order. If, to offer a somewhat schematic overview, the eighteenth-century novel is unable to conceive of conscious rebellion on the part of the heroine, and the nineteenth-century novel traces an inward awakening and resistance which is, however, crushed by an intransigent social order, then the contemporary narrative of female self-discovery plots a story of resistance and survival made possible by the mediation of the women's movement, which provides an ideological framework sanctioning the self-conscious affirmation of a gendered identity, but whose ultimate effects on social structures and institutions—transformation or accommodation—remain as yet far from clear.

The Feminist Bildungsroman

The *Bildungsroman,* it has been argued, has acquired a new function in charting the changing self-consciousness of women accompanying their gradual entry into the public domain. Whereas the male *Bildungsroman* survives only as parody, or in the form of a purely inward development which renounces all social activity, women's literature has traced a trajectory in the opposite direction, "from the world within to the world without, from introspection to activity."[23]

> Women's increased sense of freedom in this century, when women's experience has begun to approach that of the traditional male *Bildungs-held,* finds expression in a variety of fictions. Although the primary assumption underlying the *Bildungsroman,*—the evolution of a coherent self—has come under attack in modernist and avant-garde fiction, this assumption remains cogent for women writers who now for the first time find themselves in a world increasingly responsive to their needs. It is no wonder, then, that the novel of development has become . . . "the most salient form of literature" for contemporary women writing about women.[24]

The contemporary narrative of female self-discovery which describes a protagonist's journey from the enclosed realm of the familial home into the social world bears obvious resemblances to the tradition of the *Bildungsroman* as a male bourgeois genre. Equally important, the specific social conditions and ideological coordinates shaping contemporary feminist literature result in significant differences; the dominant function of gender in defining identity complicates the dialectic of individual and society which underlies the *Bildungsroman* genre by introducing the notion of the female community as a mediating structure. Consequently, the narrative trajectory and thematic preoccupations of the feminist *Bildungsroman* reveal distinctive features which do not conform to the typically resigned and conciliatory stance of its literary predecessors.

Although the term *Bildungsroman* has gradually acquired a broader currency as a generic designation for those narratives which trace a process of individual self-development within society, most extended definitions and surveys of the genre have been limited to a discussion of the *Bildungsroman* as a specifically German phenomenon, depicting a "regulated development within the life of the individual," in which the immature protagonist finally comes to an acceptance of his place in the community through a reconciliation of individual and social demands.[25] The *Bildungsroman* as idea describes a process of unfolding, a harmonious and organic development of innate capacities which exemplifies a characteristically German and eighteenth-century view of education. If the category of the *Bildungsroman* is to acquire a more general taxonomical value, however, it becomes necessary to define the category broadly enough to accommodate historical and national variations and to transcend the specifically German connotations of *Bildung,* while still retaining the distinctive features of the genre as the prototypical narrative of individual development in society, which distinguishes it from related forms such as the confession or the picaresque novel.[26] For my present purposes, the *Bildungsroman* can be construed as *biographical,* assuming the existence of a coherent individual identity which constitutes the focal point of the narrative; *dialectical,* defining identity as the result of a complex interplay between psychological and social forces; *historical,* depicting identity formation as a temporal process which is represented by means of a linear and chronological narrative; and *teleological,* organizing textual signification in relation to the projected goal of the protagonist's access to self-knowledge, which will in practice be realized to a greater or lesser degree.

These criteria are met by a number of contemporary feminist novels, in which female self-discovery is depicted as a process of confrontation and dialogue with a social environment. Although the text often emphasizes internal growth and self-understanding rather than public self-realization, only by moving out into the world can the protagonist become critically aware of the limitations of her previously secluded existence and her unquestioning acceptance of the circumscribed nature of women's social roles. The protagonist of Lessing's *The Summer before the Dark,* for example, undergoes an intensive learning process in a period of a few months; moving from the settled and comfortable life of a middle-class housewife into the workplace, then experiencing a brief extramarital affair, she concludes her voyage in an anonymous London apartment, where she attempts to bring to light and examine critically the stereotypes of femininity by which her entire life has been defined. In Marge Piercy's *Fly away Home* the heroine accidentally discovers the property speculation in which her husband is involved and is drawn into a group of activists fighting to prevent the acquisition and demolition of housing by business interests. Her gradual politicization and acceptance of social responsibility is accompanied by a recognition of her own previous blindness to her husband's business activities outside the secluded idyll of family life and an increasing sense of unease within a heterosexual relationship defined by her own subordination.

The experiences undergone by the protagonist, while often difficult and painful, are presented as the necessary steps to maturation; her encounters with the outside world help to shape and define the parameters of subjectivity. External exploration both parallels and contributes to the discovery of the interior self. Individual development requires some kind of recognition of the contingency and uncertainty of experience; this form of knowledge is counterposed to the deceptive mythology of romance, the ideological fiction of idyllic married bliss which provides an already written script without space for the articulation of dissent. The heroine's move into society thus functions as an entry into historical time, into an existence defined by contingency and change, which is contrasted to the static, dreamlike atemporality of an existence structured by repetitive domestic tasks within the private sphere of the familial home. Self-understanding is portrayed as gradual and accumulative, an irreversible process of development through successive stages. The unfolding of the text is directed toward this goal of retrospective self-knowledge, and all aspects of the text gain their significance in relation to the developmental plot.

The text's historical and teleological structure engenders an ironic distance between the perspectives of narrator and protagonist, which is a defining feature of the *Bildungsroman* as genre. Unlike the Romantic feminist text, which privileges the lost innocence of the protagonist as source of authenticity, the *Bildungsroman* critically underlines her ignorance and inexperience, emphasizing the discrepancy between the heroine's insufficient interpretation of events and the narrator's own superior understanding. In Fay Weldon's *Praxis,* for example, the narrator is the heroine herself in old age, recounting her own life history while sardonically underscoring her own naiveté as a young woman, her unquestioning subordination of her desires and ambitions to those of lovers and husbands. Similarly, at the beginning of *The Summer before the Dark* an omniscient narrator predicts the course of the protagonist's future development, commenting: "By the time it was all over with, she would certainly not have chosen to have had it differently: yet she could not have chosen for herself in advance, for she did not have the experience to choose, or the imagination."[27] This disparity between the perspectives of narrator and protagonist gradually disappears during the course of the developmental narrative, the two perspectives finally converging at the conclusion of the text, which typically serves to explicitly sanction the knowledge gained by the protagonist. Thus, for example, the final words of *Praxis* serve as an indication of the ultimate success of the heroine in overcoming the sense of isolation and unreality which has characterized her earlier life and in attaining a sense of public and communal identity: "The wall which surrounded me is quite broken down. I can touch, feel, see my fellow human beings. That is quite enough."[28] The education of the protagonist is simultaneously that of the reader: the feminist *Bildungsroman* is a didactic genre which aims to convince the reader of the legitimacy of a particular interpretative framework by bringing her or him to a cumulative and retrospective understanding of the events narrated in the text.[29]

While retaining the distinctive structural features of the genre, the feminist *Bildungsroman* differs in important ways from its literary predecessors. For instance it has often been pointed out that the traditional male *Bildungsroman* is an essentially conservative genre; the hero's passionately held, if often naive ideals, are gradually worn away through encounters with the sobering forces of reality, and the conclusion signals an integration into society which necessitates a more or less resigned acceptance of the existing social order. The feminist text, however, reveals a rather different trajectory; the journey into society does not signify a surrender of ideals and a recognition of limitations, but rather constitutes the precondition for oppositional activity and engagement. One obvious reason for this upward curve traced by the feminist *Bildungsroman* is that its starting point is more unambiguously identified as negative within the framework of values established by the text. The beginning of the traditional *Bildungsroman* is clearly gender determined; the hero is free to journey into the world in his quest for self-knowledge. The situation of the contemporary female protagonist is quite different in being marked by acquiescence, dependency, and powerlessness. In *The Summer before the Dark,* for example, Kate Brown reflects upon her own history: "Looking back over nearly a quarter of a century, she saw that that had been the characteristic of her life—passivity, adaptability to others."[30] Consequently, the move from the sphere of the family into society, from the private into the public world, is a potentially far more liberating process than is the case for the male *Bildungsroman* protagonist, who possesses from the start a more confident sense of self which the heroine has to struggle painfully toward by freeing herself from the subordinate role she has occupied in the heterosexual relationship.

Whereas the male *Bildungsroman* is often defined as a novel of apprenticeship and typically depicts the childhood and early manhood of the protagonist, the feminist *Bildungsroman* thus embraces a much wider range of ages. It is often only *after* the experience of marriage that the heroine is able to see through and reject the seductive myth of romance as the key to female self-identity, so that the journey to self-discovery frequently occurs at a relatively late stage in the protagonist's life. Franco Moretti remarks that the nineteenth-century *Bildungsroman*'s concentration upon youth as the most decisive stage of a life history reveals the genre as the symbolic form of a modernity characterized by increasing mobility, instability, and impetus toward the future, even as the literary representation of this restlessness is circumscribed by the necessary impermanence of youth and the acceptance of constraints which accompanies "maturity."[31] If the *Bildungsroman* emerges in a rapidly changing society in which youth for the first time becomes problematic, its renaissance is clearly linked to the present questioning of gender categories, with all the multiple ramifications this involves for the representation of personal and social relations. Marriage, as that mark of narrative closure which exemplifies the merging of individual and social interests, is now explicitly revealed not as the endpoint of female *Bildung,* but as its very antithesis, so that female "youth"—the period of interior and exterior discovery and development—is located at quite different points within a female social biography. The goal of the protagonist's journey and the text is an identity which is more or less explicitly defined in terms of a notion of broader female community, and it is this which can be said to identify the genre as distinctively feminist.

Community and Society

The figure of a female friend or lover invariably plays a symbolically important role in the protagonist's development. This transference of allegiance from a heterosexual relationship to one of intimacy between women involves overcoming the negative value which women have been conditioned to place upon their own sex; the recognition of the other woman serves a symbolic function as an affirmation of self, of gendered identity. In Grace Bartram's *Peeling,* for example, the heroine's gradual reconciliation with an estranged daughter and acceptance of her daughter's lesbianism serves as an index of her own increasing sense of self-worth. Margot Schroeder's *Der Schlachter empfiehlt noch immer Herz* describes the protagonist's journey toward self-understanding as one of developing commitment to both political action and emotional and sexual intimacy with her friend and coworker Kathrin. And in *The Summer before the Dark* it is two female friends who are the most important guiding figures in the heroine's critical examination of the unquestioned assumptions by which her previous existence has been governed.

It is this mediating structure of the female community, whether actually present in the form of a group of women or symbolically actualized in the figure of a single female companion, which shapes the cautiously positive conclusion of the feminist *Bildungsroman,* insofar as it serves to attenuate the clash between individual ideals and oppressive social forces which typifies the novel of bourgeois individualism. On the one hand, this model of female community provides a means of access into society by linking the protagonist to a broader social group and thus rendering explicit the political basis of private experience. On the other, it also functions as a barrier against, and a refuge from, the worst effects of a potentially threatening social order by opening up a space for nonexploitative relationships grounded in common goals and interests. The feminist *Bildungsroman* thus combines the exploration of subjectivity with a dimension of group solidarity which inspires activism and resistance rather than private resignation, and makes it possible to project a visionary hope of future change: "It was a vision of community. Of the possible. Of the person merged with the group, yet still separate. Of harmony."[32]

The comfort and strength which the protagonist gains from the company of women does not simply derive from present-day feminism, but has its roots in a long-standing tradition of female friendships which emerges as an insistent theme in women's writing.[33] At the same time, however, the centrality of community in contemporary feminist literature must also be situated in relation to the self-conscious affirmation of collective identity characteristic of contemporary social movements. The notion of community emerges as an equally insistent theme in recent black writing, which explicitly relates the destiny of the individual subject to that of the group.[34] In Walker's *The Color Purple,* for example, the motifs of black and female community are closely intertwined; Celie's increasing sense of purpose and identity is accompanied by identification with such strong female figures as Shug and Sofia and simultaneously entails an acceptance of black community and ancestral roots, symbolically enacted in Nettie's voyage to Africa.

This representation of a female collectivity in the feminist narrative and indeed in feminist discourse itself typically draws upon a crucial opposition between "community" and "society" as involving qualitatively different modes of human interaction. This long-standing distinction has been elaborated and synthesized by the German sociologist Ferdinand Tönnies, whose typology of *Gemeinschaft* and *Gesellschaft* counterposes two "ideal types" of association between individuals, types manifested in varying proportions in actual social formations.[35] In *Gemeinschaft*, exemplified in its purest form in the traditional agrarian or feudal community, associations between individuals possess a strongly personal dimension and are grounded in shared interests and traditions, bonds of kinship or friendship, or other meaningful symbolic ties which generate a sense of collective communal identity. By contrast *Gesellschaft*, as the type of association governed by rational will, is most clearly exemplified in the division of labor and differentiation of society which develops under capitalism; human relations for the most part no longer possess a meaningful collective basis, but are fundamentally alienated and abstract, subordinated to instrumental and quantitative goals.

Whatever the ultimate analytical value of such a distinction, some form of polemical opposition between an alienated *Gesellschaft* and a vision of harmonious community grounded in nonexploitative relations has inspired a number of oppositional political movements, including anarchism and utopian socialism. Elements of this distinction reemerge within contemporary feminist literature and culture, which assume that relations between women can attenuate, and in the more naive versions transcend, the iron cage of a modernity now explicitly defined as not only capitalist but fundamentally androcentric in both its ideologies and its institutions. The appeal to an ideal of "sisterhood" envisages the possibility that social relations between women may imitate kinship relations, forging personal bonds which may serve to challenge the instrumental rationality of social relations in a male-defined public sphere. Such models of female community do not simply function as a utopian vision projected into an unforeseeable future, but are perceived as a potential reality within the present social order, prefigured in the feminist narrative in the dominant role of women in the protagonist's development. In other words, *Gemeinschaft* is located within *Gesellschaft*, not merely in the form of a defensive enclave, but as an oppositional community which seeks to challenge and alter the basis of existing social values.

The feminist *Bildungsroman* thus narrates a story of development toward coherent selfhood through a process of moving into a wider community. Its temporal structuring of narrative reveals an essentially optimistic view of history as progressive emancipation, charting a process of learning through dialogue with and engagement in society. In this sense, it can be suggested that the genre charts women's movement into the urban and public spaces of a modernity from which they have been excluded. Integration does not, however, necessarily signify reconciliation, and the move outward into society can assume more or less radical contours. Unlike bourgeois enlightenment, feminism does not perceive itself as representing all humanity, but retains an emphasis upon the particularity of female experiences and interests. Women's relationship to society is thus mediated by a female community which allows for both integration and separation, which enables public activity yet asserts the irreducible reality of gender difference.

The resulting interactions and antagonisms between the values of female community and the structures and norms of a larger, male-defined society emerge as a defining feature of the feminist *Bildungsroman* as genre, with significant variations apparent in the degree of emphasis given to either one or the other side of this dialectic. In the United States, where liberal feminism has acquired a relatively broad basis of support, the feminist novel frequently integrates a narrative of individual self-development into a panoramic representation of the broader social world. In both *The Women's Room* and *Small Changes,* for example, 1968 is an important year; the fate of the female protagonist and of the community of women is intimately interwoven with the broader political conflicts and social upheavals of the late sixties and seventies. This realist spatiotemporal dimension is lacking in the German feminist *Bildungsroman,* in which society as a whole tends to remain an abstraction, a shadowy authoritarian force with which dialogue is scarcely possible. The women's movement in Germany has been particularly closely identified with a distinctive student and alternative subculture, and this is reflected in the feminist novel, which rarely goes beyond the confines of an idealized female community in which the protagonist can develop. Within its boundaries, the protagonist's oppositional radicalism remains uncompromised, but at the expense of any sustained exploration of the interrelations and interactions between feminism and the rest of society.[36]

The Novel of Awakening

Not all narratives of female self-discovery conform to the *Bildungsroman* model; some texts trace a voyage inward rather than outward, in search of a hidden female self. Self-discovery is not portrayed as a historical process, but takes the form of an abrupt and visionary apprehension of underlying unity which leads to an overcoming of ironic and alienated self-consciousness. The conceptualization of female identity as an essence to be recovered rather than a goal to be worked toward is reflected in a literary structure which foregrounds the symbolic and lyrical dimension of the text rather than the chronological development of narrative.

Whereas the *Bildungsroman* depicts the shift from the confines of the domestic sphere into the public world as an emancipatory, if often problematic process, what I term the "novel of awakening" is grounded in a moral and aesthetic revulsion against the very nature of contemporary social reality, which is perceived as alienating and debased.[37] It is not social integration which is the heroine's goal, but the recovery of a qualitatively different sense of self. Some form of symbolic or literal departure from society is the precondition for the attainment of a meaningful identity, which requires a radical rupture with the heroine's past history and with established modes of perception. The voyage undertaken by the protagonist is primarily an individual and interior one which puts her in touch with a lost sense of self, although, as in the *Bildungsroman,* this quest often possesses a communal dimension.

The protagonist of *Gaining Ground,* for instance, suddenly chooses to abandon her previous life and to leave her family in order to live a solitary existence in the Canadian wilderness, where she undergoes a gradual process of spiritual regeneration. After nine years of solitude, she is confronted by her daughter, who attempts to bring her back to civilization; she refuses. The break between self and world is absolute; the heroine cannot risk jeopardizing her new sense of peace by returning to the modern world. *Häutungen* depicts a similar act of withdrawal as the protagonist moves from male to female lovers into final isolation. Having ventured into the world, she encounters only male aggression; social interaction brings about not learning and enrichment but only compromise and alienation: "The further I ventured out into the world, the older I became, the more I lost myself."[38] The heroine's response is a retreat into the self; the final pages of the text describe a woman absorbed in the changes in her own body, oblivious to the outside world, lost in an almost autistic introversion.

The withdrawal from society may, however, be explicitly acknowledged as temporary; as outsiders, women must first search elsewhere for the symbolic identity which will enable them to participate in the social world. In *Surfacing* the heroine, returning to the Canadian wilderness of her childhood, is remote, alienated, deprived of the ability to feel: "At some point my neck must have closed over, pond freezing or a wound, shutting me into my head; since then, everything has been glancing off me."[39] Remaining alone in the wilderness after her companions have departed, she ritually sacrifices her clothes and possessions, tokens of a civilization which she must renounce, and immerses herself in the natural world, experiencing a mystic vision of her dead mother as herald of sacred truths. But the text ends with the protagonist's decision to return to the city and her lover, recognizing that withdrawal does not constitute a meaningful option: "This above all, to refuse to be a victim. Unless I can do that, I can do nothing."[40] There can be no return to a naive mythic state of being, merely a brief illumination, a moment of intense feeling which can call into question the all-pervasiveness of ironic consciousness. "No gods to help me now, they're questionable once more, theoretical as Jesus. They've receded, back to the past, inside the skull, is it the same place . . . from now on I'll have to live in the usual way, defining them by their absence."[41]

This kind of self-discovery narrative is clearly modeled on the conventions of the romance quest;[42] the protagonist moves away from a corrupt society, undergoes some form of powerful transfiguration or illumination of consciousness in exceptional circumstances, and must decide whether or not to return to the community to pass on this knowledge. In all cases, however, self-discovery, whatever its ultimate consequences, is represented as a coming to consciousness of a latent female self. Identity is not a goal to be worked toward, as in the *Bildungsroman,* but a point of origin, an authentic and whole subjectivity from which the protagonist has become estranged; the protagonist's journey is a circular one in which the destination coincides with the starting point. It is thus not *irony* which characterizes the text, but *nostalgia.*[43]

This discovery of female self can best be described as a process of awakening rather than learning, a recovery of what has always been present but suppressed. Awakening is of course a purely inward and individual experience, not a social and public act; unlike the notion of *Bildung,* as a gradual development over time, it marks a circumscribed moment, a threshold between two states. The protagonist's transfor-

Banana Bottom is an awakening novel ✓

mation of consciousness is often depicted as a mysterious, unforesee-able, cataclysmic experience, a sudden illumination unmotivated by past events. The protagonist of *Gaining Ground* experiences a mystical certainty: "This was the ending, here. Like driving head-on into a brick wall, knowing it was over, reduced to the core of person that does not think or know, no chance given for regret or sorrow or second thoughts, in the brilliant last moment."[44] Awakening thus signifies a disjunctive moment, a shift from one mode of being into a radically altered one; the metaphorical transition from a sleeping to a waking state, also described in terms of death and rebirth, reveals a discontinuous model of experience which evokes an explicit contrast between alienation and authenticity. In *Gaining Ground* the heroine refers to the death of her old self, "there was no past here";[45] the protagonist of *Praisesong for the Widow* awakes from uneasy dreams, "like a slate that had been wiped clean, a *tabula rasa* upon which a whole new history could be written."[46] Often, the experience of dreams and hallucinations symbolizes the disorientation of the hero-ine, the undermining of her established value systems and conceptions of reality which marks the transition from one stage of consciousness to another. The repudiation of past history—the heroine's previous social and public existence—is portrayed as an absolute one, often symbolically expressed through some form of ritual purification in which the heroine strips herself of the clothing and possessions which represent her "civilized" self.

This refusal of history in turn influences the structure of the literary text, in which the historical and chronological dimension of narrative is subordinated to the delineation of symbolic space. The text is concerned less with a detailed representation of a social environment than with the evocation of a symbolic realm which echoes and affirms the subject's inner being. In *Gaining Ground,* for example, the harmonious and ordered rhythms of nature function as a mirror for the heroine's newly acquired sense of inner peace, even as this is subjectively experienced as a loss of self, a mystical immersion in the greater unity of nature. In *Häutungen* metaphors of inner space play an important role; the heroine's progressive withdrawal into the refuge of her room is echoed by her preoccupation with the inner cavities of her own body. The womb as both source and center echoes the text's central metaphor of "shedding" surface layers to find an authentic inner self. And the island of Carriacou, which concludes the protag-onist's journey in *Praisesong for the Widow*, is explicitly acknowledged as the symbolic goal of her journey toward black identity rather than a geographical reality: "Everything fleeting and ephemeral. The island more of a mirage than an actual place. Something conjured up perhaps to satisfy a longing and need."[47]

Recovering the Lost Paradise: Romantic Topoi in Feminist Literature

It is evident that this kind of self-discovery narrative reveals a clear debt to Romanticism in its structures and themes. Discussing the recent resurgence of Romantic elements within contemporary culture, Robert Sayre and Michael Löwy summarize their import as follows: "The Romantic vision is characterized by the painful conviction that present reality lacks certain essential human values, values which have been 'alienated' . . . The nostalgia for paradise lost is most often accompanied by a *quest for what has been lost* . . . the phenomenon involves an active response, an attempt to rediscover or recreate the lost paradise."[48] The temporal structure underlying Romanticism is shaped by the myth of the Fall; the condition of humanity is perceived as a degeneration from an original state of innocence and spiritual grace. A nostalgic vision of an authentic subjectivity opposed to and subversive of the norms and values of modern social existence is strongly in evidence in the novel of awakening, which typically contains a number of explicitly Romantic motifs.

The historical present is invariably represented in a critical light as a society governed by materialist and rationalist values; civilization, technology, urban culture are counterposed against the sphere of nature as a potential site of spiritual regeneration. This conception of nature is itself of course the cultural product of an industrialized and urbanized society, which creates an idealized image of the natural world onto which it projects its fantasies of an organic, harmonious, and nonalienated existence. In *Surfacing* the protagonist, seeking salvation in the wilderness, encounters hunters from the city, intruders violating the countryside. Her own companions, self-styled radicals who have rejected their families and their past, appear false and superficial, their pseudosophistication concealing an inner emptiness and inability to feel. "How did we get bad?"[49] she asks, and writes of people, "They are evolving, they are halfway to machine, the leftover flesh atrophied and diseased, porous like an appendix."[50]

It is only her inarticulate lover who offers any hope for the future: "What will preserve him is the absence of words."[51] In *Praisesong for the Widow* wealthy black widow Avey Johnson comes to recognize the spiritual impoverishment of an existence lived in accordance with the values of a white male-dominated society. Abandoning the luxurious cruise ship on which she has been taking a Caribbean holiday, she is drawn to join a large group of islanders who are returning home to celebrate a tribal festival. The violent sickness which overcomes her in a primitive boat on the rough seas acts as a symbolic purging of her own uncritical acceptance of the materialism of American society and her denial of black roots, of community and spirituality.

Redemption, then, requires some form of refusal of modern civilization, which is realized on a subjective level in an attempt to transcend the bifurcated nature of modern consciousness: "I'd allowed myself to be cut in two . . . I was the wrong half, detached, terminal. I was nothing but a head, or no, something minor like a severed thumb; numb."[52] *Gaining Ground* traces the protagonist's overcoming of ironic self-consciousness and the acquisition of a sense of harmony in which the world and self are experienced as one: "I was wholly the sensation."[53] The heroine's new "faith" is portrayed as an instinctive and fatalistic conviction which is impervious to rational argumentation. Similarly, the spiritual regeneration of the protagonist of *Surfacing* takes place after the "failure of logic." "From any rational point of view I am absurd; but there are no longer any rational points of view."[54] Female self-discovery is frequently portrayed as the surrender of the veneer of civilization and the rediscovery of "natural" instincts: "I tried for all those years to be civilized but I'm not and I'm through pretending."[55] "I did not think. I sensed and then I acted . . . The instincts . . . could not be wrong."[56] In this Romantic reaction against culture, childhood often functions as a symbol of a lost innocence and spontaneity which women must seek to regain. *Häutungen* associates the erotic pleasure of childhood with a vision of the creation of the world, an image of unself-conscious sensuality, which is contrasted to the anxiety and alienation typical of the protagonist's adult heterosexual experiences. And in *Surfacing* the protagonist's unborn child embodies her hopes for the future: "I can feel my lost child surfacing within me . . . I will never teach it any words."[57]

The recurring suspicion of language as a deceptive and corrupting medium reflects this nostalgic yearning for a prelapsarian innocence;

by its very nature, language fragments and distorts, threatening the unity and immediacy to which the heroine aspires. "In telling it I would lose it. And in any case I would not find the words."[58] Speaking is necessarily a compromise, a betrayal of self: "The animals have no need for speech, why talk when you are a word?"[59] Speechlessness thus often operates as an index of authenticity and as a refusal of the compromised world of social communication; the heroine's silence is intended to convey the intense and complex nature of female subjectivity, which is contrasted to the glib eloquence of the male. "His eloquence hinders me. I hear didactic torrents of words in a language which will never be sufficient for my concerns."[60]

Underlying these Romantic motifs is the desire to escape the burden of historical consciousness by means of a return to some kind of mythic apprehension of being. A conception of time as circular and repetitive, in tune with the rhythms of the natural world, is expressed in *Gaining Ground:* "My days and seasons have spun gently, unbroken, no time, only rhythm. I am rooted in a moment, and in a pattern of moments."[61] Unlike the *Bildungsroman,* the Romantic feminist text denies the relevance for women of a model of history as progress and development. Instead, history is identified with the negative aspects of a modernity predicated upon abstract rationality and a repressive logic of identity and sameness. Thus "everything from history must be eliminated" before the protagonist of *Surfacing* is ready to apprehend sacred and spiritual truths;[62] mythic and nonrational consciousness is perceived to constitute the only appropriate modality for a "feminine" identity which has been excluded from public history.

The motifs sketched out above are not of course confined to literary texts, but reflect a more general resurgence of Romantic ideologies within Western societies in recent years. In the context of the women's movement, they are most clearly exemplified in "cultural feminism," which has been associated in the English-speaking world with such authors as Susan Griffin, Adrienne Rich, and Mary Daly. Their writings reveal a similar dichotomization of nature and culture which relies on a notion of authentic female being and which frequently appeals to a narrative of femininity as a fall from grace, exemplified in the nostalgic vision of a matriarchy of the distant past as a lost golden age. In Griffin's *Women and Nature,* for example, the pseudo-objectivity of a male discourse identified with the domination of science and rationality in Western societies is counterposed against the lyrical voices of women and nature speaking in unison. Similarly, Rich expresses a Romantically inspired view of an authentic female experience underlying patriarchal ideology and articulates the same rejection of the mind-body split as a product of male dualistic thought.[63] Such arguments typically embroil themselves in logical contradictions; the very critique of the nature-culture opposition as a product of patriarchal thought itself invokes and reinforces such oppositions through its appeals to a kind of substratum of female identity below the veneer of patriarchal conditioning.[64]

I have already argued that Romantic feminism is both theoretically naive as an account of and explanation for women's oppression and politically unsatisfactory in its celebration of an ideology of the feminine and a withdrawal into a women's sphere. Nevertheless, simply to dismiss its stance as reactionary or essentialist is to fail to engage with the Romantic feminist position and to consider its broader social significance. Griffin, Dworkin, Daly, and Rich are among the most influential of contemporary feminist writers, and may cater to needs which socialist feminism, for example, should consider more seriously, even if it does not necessarily consent to the particular means by which they are articulated. While as a political and theoretical account of gender relations cultural feminism is problematic, as a poetic discourse it gives voice to a powerful experience of cultural dislocation. The Romantic feminist vision is the product of a psychological and aesthetic (rather than political) conception of liberation, less concerned with strategic means for ending the oppression of women than with expressing a paradisal longing for harmony fueled by a revulsion against the conditions of life under contemporary capitalism.

It is the Romantic feminist text, whether in the form of fiction or essayistic prose, which has expressed the most forceful condemnation of existing social values, going beyond issues of political and economic equality to renew the questioning of the very basis of contemporary ideologies of modernity and progress. The longing for unity and wholeness which emerges as a recurring theme in feminist literature, while often expressed in rather naive terms, springs from a perception of the destructive effects of social fragmentation and erosion of community. The Romantic desire for a harmonious relationship between humanity and nature reemerges as a highly relevant and by no means outdated theme as the potentially catastrophic effects of ideologies of progress which have unleashed uncontrolled technological and industrial development have become increasingly apparent. Similarly, the affirmation of gendered identity and the reappraisal of the value of myth and tradition need to be

148

understood as one form of critical response to the erosion of cultural ✓
identities by the universalizing logic of a capitalist consumer culture.

The concern with subjectivity, spirituality, and myth which
emerges as a significant dimension within feminist literature and
culture cannot therefore be unconditionally dismissed as "regressive,"
but calls attention to needs which have been suppressed by prevailing
ideologies of modernity and progress and which socialist politics has
typically failed to address. But the means by which these needs are
articulated are often politically ambivalent. Thus the feminist protest
against social fragmentation and the breakdown of community, the
objectification of women as sexual commodities, the purposeless
dynamic of technological change, springs from a deep dissatisfaction
with existing social conditions yet can easily result in a false reconciliation of existing contradictions through a mystification of femininity and an uncritical celebration of irrationalism, which has
strongly conservative implications.

In this context, a more detailed consideration of individual texts
would be necessary to specify more precisely their political significance. Gender is not the only relevant issue here; the critique of
social values is also influenced by quite specific national and cultural
contexts. In the Canadian novel, for example, the nature-culture
opposition serves to demarcate national as well as gender boundaries;
the celebration of wilderness, of "nature as monster" in *Surfacing* and
Gaining Ground, can also be read as the celebration of a distinctive
cultural identity in the face of the homogenizing and imperialistic
tendencies of an American culture which is identified with the most
negative aspects of modernity. Sherrill Grace has traced the preoccupation with wilderness as a distinctive theme in recent Canadian
women's writing which grows out of a long-standing fascination
with the representation of landscape in the Canadian literary
tradition.[65] Similarly, a text such as *Häutungen* reveals the clear
influence of a tradition of German idealism in its celebration of female
subjectivity as a withdrawal into inwardness. As Marlis Gerhardt
points out, "Verena Stefan . . . communicates . . . an ideological
message which is deeply rooted in the tradition of German irrationalism. Characteristic of this is e.g., the flight from society, the
retreat to 'Mother Nature' and the idea of a non-theoretical, 'unmediated knowledge.' "[66] The celebration of authentic inwardness in
German feminism forms part of a more general post-1968 cultural
shift within West German literature toward a concentration upon
emotion, spirituality, and subjective identity, a concentration

strongly in evidence in the work of both female and male writers.[67] In contrast to this Romantic individualism, which refuses the social world, the celebration of spirituality in contemporary Afro-American writing often contains a strongly collective and activist dimension, as in *Praisesong for the Widow,* where the protagonist's enlightenment places her under an obligation to pass on the sacred truths she has discovered to the community as a whole, in particular to those young blacks who seek to conform to all aspects of the dominant white culture, "unprotected, lacking memory and a necessary distance of mind."[68]

The Status of Female Identity

The main types of feminist self-discovery narrative which I have discussed offer clear points of comparison with the conflicting tendencies underlying oppositional movements: on the one hand, a desire for integration and participation within a larger social and public community as a means of overcoming a condition of marginalization and powerlessness, on the other, an insistence upon a qualitative difference of cultural perspective as a means of articulating a radical challenge to dominant values and institutions, a stress on difference which resists assimilation into the mainstream of social life. This hesitation between alternative models of liberation is rendered more acute in the context of feminism by the historical location of women within the private sphere, resulting in prevailing ideologies of femininity as the sphere of otherness, of antireason and anticulture, which continue to exercise a powerful influence upon feminists and nonfeminists alike. Hence, as Kristeva points out, the development of the women's movement has been shaped by two distinct paradigms or temporal modalities: first, the insertion of women into history through identification with and participation in the public and social sphere, and second, a refusal of linear temporality, a distrust of the political domain and a preoccupation with giving symbolic realization to the specificity of feminine psychology as irreducible difference.[69]

In all cases, however, the feminist self-discovery narrative represents a concern with questions of identity and autonomous selfhood, tracing a distinctive plot which marks out some form of movement from alienation and lack to self-knowledge and a potential for self-determination. It does not content itself with a negative critique of existing gender relations and representations of women, but maps out an alternative vision of female identity. In this sense, it could be argued that the feminist narrative offers an imaginary resolution of real contradictions, in which the diverse social and ideological problems facing women in capitalist and patriarchal society are harmonized and smoothed over on the level of biographical narrative in the protagonist's attainment of a meaningful identity.

Of course, important differences are apparent in the degree of closure offered by the text. In some instances the narrative and poetic structure of the literary work is subordinated to a relatively schematic, didactic, and dualistic account of gender relations which traces an unambiguous trajectory from oppression to autonomy. In other texts the heroine's access to self-knowledge is more tentatively portrayed in such a manner as to suggest the elusive and problematic status of identity. The self-discovery genre as such, however, retains an essentially optimistic belief in the possibility of female development, even if the continuing infringement of broader social and cultural constraints upon women's lives does not necessarily allow for an unproblematically harmonious conclusion to the text. Literature can be seen in this context as regaining an affirmative function, not in the sense of serving as an apology for or legitimation of existing social relations, but in being used by women as a means of creating symbolic fictions of women's survival and resistance which clearly possess an inspiratory and exemplary status. The feminist self-discovery narrative is not interested in the issue of the fictionality of literary representation as such, but seeks to negate the cultural authority of one version of women's experience in order to put alternative versions in its place. While rejecting the atomized individualism of the bourgeois literary tradition, it proceeds from the assumption that autonomous selfhood is not an outmoded fiction but still a pressing political concern.

How a critic chooses to read such texts is ultimately a political question; like any text, the feminist narrative can be read in two ways, in terms of what it makes possible, and what it serves to obscure. From a traditional Marxist position, for example, which assumes the primacy of class conflict and economic relations of production as the means by which the real is ultimately constituted, feminist literature may be viewed as an ideological phenomenon which substitutes a false resolution of fundamental economic and social contradictions on a psychological and subjective level, thus serving an essentially conservative function. If one proceeds from the

151

assumption, as I have done, that the present struggles for representation and self-determination in the public sphere on the part of women and other oppressed groups are politically important and cannot be reduced to a function of the self-reproduction of capital, then the enabling function of feminist literature as a means to constituting alternative accounts of female identity moves into the foreground of analysis. The focus upon subjective self-transformation can be seen in this context to echo the emphasis of the women's movement on the necessity of changing consciousness through individual recognition of the all-pervasive nature of female subordination, with the consequent reconceptualization of the spheres of culture, ideology, and literature as relatively autonomous sites of struggle and resistance. Insofar as narrative constitutes one of the most important ways in which ideologies are concretized in relation to life experience, the emergence of new plots for women which emphasize autonomy rather than dependence is to be welcomed as an indication of the influence of feminism upon the cultural and ideological domain. This is not to deny the validity of aspects of the Marxist critique; one can note, for example, the class-blindness of almost the entire body of feminist literature, the discrepancy between its subjective perception of addressing the needs of all women and a model of emancipation which is for the most part restricted to an educated middle class.

The importance of subjectivity, identity, and narrative in feminist fiction in turn raises a number of more general questions about the politics of literature and the insufficiency of sterile dichotomies—of realism versus experimentalism, identity versus negativity, tradition versus modernity—which have long structured oppositional thinking about cultural practices and in which the second term is unconditionally privileged over the first. The example of feminist literature suggests that the cultural needs of subordinate groups cannot be adequately grasped by continuing to think in terms of such antithetical dualisms. Thus the reemergence and renewal of the *Bildungsroman* as a literary structure relevant to women's current experiences in relation to the politics of feminism calls into question avant-garde typologies of literary form which have simply dismissed realism as anachronistic. Similarly, the current resurgence of Romanticism is to be grasped not merely as a regressive yearning for an idealized past (although elements of such a tendency are obviously apparent) but also as a critical exposure of and response to the hegemony of a dominant modernist culture which has fetishized constant innovation and change and has effectively repressed all considerations of questions of community, tradition, and symbolic identity. The point here is not to argue that it is either possible or desirable to return to the moral or epistemological certainties of a past age, but to develop an alternative account of feminist literature and culture which is able to explain the function of identity and affirmation as well as negativity and critique in the development of an oppositional feminist culture.

CHAPTER FIVE ✍

Politics, Aesthetics, and the Feminist Public Sphere

The preceding analysis of an important body of recent feminist writing provides a basis for returning to a consideration of the broader question of the relationship between aesthetics and feminist politics. Rather than collapsing literary signification into a function of a purely pragmatic and instrumental political aesthetic, I will argue for a more dialectical position which acknowledges both the interrelations and the tensions between literature and feminist politics. A critical reconsideration of the debate between realism and modernism suggests that the myth of a revolutionary modernism is crucially dependent upon the prior assumption of a monolithic ruling ideology permeating all aspects of social life with which realism is presumed to be complicit. The uncoupling of feminist discussion about "textual politics" from such a long-standing and reified opposition opens the way to an alternative politics of the text which can critically address the emancipatory potential of a range of cultural forms in relation to the historical emergence of a feminist counterpublic sphere.

Two particularly significant insights have emerged from the investigation of feminist literature. First, I have suggested that the construction of symbolic fictions constitutes an important moment in the self-definition of an oppositional feminist community. Behind the current preoccupation with autobiographical writing lies a legitimate concern with exploring questions of personal and gender identity, and here realist forms have been extensively drawn upon to develop new woman-centered narratives which have challenged the traditional emplotment of women's lives. Subjectivity and narrative emerge as key elements of current feminist literary practice, enabling fictions which have been instrumental in the development of an oppositional feminist culture. Second, it has become apparent that the process of identity formation in feminist literature is crucially indebted to a concept of community. The individual subject is viewed in relation to and as a representative of a gendered collective which self-consciously defines itself against society as a whole. Feminist literature thus reappropriates some of the concerns first addressed by bourgeois subjectivity while rejecting both its individualism and its belief in the universality of male bourgeois experience.

On an aesthetic level, the predominance of realism in contemporary women's writing suggests the need for a reconsideration of models of literary history grounded in a progressive periodization of literary forms. The assumption that modernism is more "advanced" than realism, or that a parodistic "postmodernist" style of art has in its turn rendered modernism obsolete, becomes more difficult to uphold if the actual diversity of literary and artistic styles presently employed by different groups is taken into account. The current plurality of feminist artistic practices calls into question the ideology of modernism, which privileges the "revolutionary" nature of experimental innovation as a revolt against tradition.

The preference for realism and representation over an aesthetics of negativity in much of contemporary women's writing must itself be situated in relation to the reemergence of feminism as a political movement and women's affirmation of a collective gendered identity as a positive term in which to ground an aesthetic practice. At this point it becomes necessary to offer a more specific account of the constitution of this oppositional community by moving outside the literary text to an examination of its actual status and significance as an ideological and social formation. The category of a feminist counter-public sphere provides a useful means to theorizing the existence of an oppositional discursive space within contemporary society grounded in gender politics, making it possible to examine the mechanisms by which this collectivity is constituted, its political implications and effects, as well as its potential limitations. If, on the one hand, this feminist public sphere has exercised an important influence upon changing conceptions of the relationship between aesthetics and politics, on the other hand it is itself conditioned by and dependent upon the broader network of ideological relations and social structures within which it has emerged.

Realism, Modernism, and the "Death of the Avant-Garde"

It was argued earlier that no convincing case has yet been made for a gendered aesthetics, for the assertion that men and women write in distinctively different ways or that certain styles or structures in literature and art can be classified as inherently masculine or feminine. A feminist theory of art, then, must necessarily proceed differently, by showing how the general question of the range and potential of artistic forms in contemporary society can be related to the specific concerns of a feminist politics. Critics have often assumed that, even if experimental art cannot be described as "feminine" in any meaningful sense, it nevertheless constitutes the most appropriate because most subversive form of feminist cultural activity. They have seen the radicalism of artistic experimentation as providing the necessary corollary to a progressive politics through its subversion of existing structures of representation which are taken over unquestioned into the realist text.

The polarization of realism and modernism has been particularly pronounced in recent debates in English cultural studies. One influential source has been Barthes's distinction between the "readerly" and the "writerly" text. This distinction sets up a dichotomy between realist forms, which are passively consumed by the reader, and experimental forms, which problematize signification and involve the reader's active cooperation in the construction of meaning.[1] Another influence has been the Althusserian theory of the subject as interpellated within ideology, which has inspired a hostility toward realism and a celebration of modernist texts that foreground their own conventional status and thus by implication the constructed nature of reality.[2] Irrespective of actual content, the realist novel is perceived to be irredeemably compromised; it generates the illusion of transparency, of showing things as they really are, rather than drawing attention to its own signifying practice and the workings of ideology in the construction of meaning and the unified subject. Thus Colin MacCabe states, "The classic realist text cannot deal with the real in its contradiction because of the unquestioned status of the representation at the level of the dominant discourse."[3]

This critique of realist narrative as a form which conceals its own ideological status by presenting itself as a mirror of reality has gained wide-spread support; Catherine Belsey asserts that realism "is a

156

predominantly conservative form,"[4] while Rosalind Coward, considering the question of what constitutes a feminist novel, argues: "Nor can we say that the structures of the realist novel are neutral and that they can just be filled with a feminist content."[5] The development of a feminist antirealist aesthetic has been significantly encouraged by the already noted influence of Lacan and Derrida; the function of a feminist art is perceived as primarily negative and subversive, a critical dismantling of existing ideological and discursive positions. Consequently a "conservative" realism is counterposed against a "radical" modernist or avant-garde art, which is perceived to challenge rather than affirm dominant modes of representation.

This assertion that modernist art can be counterposed to realism as a more advanced form which disrupts ideological closures initially appears plausible but on closer examination reveals a number of problems which make it a tenuous basis for the development of a feminist cultural politics. To begin with, the proposition that realism is a "closed" form which imposes single and transparent meanings upon the reader, in which, as MacCabe argues, "everything becomes obvious,"[6] can easily be challenged by pointing to the large numbers of realist texts—including an entire canon of nineteenth-century European and American novels—which continue to generate an inexhaustible supply of different and often highly contradictory readings. Polemically, one could in fact argue that realist works may allow for a *greater* richness and diversity of interpretation than modern experimental texts, which are interpreted with monotonous regularity as metalinguistic propositions about the impossibility of representation.

What is ignored here is that distinctions between texts are not merely constituted through stylistic differences—experimental versus nonexperimental language—but are fundamentally determined by difference of social function as constituted in the context of reception. As Pierre Macherey points out, "The writer's language is new, not in its material form, but in its use";[7] it is in being read *as literature* that the formal dimension of the text emerges as the primary object of the reader's attention, allowing for a receptivity to its potential ambiguities and indeterminacies which makes possible multiple rereadings. It is, in other words, because of the prior existence of prevailing conceptions of the autonomy of literature and art that certain texts are understood to contain a formally mediated distance to the ideological positions which they represent, not because of the uniquely privileged status of any single linguistic or artistic form as such. Consequently, an analysis of the socially constructed category of art must play a crucial role in attempting to assess the question of the relationship between aesthetic form and political effect as it relates to the specific problem of a feminist aesthetics. While on the one hand modern literary texts freely subvert norms of communication and standardized codes of representation, on the other hand this capacity cannot be automatically hailed as subversive if it has itself become established as a typical feature of modern art which may bear little relationship to the reader's experiences outside the text. Both realism and modernism are aesthetic *conventions,* and as such need to be situated in relation to the mediating frameworks and ideological assumptions governing the reception of literature and art in modern society.

From this perspective it is possible to indicate some of the difficulties which arise from a privileging of modernism as the foundation for a political aesthetic. A sociological critique would center on the failure to deal with art and literature as socially constructed "frames" which mediate the response to a particular text. The modernist view of art as the self-problematization of signification is itself grounded in a particular historical development; conceptions of the specificity of literature whereby the formal properties of the literary text negate, transcend, deconstruct, or otherwise relativize its content are the product of the modern understanding of art and need to be examined in relation to the ideological functions which they serve. Although the relative autonomy of literature, as exemplified in its freedom from everyday linguistic constraints, may potentially serve a critical function in defamiliarizing or relativizing fixed ideological positions, this function is often gained at the cost of a mystification of the experimental text as an esoteric site of subversive impulses. Thus entire academic industries are based upon the exegesis of modern art, which acquires an enigmatic aura that can be deciphered only by the expert: "In a way analogous to religion, the work of art alludes mysteriously to a superior but now essentially opaque and unknowable order."[8] A feminist aesthetic theory, then, must take into account this institutionalized status of art as exemplified in existing ideological and discursive frameworks. How does this privileged status of the text influence the potential social effect of any particular work? Can a comprehensive politics of the text be grounded in a hypostatization of a modernist aesthetic which draws attention to the polysemic nature of linguistic signifiers but which at the same time, in Lunn's phase, remains at "an excessive distance in its esotericism from the vital and mundane problems of the nonintellectual population"?[9]

From a historical perspective, it can be argued that while modernism, and indeed realism itself, once posed a challenge to existing aesthetic conventions, the "revolutionary" effects of changes in formal techniques grow ever more short-lived. As previously noted, theorists such as Kristeva, who proclaim the subversive power of formal experimentation, fail to consider that the breaking of conventions itself becomes conventional, and the shock effect of any challenge to existing structures of representation is necessarily of limited duration. No form of art can hope to escape the constraints of signification; the text's defamiliarizing effect is inevitably exhausted as it in turn comes to embody the new aesthetic norm at the level of both production and reception. Peter Bürger has argued that the historical avant-garde of the early twentieth century (Dada, surrealism, Russian constructivism) signaled a fundamental caesura in this historical succession of aesthetic styles by its iconoclastic protest in the form of a disruptive and nihilistic "anti-art," which sought to demystify the aura of the artwork as a privileged repository of cultural meaning. This protest was, however, ultimately unsuccessful; rather than dismantling the category of the aesthetic, the works of the avant-garde in turn became venerated exhibits in the museum and were assimilated into the infinitely flexible "institution of art."[10] Contemporary art can only either repeat these acts of provocation—which have now become ritualized forms of transgression that no longer shock by their novelty—or reappropriate and recombine more traditional forms; neither option appears in itself to offer a convincing solution to the problem of a revolutionary aesthetic in a post–avant-garde era. Bürger's analysis is intended as a rebuttal of the Marxist aesthetics of Lukács and Adorno: the belief that the modernist work constitutes the most advanced state of artistic development (Adorno) is merely the mirror image of the Lukácsian understanding of modernist art as decadence. In a post–avant-garde era, however, it is no longer possible to attribute a fixed political meaning to any particular aesthetic style. The neutralization of the protest of the avant-garde makes it clear that the problem of the political ineffectiveness of art cannot be overcome by developing a more "revolutionary" style, but is conditioned by prevailing ideologies of reception resulting from the separation of art from social life in bourgeois society. The possibility of a normative political aesthetic, the belief that certain artistic forms are inherently more radical than others, is thus invalidated and needs to be replaced by a sociologically based analysis of the reception of artworks in relation to specific audiences.[11] This question of reception emerges as the crucial issue in theorizing the distinctive features of feminist culture, whose importance lies not in the development of uniquely "feminine" or "subversive" styles of art, but rather in its effectivity in engendering a relatively widespread and influential politicization of processes of reception as well as production which has affected the reading of both avant-garde and more popular texts.

Bürger's account is one significant example of the increasing dissatisfaction with theories of "revolutionary" art permeating contemporary Western societies: "The familiar ideas of what constitutes a critical art . . . have lost much of their explanatory and normative power in recent decades."[12] One reason for this increasing skepticism regarding the relationship between aesthetic and political innovation may be, as Bürger's analysis suggests, a growing sense of the "death of the avant-garde," the ease with which the iconoclastic gestures of experimental art appear to have been accepted and neutralized within the cultural institutions of modern society. The belief in the oppositional function of experimental aesthetic strategies is further undermined by the absorption of many of these techniques into contemporary mass culture forms. The avant-garde celebration of the new as the most advanced can be seen in this context merely to echo the fetishization of novelty and fashion which is the hallmark of a capitalist consumer culture built upon constant innovation and instant obsolescence. As Andreas Huyssen suggests, the theory of a subversive textual politics reveals an overemphasis on the transgressive function of the experimental text in modern society: "To insist on the adversary function of *écriture* and of breaking linguistic codes when every second ad bristles with domesticated avantgardist and modernist strategies strikes me as caught precisely in that very overestimation of art's transformative *function* for society which is the signature of an earlier, modernist, age."[13] The celebration of a fragmented, pleasure-oriented textuality may in this context merely reiterate rather than challenge the logic of a hedonistic, consumption-oriented late capitalist society, in which the unified, repressed self of bourgeois liberalism often targeted by radical critics is in many respects already anachronistic. E. Ann Kaplan, for example, has demonstrated in a recent study how avant-garde strategies of self-reflexivity and narrative fragmentation have become standardized features of contemporary music television, suggesting that such techniques serve to stimulate processes of consumption and hence to affirm the status quo rather than subvert it.[14]

Feminist theories of "textual politics" grounded in a modernist aesthetics—for example, the celebration of the writings of Virginia Woolf as radically subversive of patriarchal ideology—are thus open to criticism on the grounds that they continue to draw upon static oppositions between realism and modernism without taking into account the changing social meanings of textual forms. The assumption that the political value of a text can be read off from its aesthetic value as defined by a modernist paradigm, and that a text which employs experimental techniques is therefore more radical in its effects than one which relies on established structures and conventional language, is too simple. Such an assumption takes for granted an equivalence between automatized language and dominant ideology and between experimentalism and oppositionality, an equation which is abstract and ultimately formalist in its failure to theorize the contingent functions of textual forms in relation to socially differentiated publics at particular historical moments. The supposedly revolutionary function of experimental techniques is increasingly questionable in late capitalist society, while the "conservative" status of realism as a closed form which reflects ruling ideologies has been challenged by its reappropriation in new social contexts, for example by oppositional movements such as feminism. It is thus increasingly implausible to claim that aesthetic radicalism equals political radicalism and to ground a feminist politics of the text in an assumption of the inherently subversive effects of stylistic innovation.

Thus I am not in favor of adopting the reductionist and easily criticized position that rejects all aesthetic differences between texts—it would be absurd to deny that *The Waves* is a more formally self-conscious work than an example of feminist confession; but I do suggest that this distinction does not provide sufficient grounds for hailing modernism as a *politically* more radical form vis-à-vis feminist interests without taking into account frameworks of reception as they mediate the potential effects of any particular text in relation to the politics of the women's movement as a whole. Radical impulses are not inherent in the formal properties of texts; they can be realized only through interactions between texts and readers, so that it becomes necessary to situate the modernist text in relation to the interests and expectations of potential audiences. In the context of the women's movement, the necessity and importance of a feminist avant-garde must be balanced against an equal need on the part of oppositional movements for texts which address the particularity of their social experience more explicitly and unambiguously, a need that has often resulted in a preference for realist forms which emphasize the denotative rather than aesthetic dimension of the text. One of the strengths of feminism has been precisely this partial reintegration of literature into the everyday communicative practices of large numbers of women by describing and commenting on women's experiences of gender relations. The political implications of modernism, by contrast, remain somewhat more ambiguous; its conception of the text as a privileged and subversive space which undermines truth and self-identity has a potential tendency to limit direct political effects, precisely because it presupposes the separation of the polysemic artwork from the sphere of everyday social practices. In other words, prevailing conceptions of literature which make it possible to identify the literary text as a site of resistance to ideology by virtue of its formal specificity simultaneously render problematic attempts to harness such an understanding of literary signification to the necessarily more determinate interests of an oppositional politics.

Pauline Johnson's discussion of Woolf's modernism explicitly acknowledges these ambivalent political implications of a modernist aesthetic which relocates freedom within the space of the literary text and which may thus serve a compensatory as well as a critical function:

> Although the ideal subjectivity posited by Woolf empowers her fiction with a strongly critical standpoint, the merely aesthetical character of this ideal means that her critique ultimately fails to project a practical imperative . . . The alternative vision proposed in her art functions as a compensatory, substitute gratification which siphons off and renders harmless the radical need for changed gender relations to which her works, in their passionate critique of existing relations between the sexes, also give expression.[15]

Johnson goes on to argue that modernism nevertheless provides a more appropriate basis for a feminist aesthetic than the postmodern pluralism which she detects within aspects of current feminist theory and practice, in that only the difficult modernist text can provide an authentic site of resistance and critique. While I do not disagree with Johnson's criticism of an aesthetic relativism which claims to renounce all judgments as "hierarchical," her argument reveals in my view the insufficiency of a continuing uncritical adherence to paradigms established by the Frankfurt School (Johnson explicitly draws on Marcuse). Insofar as the emergence of new social movements (of which feminism is the most influential) has been instrumental in problematizing the assumptions behind Critical Theory's sweeping and pessimistic condemnation of advanced capitalism as a one-dimensional society, the Frankfurt School's categories of analysis cannot simply be taken over unmodified into a feminist aesthetic theory. The privileging of a modernist aesthetic as a site of freedom within Critical Theory is crucially dependent upon a prior diagnosis of the modern world as a totally administered society with no possibility of genuine opposition or dissent. If, however, this originating premise is rejected, the dichotomy of authentic art versus degraded mass culture loses much of its rhetorical force.

Thus it has often been noted that the quest for a Marxist aesthetic has been inspired by the erosion of the revolutionary potential embodied in the industrial proletariat, resulting in a relocation of resistance in the work of art as alternative bearer of historical meaning.[16] Adorno's advocacy of modernism, it must be remembered, springs from a social pessimism which is unable to identify any contemporary agent of political change; given the prevailing technocratic logic of an administered society, the dissonant, fragmentary nature of modern art offers passive resistance to the all-pervasive commodification of experience. Adorno does not assign such art any direct social function or political effect; rather it embodies a form of critical negativity whose autonomy is guaranteed by its esoteric and difficult character. Modernist art, in other words, possesses a redemptive function as the sole authentic site of critical resistance in a reified social world in which any notion of collective action has become problematic.[17]

Feminism, however, rejects such pessimism in its identification of women as an oppressed class which embodies a potential force for social change, affirming the emancipatory potential of a diversity of current feminist political and cultural practices in relation to the significant gains made by the women's movement in the last twenty years. Feminist criticism does not need to deny the formal complexity of the modernist artwork but to problematize the assumption that "high" art embodies the only authentic site of critique in an alienated society. Feminism in fact offers one of the most persuasive political alternatives to current formalist textual theories, since it can ground its analysis in relation to an active social agent rather than resorting to the experimental text as a source of subversive impulses. Given that existing discussions of the question of feminist aesthetics have only become *possible* because of the recent reemergence of the women's movement and its influence upon the spheres of culture and ideology, it is surprising that there has been relatively little emphasis upon the social dimension of feminist literature and art. It is precisely the vitality and visibility of women's current artistic and critical practice across a range of forms and genres, not the positing of an abstract theory of a "subversive" aesthetic, which must provide a basis for a discussion of feminism's political function in culture.

The Feminist Counter-Public Sphere

To develop a more adequate theorization of the relationship between feminist politics and literature it is necessary to move beyond the bounds of textual analysis to consider the status and effects of the women's movement as a force for change in the public realm. The concept of a feminist public sphere provides a model for the analysis of diverse forms of recent artistic and cultural activity by women in relation to the historical emergence of an influential oppositional ideology which seeks to challenge the existing reality of gender subordination. Such a model makes it possible to situate the debate over literary forms in relation to the conflicting needs of different sections of the women's movement rather than simply assigning an abstract political value to particular techniques.

What exactly is a feminist public sphere? The concept draws upon the model of the bourgeois public sphere theorized by Habermas in *Structural Changes in the Public Sphere*. Habermas defines the bourgeois or classic public sphere as a historically determined formation which emerges from the specific conditions of late seventeenth- and eighteenth-century society, its participants male property owners and the enlightened aristocracy. It represents the first emergence of a critical and independent public domain that perceives itself as distinct from state interests, a discursive community bound by shared assumptions which define its boundaries and validate its claim to authority as the locus of informed public opinion. Primary among these is the belief in rationality, which is intended to equalize all participants within the discourse; it is critical reason that henceforth provides the legitimation for argument on politics and culture, not tradition, religious dogma, or social privilege. The acknowledgment of the essentially rational nature of the individual thus fulfills an emancipatory function in equalizing all participants in public discourse. Within the boundaries of the public sphere differences in rank and class are in theory subordinate to the demands of critical reasoned debate. "Access is guaranteed to all citizens."[18]

At the same time, of course, the possibility of participation in this discursive community is predicated upon historically determined factors of gender and class; the eighteenth-century public sphere, which perceives itself to be grounded in rational and universal principles, is in reality limited to an educated male bourgeoisie and enlightened nobility. The bourgeois public sphere is thus characterized by a blindness to the actual and unequal material conditions which render its own existence possible and holds fast to the illusion that humanity is adequately represented by the male property-owning public. Nevertheless, according to Habermas, the emergence of the bourgeois public sphere represents an emancipatory moment which cannot be reduced to false consciousness. In discussing the notion of universal rationality through which the bourgeois public sphere defines itself, he argues that while it is not really given, it is nevertheless an influential concept which helps to generate the first relatively autonomous discursive space which can define itself critically against state power.[19]

The consensual basis and critical function of the bourgeois public sphere slowly disintegrates under the dynamic of capitalist growth and the development of an industrialized mass society. The resulting intervention of the state in the regulation of economic affairs and the growth of ever more powerful state bureaucracies leads to a blurring of the distinction between civil society and the state upon which the bourgeois public sphere depends and a consequent depoliticization of public discourse. Although a rapid expansion takes place in education, literacy, and communication, the extension of the public sphere into ever larger sectors of society is accompanied, Habermas argues, by a progressive loss of critical function as its institutions become integrated into late capitalist society; the commodification of the mass media and the influence of state bureaucracies on individual life experience (the colonization of the life world) makes it increasingly impossible to identify any independent arena for the critical and informed formation of public opinion.

Political developments since the writing of Habermas's work in 1962—most notably the radicalization of student groups in the 1960s and the growth of new social movements in the 1970s and 1980s—have since inspired theorists to posit the growth of counter-public spheres, understood as critical oppositional forces within the society of late capitalism which cannot be adequately comprehended in terms of such a pessimistic thesis of one-dimensionality.[20] The social function and ideological self-understanding of such public spheres reveal, however, a significant shift, insofar as their emancipatory project no longer appeals to an idea of universality but is directed toward an affirmation of specificity in relation to gender, race, ethnicity, age, sexual preference, and so on. They seek to define themselves *against* the homogenizing and universalizing logic of the global megaculture of modern mass communication as a debased pseudopublic sphere, and to voice needs and articulate oppositional values which the "culture industry" fails to address. These new sites of oppositionality are multiple and heterogeneous and do not converge to form a single revolutionary movement; the current plurality of public spheres is united only by a common concern to establish "qualitatively new forms of social and political relations in which . . . mutuality, discussion, and concern with concrete needs predominate."[21]

The women's movement has offered one of the most dynamic examples of a counter-ideology in recent years to have generated an oppositional public arena for the articulation of women's needs in critical opposition to the values of a male-defined society. Like the original bourgeois public sphere, the feminist public sphere constitutes a discursive space which defines itself in terms of a common identity; here it is the shared experience of gender-based oppression which provides the mediating factor intended to unite all participants beyond their specific differences. "As with the classical public sphere, distinctions of class may be temporarily suspended, though not ignored, within this new domain; the shared fact of gender works to equalize all participants within it."[22] The consciousness of membership in an oppressed group engenders a solidarity rooted in collective identity and in theory grants all participants equal status; the "we" of feminist discourse is intended to represent all women as collective cosubjects. As a consequence, the women's movement can accommodate disparate and often conflicting ideological positions, because membership is conditional not on the acceptance of a clearly delineated theoretical framework, but on a more general sense of commonality in the experience of oppression. Hence the importance that literature has assumed in the development of an oppositional women's culture; the feminist novel focuses upon areas of personal experience which women are perceived to share in common beyond their cultural, political, and class differences. The feminist public sphere exemplifies a repoliticization of culture which seeks to relate literature and art to the specific experiences and interests of an explicitly gendered community.

Unlike the bourgeois public sphere, then, the feminist public sphere does not claim a representative universality but rather offers a critique of cultural values from the standpoint of women as a marginalized group within society. In this sense it constitutes a *partial* or counter-public sphere; as in the case of other oppositional communities defined in terms of racial or ethnic identity or sexual preference, the experience of discrimination, oppression, and cultural dislocation provides the impetus for the development of a self-consciously oppositional identity. Yet insofar as it is a *public* sphere, its arguments are also directed outward, toward a dissemination of feminist ideas and values throughout society as a whole. The tension between universality and particularity defining the logic of the feminist public sphere here becomes apparent. On the one hand it is gender-specific, appealing to the experiences of women who find their interests distorted or excluded in the existing forms of a male-dominated culture. Thus feminist culture has frequently focused upon the representation of experiences exclusive to women, such as female sexuality, lesbian relationships, and the experience of motherhood. On the other hand the feminist public sphere also constitutes a discursive arena which disseminates its arguments outward through such public channels of communication as books, journals, the mass media, and the education system. This gradual expansion of feminist values from their roots in the women's movement throughout society as a whole is a necessary corollary of feminism's claim to embody a catalyst of social and cultural change. While feminist discourse originates from women's experiences of oppression and recognizes their ultimate authority in speaking of its effects, feminism as a critique of values is also engaged in a more general and public process of revising or refuting male-defined cultural and discursive

167

frameworks. The feminist public sphere, in other words, serves a dual function: *internally,* it generates a gender-specific identity grounded in a consciousness of community and solidarity among women; *externally,* it seeks to convince society as a whole of the validity of feminist claims, challenging existing structures of authority through political activity and theoretical critique.

A further tension endemic to the operation of a public sphere is the disparity between its ideal and its real status, that is, between its self-understanding as a representative forum for all women and an actual practice which has been significantly limited by the factor of access to education, and hence dominated by white middle-class interests. Here there are obvious parallels to the bourgeois public sphere; the ideal of a free discursive space that equalizes all participants is an enabling fiction which engenders a sense of collective identity but is achieved only by obscuring actual material inequalities and political antagonisms among its participants. The self-recognition of women as an oppressed group is an emancipatory step which makes possible the recognition of and struggle against sexism, but this step is often attained by a suspension of other forms of difference, an erasure felt most painfully by those whose unequal status and particular needs are suppressed by the fiction of a unifying identity. Recent years have seen a proliferation of critiques of first-world middle-class feminism which have exposed its blindness to or complicity with other forms of exploitation and oppression; Bell Hooks comments, "white women who dominate feminist discourse today rarely question whether or not their perspective on women's reality is true to the lived experiences of women as a collective group. Nor are they aware of the extent to which their perspectives reflect race and class biases."[23] As a result, it has become apparent that female community cannot simply transcend existing power structures but is deeply implicated within them, and that the exclusive focus upon gender politics can serve to obscure other, equally fundamental structural inequalities within late capitalism.

It must also be noted, however, that the very possibility of Hook's own critique presupposes a preexisting ideal of a public sphere which claims to represent all women and can thus be criticized and made answerable for its failure to do so. Some form of appeal to collective identity and solidarity is a necessary precondition for the emergence and effectiveness of an oppositional movement; feminist theorists who reject any notion of a unifying identity as a repressive fiction in

168

favor of a stress on absolute difference fail to show how such diversity and fragmentation can be reconciled with goal-oriented political struggles based upon common interests. An appeal to a shared experience of oppression provides the starting point from which women as a group can open up the problematic of gender, at the same time as this notion of gendered community contains a strongly utopian dimension. Feminism thus oscillates between its appeal to an ideal of a unified collective subject drawn from the primary distinction of male versus female and the actual activities and self-understanding of women, in which gender-based divisions frequently conflict with a whole range of other alliances, such as those based on race or class, and work against any unproblematic notion of harmonious consensus.[24] The ideal of a communal gendered identity generated by the feminist public sphere is thus both empowering and constricting; it can be viewed negatively as ideology, insofar as it fails to come to grips with the material reality of a class- and race-divided society, but also positively, in that changes in worldview resulting from the feminist emphasis upon the specificity of gender politics and the problems which women share as women can serve an important critical function in making women more aware of and less amenable to their own exploitation.

It thus becomes possible to locate the diverse forms of contemporary feminist literature and culture in relation to the contradictory tensions generated by the feminist public sphere, which simultaneously affirms and problematizes the very ideal of gendered identity that defines it. I have argued that women's use of supposedly "outdated" forms such as the autobiography or the *Bildungsroman* cannot simply be interpreted as anachronistic or regressive; the important and wide-spread reappropriation and reworking of such textual models indicates that the project of modernity is indeed an unfinished history, that concerns with subjectivity and self-emancipation encoded within such narrative structures possess a continuing and often urgent relevance for oppressed social groups. Simultaneously, an important strand within the women's movement, primarily associated with the work of feminist artists and intellectuals, has sought to examine more critically the taken-for-granted assumptions behind everyday feminist thought, drawing upon experimental techniques to explode notions of a stable subjectivity and an unproblematically given female "reality." The range of feminist practices draws attention to the ambivalent siting of feminism as both affir-

169

mation and critique of female identity, neither aspect of which can be exclusively privileged at the expense of the other. Yet even the most experimental feminist text which deconstructs fixed identities is made possible by and operates within the boundaries of a historically given oppositional public sphere defined around the idea of female gender. The very critique of the concept of an oppositional gendered identity simultaneously affirms its prior existence—not as an ontological given, but as an actually existing discursive formation which has generated a range of diverse and contradictory political and cultural activities.

The complex interaction and interpenetration between feminist ideology and the broader social domain can be illustrated through an examination of the diverse institutional locations of the feminist public sphere. At one end of the scale, the women's movement is one of the main forums for political activity which operates on a grass-roots level outside existing institutional frameworks and has generated an infrastructure of decentralized collectively organized projects, such as women's groups, feminist publications, day-care and health centers, and bookstores. At the other end, a major site of feminist activity has also been within existing state institutions, including bureaucracies and universities, promoting such issues as affirmative action and the introduction and development of women's studies as an academic discipline. There exists another range of feminist activities, such as women's refuges and advisory centers, which often function with a degree of autonomy but within the framework of existing social welfare bureaucracies. Thus Myra Ferree and Beth Hess discuss "bureaucratic" and "collectivist" modes as interweaving strands within feminism, rather than as distinct branches, and refer to the blurring of distinctions between self-help collectives and the bureaucratically organized lobbying organizations within the women's movement.[25] Similarly, feminist cultural activity has developed on a number of distinct but often interconnecting levels, from the small autonomous writers' or film-makers' groups to the increasingly prevalent dissemination of feminist ideas through journalism, television, bestselling novels, and commercial films. The women's movement can thus be seen to function as a "structural chameleon,"[26] which allows women to exercise a variety of options for political and cultural change on diverse terrains.

As such examples make clear, the present status and influence of the women's movement cannot be adequately accounted for by the notion of a unified and autonomous counter-public sphere which remains separate from the rest of society. Given the complex interpenetrations of state and society in late capitalism, one can no longer postulate the ideal of a public sphere which can function outside existing commercial and state institutions and at the same time claim an influential and representative function as a forum for oppositional activity and debate. Instead, the category of the feminist public sphere needs to be understood in terms of a series of cultural strategies which can be effective across a range of levels both outside and inside existing institutional structures, for example, by exploiting the contradictory critical spaces within the education system.[27] Rather than a uniform interpretative community, then, it is perhaps more appropriate to speak of coalitions of overlapping subcommunities, which share a common interest in combating gender oppression but which are differentiated not only by class and race positions but often by institutional locations and professional allegiances, and which draw upon a varied range of discursive frameworks. Within the academy, to take one example, feminism does not exist in the form of a single, holistic, and self-contained body of knowledge; rather, it manifests itself in a diversity of intellectual constructs which work both within and against existing disciplinary knowledges; the latter provide conditions of possibility for the development of feminist philosophy, literary criticism, and similar fields, which simultaneously work against the grain of the intellectual traditions on which they draw, challenging many of the institutionalized premises of academic discourse and seeking to establish connections between previously distinct forms of knowledge.

This acknowledgment of the multiple locations of oppositional feminist practice works against the notion of a privileged political subject, for example, the belief that the activist who works "outside the system" is necessarily more radical than the feminist who works within an institution; on the contrary, it becomes clear that there exists no "outside," no privileged Archimedean standpoint which can remain free of ideological and discursive structures. This does not deny, however, that certain forms of political activity and organizational structures may prove more conducive to feminist interests and goals than others. Bureaucracies, on the one hand (and here I draw on the European and Australian rather than American experience), have in recent years proved relatively progressive sites for the promotion of feminist interests through legislation, educational reforms, and so on, which have at times been in advance of mainstream public opinion. On the other hand, as Nancy Fraser argues, the administrative logic of the bureaucracy can be seen as ultimately antithetical to feminist interests in its quantification and decontextualization of human needs. Citing women's refuges as one example, Fraser suggests that their original nonhierarchical structures, in which no clear distinction existed between women seeking refuge and staff who had themselves previously been battered, was significantly modified as these shelters became recipients of state funding, with a corresponding influx of professionalized social workers and the consequent positioning of battered women as passive clients of the bureaucratic welfare system.[28]

This example clearly reveals the contradictory relationship between feminist interests and established structures; an urgent need for public funding and access to institutional resources for projects related to women's interests typically results in an increasing degree of accountability to structures which are fundamentally hierarchical and non-participatory. Thus obvious risks result from the mainstreaming and institutionalization of feminism, which has often been deeply suspicious of conventional political processes and the power structures they engender; feminism as a critique of values can find itself trivialized as a fashionable lifestyle to be marketed like any other commodity, and women working within bureaucratic or private enterprise structures may find that attempts to undermine or subvert existing hierarchies have the opposite effect of appearing to legitimate their authority. In this sense, it remains a difficult and as yet unresolved question whether the significant cultural impact of feminism will translate itself into a major transformation of political and economic structures, or whether, viewed more pessimistically, the logic of advanced capitalism is such as to simultaneously engender and place significant constraints upon the subversive consequences of oppositional ideologies. It must be stressed, however, that institutional structures do not constitute monolithic entities but, to differing degrees, provide possibilities for resistance, for challenges to or modifications of existing frameworks. In this context, there is a need to temper idealism with a pragmatism which concerns itself with gaining access to limited resources and struggling to achieve more systematic processes of change, even if this requires in practical terms a certain dilution of ideological positions.

An extension of this analysis to the sphere of cultural production and reception reveals similar tensions between the oppositional impetus of feminist literature and art and its subjection to institutional interests and the constraints of the market. In the specific case of literature, for example, one can differentiate, following Peter Hohendahl, between two dimensions of the literary institution: the level of organization—the material apparatus of publishing houses, the book trade, libraries, bookshops, through which books are produced and distributed—and the level of institutionalization, the various forms of discourse about literature, such as reviews, criticism, literary theory, and so on. "The organization, therefore, remains bound to the relations of production, whereas institutionalization occurs in the realm of ideology as the establishment of norms, conventions, and practices that pre-form the way in which participants in literary communication understand and use works and genres."[29] Feminism's influence has clearly occurred primarily at the latter level, in influencing institutionalized norms of interpretation and the ways in which literature is written and read; feminist literature and criticism has offered the most sustained recent challenge to the idealist mythology of literature as a self-contained and transcendental sphere. Feminism has been less effective in altering the organizational structures through which these ideologies are produced and disseminated, although various attempts have been made to circumvent the more overt pressures of the market by setting up independent feminist presses, journals, and so on. But with the important exception of state-financed television and radio broadcasting and various forms of arts funding, feminist art and culture is necessarily subject in differing degrees to the constraints of the market, with all the potential difficulties that result from conflicts of interest between feminist authors and the profit-oriented structures through which texts are produced and distributed.

Literature of course constitutes only one small section of cultural production, even if it has been a relatively influential one in the generation of an oppositional feminist culture, and an awareness of the multiplicity of potential audiences constituted within a feminist public sphere provides a standpoint from which to affirm the importance of a wide-ranging feminist "cultural politics." It is in this context that feminist theorists need to acknowledge the importance of the mass media and of feminist influence in channels which can potentially reach vast audiences. I have already criticized a "purist" tendency within feminist theory, which assumes that the only legitimate feminist cultural activity renounces all popular conventions and is situated outside existing commercial cultural institutions. The increasingly overt commercialization of modern art makes it difficult to hold onto any such distinction between a "commercial" mass culture and an "uncompromised" avant-garde.[30] Of course, experimental art forms, even if they do not possess any inherently "revolutionary" value, can nevertheless play an important role in the development of a critical feminist presence in "high" art. In the context of the visual arts, for example, one can point to the resonances generated by such works as Judy Chicago's *The Dinner Party* and Mary Kelly's *Post-Partum Document,* which have served to crystallize distinctive and very different conceptions of gender identity and to generate extensive controversy as to the nature and goals of feminist art. But the point is that a reception-based model of a feminist "cultural politics" grounded in the recognition of the plural audiences constituted within the feminist public sphere does not justify giving particular priority to an avant-garde aesthetic and requires that equally serious attention be paid to the political potential of more popular forms such as television, rock music, popular novels, and women's magazines. This is particularly important given the enormous female participation in the consumption of mass culture forms, most obviously apparent in the case of such specifically "feminine" genres as romance fiction and soap opera, and a consequent need to reevaluate a long-standing and dismissive association of the popular with the feminine, an association which has been in evidence since the original emergence of a female reading public in the eighteenth century. In recent years important work has begun in the area of women's popular culture, taking seriously the pleasures which it offers to female audiences while simultaneously subjecting the ideological dimension of such pleasures to critical analysis.[31] As a result, the value of formal innovation in feminist cultural production must be balanced against the importance of communicating a degree of political awareness to large audiences of women: "A small popular change is *relatively* just as significant as a large minority change. There may be at least as much potential for change in a TV soap opera as in agit-prop theatre."[32] The model of a feminist public sphere provides a theoretical justification for feminist interest in *both* popular and more esoteric forms in relation to the cultural interests and needs of different segments of an actual or potential feminist public while avoiding the problems inherent in existing attempts to theorize a "feminist aesthetic."

The Dialectic of "Feminism" and "Aesthetics"

One of the most important achievements of the women's movement has been to repoliticize art on the level of both production and reception, and to question ruling ideologies of the text as a self-contained artifact which recur in both modernist aesthetics and formalist criticism. This repoliticization of the aesthetic sphere does not imply, in my view, that aesthetic categories are to be interpreted as a direct reflection of the interests of a political ideology, or that literary meaning is limited to its current political use-value for the women's movement, assumptions that lay themselves open to the obvious charge of reductionism. Rather, as evidenced by the current debates between American and French feminists, there exists a symptomatic tension in feminist literary theory between a pragmatic position, which seeks to repoliticize the literary text by reinserting it into the sphere of everyday communicative practices, and a simultaneous awareness of the potential limitations of a purely functionalist aesthetic, which stresses immediate political effects and is unable to address the specificity of literature as a site of plural signification and aesthetic pleasure which may resist as well as transmit dominant ideological positions.

Thus the assumption that literary meaning can in all cases be reduced to its immediate function in the transmission of an unambiguous political content fails to take into account the distinctive features of literary modes of signification, instead reading fiction as a one-dimensional articulation of existing ideological systems. The historical emergence of the category of literature as a relatively autonomous domain within bourgeois society allows a recognition of literary texts as polysemic symbolic structures governed by a high degree of self-referentiality; literature comes to function as a form of metalanguage which may problematize referential meaning rather than transmit it, critically reflecting upon or playfully parodying the aesthetic conventions governing its own discourse. The increasing separation of the spheres of "fact" and "fiction" embodied in the self-differentiation of literature as a distinctive sphere governed by its own techniques and conventions makes it impossible to assume any automatic or self-evident equation between literary value and instrumental political value. This does not of course negate the possibility that particular individuals may find their own aesthetic responses entirely determined by moral or political factors, causing them to reject as works of art those texts which they consider "ideologically unsound." But any attempt to assert the *necessary* identity of political and aesthetic value in the context of a theory of feminist aesthetics runs into obvious problems, given the impossibility of revoking the relative autonomy of literature and art in modernity as embodied, for instance, in the capacity of readers to experience pleasure from texts they do not necessarily concur with on political grounds or texts whose ideological stance may not be immediately obvious.

In other words, while the relative autonomy of art is the product of a sociohistorical development, it does not follow that the differentiations which it serves to identify can be voluntaristically abolished or simply collapsed back into a socioeconomic or gender-determined base. Janet Wolff points out that critiques of aesthetics frequently rely upon a version of the "genetic fallacy" and assume that an account of the historical and social determinants of a particular cultural formation constitutes an adequate basis for invalidating its claims. Wolff herself states that "the sociology of art and the social history of art convincingly show the historical, ideological and contingent nature of a good deal of 'aesthetics' and of many, if not all, 'aesthetic judgements' "; nevertheless she argues against a reductionist standpoint which reads aesthetic categories as a direct expression of ideological interests, asserting the "irreducibility of 'aesthetic value' to social, political or ideological co-ordinates."[33] To argue that art possesses a relative autonomy *within* society is not to suggest that it is independent *of* society, to employ Macherey's distinction,[34] or to argue that aesthetic judgments occur in some ideology-free suprahistorical realm. On the contrary, aesthetic judgments are necessarily and invariably mediated by the social and ideological contexts in which they occur. Thus, for example, the boundaries which separate what is considered art from nonart are shifting, unstable, and historically contingent and will be influenced by the ideologies and tastes of particular eras and social groups. Wolff has documented some of the numerous social, political, and ideological factors which have shaped the construction of artistic and literary canons.[35] Consequently, the criteria determining aesthetic judgments and values are by no means unproblematic and can be challenged or revised by oppositional movements capable of exposing their ideological basis.

Thus it has been possible for feminism to reveal numerous convincing instances of the influences of sexism on the evaluation of literary and artistic texts; a misogynist culture has shaped the practice of literary criticism at both individual and institutional levels. As

Nina Baym points out, "I cannot avoid the belief that 'purely' literary criteria, as they have been employed to identify the best American works, have inevitably had a bias in favor of things male—in favor, say, of whaling ships rather than the sewing circle as a symbol of the human community."[36] Consequently, feminist critics have succeeded in exposing and challenging the male prejudices which have denigrated women writers and artists and which have trivialized texts dealing with female concerns and centering on the domestic sphere. Any such approach is, however, unlikely to provide a convincing argument for the gender-based nature of *all* aesthetic judgments. Thus Michèle Barrett has questioned the assumption that a straightforward unilinear determining relationship can be established between aesthetic categories and sociopolitical structures, where the first term is reducible to an epiphenomenal function of the second.[37] Clearly, no text can in principle be exempt from an aesthetic reading, and all texts, whether "fictional" or "factual," are permeated to some degree by metaphor, narrative, and other figurative devices. Nevertheless, there remain important differences between texts in terms of their foregrounding of this poetic and self-referential dimension of signification, attained by means of the text's relative distance from the pragmatic constraints of everyday communicative practices. Because aesthetic criteria are produced within specific social and historical contexts, in other words, it does not follow that they are either completely arbitrary or can be construed as a one-dimensional reflection of gender or class biases.

The rejection of a reductionist aesthetic which seeks to subsume all forms of artistic production into a direct expression of particular ideological interests does not imply that a rigid division can be established between "art" and "ideology" as separate and antagonistic spheres. The relationship is more appropriately conceptualized in terms of a continuum in which the aesthetic function may be more or less dominant but always intermeshes with the ideological conditions governing the text's own historical location.[38] Thus the distinction between "high" and "popular" cultural texts cannot be adequately grasped in terms of an antithetical opposition between "exceptional" texts which liberate multiple levels of meaning and formulaic fictions which merely serve to reinforce repressive ideological structures. Even the most overtly stereotypical and conventional of texts may articulate moments of protest and express utopian longings, while the most fragmented and aesthetically self-conscious of texts cannot

177

escape its own ideological positioning. In turn, the relative significance and value assigned this aesthetic dimension is by no means constant and will change according to the priorities of particular social groups. At certain historical moments the urgency of political struggles may take priority over aesthetic considerations, which will be subordinated to specific didactic and ideological goals; in other instances (the example of Eastern bloc countries comes to mind) it becomes (politically) important to resist the instrumentalization of literature and to assert the validity of artistic experimentation and aesthetic pleasure and knowledge as legitimate goals in their own right.

In this context, one must realize that the ideological function of aesthetic autonomy in modern Western societies is a fundamentally ambivalent one, a crucial point ignored by those theorists who assume that it embodies a straightforward expression of ruling-class interests. On the one hand, an acknowledgment of aesthetic specificity has helped to encourage a mystification of art as a quasi-transcendental sphere, obscuring the historical and ideological determinants affecting the production of art and the dissemination of aesthetic values, and perpetuating the myth of the great artist as solitary genius. On the other hand, however, it has also formed the basis of a number of oppositional readings of literature; the formal complexity of the text is perceived to serve a potentially critical function by distancing and defamiliarizing the ideological frameworks within which it operates. A conception of literary discourse as a site of resistance to or subversion of ideology has been frequently drawn upon by both Marxist and feminist critics; the ambiguities and dissonances within the text reveal contradictions which enable a critical reading of prevailing ideologies. The text's relative autonomy, as embodied in its formally mediated relationship to ideology, can be appropriated by both conservative and radical positions, depending upon whether its affirmative/compensatory or its negative/contestatory function is foregrounded. Because the notion of aesthetic autonomy has been used by conservative critics to defend an ahistorical and apolitical reading of culture, feminism is not thereby obliged to respond by adopting a reductive theory of literary meaning. Rather, there is a need to acknowledge the formal complexity of the literary or artistic text while at the same time continuing to stress the socially mediated nature of both the text and responses to it.

This point has in fact been tacitly recognized in the interpretative

178

practices of much contemporary feminist criticism. Whereas the earliest feminist readings concentrated upon the critique of sexist images in literature, an issue which still possesses relevance, particularly in the context of a theory of reception that relates texts to ordinary readers, it has become apparent that literary texts are governed by complex structural relations, which cannot always be reduced to a one-dimensional reflection of patriarchal ideology. Like Marxism, feminism has become increasingly aware of the problems involved in a reductionist approach to the analysis of culture, and feminist critics have consequently sought to address the specificity of literary signification by exploring the formal dissonances and contradictions within the individual work. At the same time, this potential "openness" of the text, which defamiliarizes fixed ideological positions, does not in itself generate a specifically feminist knowledge: the polysemic work that allows for a feminist reading can by the same logic be equally well appropriated for a conservative one. The value of a text as art, if one means by this a self-reflexive symbolic structure which generates multiple meanings and is not directly reducible to ideological interests, does not therefore constitute a sufficient basis for the specific needs and interests of a feminist politics of culture, which also needs to situate itself more concretely in relation to the ideological dimension of the text and the praxis-oriented interests of an oppositional feminist public sphere.

There remains, then, both an interaction and an inevitable tension between the spheres of "feminism" and "aesthetics." As Patrocinio Schweickart argues, feminist criticism is a necessarily contradictory enterprise; it produces tensions and problems which cannot be resolved by thinking either dualistically (whereby literature and ideology are separate spheres) or monistically (whereby literature is indistinguishable from political ideology): "Feminist criticism must not imply the subordination of feminism to traditional literary criticism, or the subordination of aesthetic and literary concerns to politics, or a compromise between these opposing interests. Feminist criticism should be a dialectical mediation between them."[39] My own analysis has tended to stress the "feminist" side of the dialectic, given my interest in the politics of feminist fiction and my concern to show that this issue can be adequately addressed only by relating literary practices to the goals and interests of the women's movement, rather than relying upon an abstract fetishization of aesthetic modernism as a source of subversion. Instead of limiting itself to a reading of a few "great works," whether those of Virginia Woolf or other canonical writers, feminist analysis can more usefully attempt to embrace an understanding of the full range of literary forms written and read by women in relation to a broader theorization of women's position in culture and society. In the case of feminist literature, this has entailed an investigation of the social importance and strategic value of contemporary women's writing in relation to the emancipatory claims of the women's movement. I have attempted to analyze some of the ways in which feminism has shaped attitudes toward the production and reception of literature and art. An investigation of some of the most representative genres of feminist literature has made it possible to elucidate in more detail the relationship between the ideological perspectives generated by feminism and the structures and themes of recent women's writing.

At the same time, it must be acknowledged that this reading offers only a partial and by no means comprehensive account of literary meaning, which cannot be collapsed into the social function it serves for a historically specific set of writers and readers without all the attendant problems of sociological reductionism. Literary theory had adequately demonstrated that literary texts, to varying degrees, possess the capacity to resist or transcend the interpretative schemata which are imposed upon them at any particular moment. Some examples of recent feminist writing foreground this polysemic dimension of literary discourse more clearly than others and continue to generate multiple resonances well beyond the immediate historical conditions of their production. The works of Margaret Atwood, for example, have inspired a large number of readings which go beyond any specific feminist "message" her texts may be said to contain. Other examples of feminist fiction that served an important purpose at the time of publication by articulating women's discovery of their oppression may appear aesthetically naive or excessively didactic at a historical distance.

The notion of a feminist aesthetics presupposes that these two dimensions of textual reception can be unproblematically harmonized, assuming either that an aesthetically self-conscious literature which subverts conventions of representation forms a sufficient basis for a feminist politics of culture (a position that can be regarded as both elitist and politically naive), or that texts which have been politically important to the women's movement are automatically of aesthetic significance, a position that taken to its logical conclusion would rate *The Women's Room* as a better work of art than the writing of Kafka, or indeed Woolf. A dialectical interaction between politics and aesthetics is compressed into an identity which attempts to construct a normative aesthetic on the basis of feminist interests.

Seen thus, the question of a feminist aesthetics, defined as a theory which would subordinate all aesthetic categories to the interests of feminist ideology, reveals itself to be something of a nonissue, a chimera which feminist critics have needlessly pursued. Rather than privileging the aesthetic, a feminist cultural politics should concern itself with addressing the potential value of forms from both high and mass culture in relation to the objectives of a feminist public sphere. Because a particular form is formally conventional, or marketed for profit, we may not automatically conclude that it is irredeemably compromised and cannot constitute a legitimate medium of opposi-tional cultural activity. The emergence of the feminist public sphere thus calls into question the dichotomy that Bürger poses in his *Theory of the Avant-Garde* and that reveals his continuing indebtedness to Adorno's position in spite of his attempts to problematize it: between an autonomous art which protests against society but remains elitist and ineffective, and the products of the mass media, which encourage identification and blur the distinction between art and life but with the loss of any critical dimension.[40] Much feminist literature is both popular *and* oppositional; the importance of the women's movement, along with other sites of resistance in contemporary society which have generated a diversity of cultural forms, calls into question the assumption underlying negative aesthetics that a literature which draws on rather than problematizes conventional forms is invariably complicit with a monolithic ruling ideology and serves as an apology for the status quo.

It should be stressed that this shift, from the pursuit of a single "feminist aesthetics" toward a situating of a range of literary and cultural forms in relation to the politics of the women's movement, does not imply any kind of uncritical assent to current feminist political and cultural practices. On the contrary, as I have tried to show, there exist problematic tendencies within feminism which need to be addressed, such as the trend toward an increasingly conservative and quietist politics grounded in a romantic celebration of a feminine sphere.[41] It is possible, moreover, that the diversity of contemporary feminism, often hailed as one of its main strengths, may well result in a gradual dissipation of its oppositional force; the women's movement appears to be splintering into conflicting factions, which may prove unable to articulate a systematic challenge to the increasing hegemony of neoconservatism in Western societies in the late 1980s. The significant ideological gains made by feminism in the last twenty years do not by any means provide grounds for unqualified optimism.

In any case, the question of the politics of feminist reading or writing is not a question which can be resolved at an aesthetic level alone; it is inextricably linked to the fate of the women's movement as a whole. I have argued that one of the most important strengths of feminism derives from the fact that it does not simply constitute an academic discourse but continues to inspire a social and cultural movement and that this issue must remain central to the discussion of the significance of feminist literature. Thus the political value and limitations of particular forms can be meaningfully assessed only in the context of a more general theoretical consideration of the relations among women, literature, and society. I am not suggesting that the function of literature is to reflect passively the already constituted needs of a female audience; on the contrary, literature and art can help to create new perceptions and new needs. In this sense there exists a dialectical relationship between audiences and texts which cannot be encompassed either by conceiving of literature as a mere reflection of existing social relations or by vaguely referring to the literary text as a form of radical intervention without specifying the text's particular relation to the social and historical contexts in which it is produced and received. My analysis has attempted to draw out the enabling function of feminist literature as a critique of values and as a source of positive fictions of female identity, while simultaneously insisting that feminist literature, like feminism itself, must be viewed not in isolation, but in relation to the social and ideological conditions within which it emerges and against which it defines itself.

Bibliography
Notes
Index

Bibliography

Primary Sources: Feminist Literature

Atwood, Margaret. *Surfacing*. London: André Deutsch, 1972.

Barfoot, Joan. *Gaining Ground* (1978). Reprint, London: The Women's Press, 1980.

Bartram, Grace. *Peeling*. London: The Women's Press, 1986.

Cardinal, Marie. *The Words to Say It,* trans. Pat Goodheart. Cambridge, Mass.: Van Vactor and Goodheart, 1983. Originally published as *Les mots pour le dire*. Paris: Grasset et Fasquelle, 1975.

French, Marilyn. *The Women's Room*. New York: Summit, 1977.

Koller, Alice. *An Unknown Woman: A Journey to Self-Discovery* (1982). Reprint, New York: Bantam, 1983.

Lessing, Doris. *The Summer before the Dark*. London: Jonathan Cape, 1973.

Lorde, Audre. *The Cancer Journals* (1980). Reprint, London: Sheba Feminist Publishers, 1985.

Marshall, Paule. *Praisesong for the Widow*. London: Virago, 1983.

Merian, Svende. *Der Tod des Märchenprinzen* (1980). Reprint, Reinbek: Rowohlt, 1983.

Meulenbelt, Anja. *The Shame Is Over: A Political Life Story,* trans. Ann Oosthuizen. London: The Women's Press, 1980.

Millett, Kate. *Flying* (1974). Reprint, London: Hart-Davis, MacGibbon, 1975.

——— *Sita*. London: Virago, 1977.

Oakley, Ann. *Taking It Like a Woman*. London: Jonathan Cape, 1984.

Offenbach, Judith. *Sonja: Eine Melancholie für Fortgeschrittene*. Frankfurt am Main: Suhrkamp, 1980.

Piercy, Marge. *Small Changes* (1972). Reprint, New York: Fawcett Crest, 1974.

——— *Fly away Home* (1984). Reprint, London: Pan, 1985.

Schroeder, Margot. *Der Schlachter empfiehlt noch immer Herz.* Munich: Frauenbuchverlag, 1976.

Schwaiger, Brigitte. *Wie kommt das Salz ins Meer.* Vienna: Paul Zsolnay, 1977.

Stefan, Verena. *Häutungen.* Munich: Frauenoffensive, 1975.

Struck, Karin. *Klassenliebe.* Frankfurt am Main: Suhrkamp, 1973.

—— *Kindheits Ende: Journal einer Krise.* Frankfurt am Main: Suhrkamp, 1982.

Walker, Alice. *Meridian.* New York: Harcourt Brace Jovanovich, 1976.

—— *The Color Purple.* London: The Women's Press, 1983.

Weldon, Fay. *Praxis.* London: Hodder and Stoughton, 1980.

Secondary Sources

Abel, Elizabeth, Marianne Hirsch, and Elizabeth Langland, eds., *The Voyage In: Fictions of Female Development.* Hanover, N.H.: University Press of New England, 1983.

Abrams, M. H. *Natural Supernaturalisms: Tradition and Revolution in Romantic Literature.* New York: Norton, 1971.

Adorno, Theodor. "Reconciliation under Duress." In Ernst Bloch et al., *Aesthetics and Politics.* London: New Left Books, 1977.

Altbach, Edith Hoshino. "The New German Women's Movement." In *German Feminism: Readings in Politics and Literature,* ed. Edith Hoshino Altbach et al. Albany: State University of New York Press, 1984.

Aronowitz, Stanley. "On Narcissism." *Telos,* no. 44 (1980): 65–74.

Atwood, Margaret. *Survival: A Thematic Guide to Canadian Literature.* Toronto: Anansi, 1972.

Barrett, Michèle. *Women's Oppression Today: Problems in Marxist Feminist Analysis.* London: Verso, 1980.

—— "Feminism and the Definition of Cultural Politics." In *Feminism, Culture and Politics,* ed. Rosalind Brunt and Caroline Rowan. London: Lawrence and Wishart, 1982.

—— "The Concept of 'Difference.' " *Feminist Review,* no. 26 (1987): 29–41.

Baym, Nina. *Women's Fiction: A Guide to Novels by and about Women in America, 1820–1870.* Ithaca: Cornell University Press, 1978.

Belsey, Catherine. *Critical Practice.* London: Methuen, 1980.

Benhabib, Seyla, and Drucilla Cornell. Introduction, *Praxis International,* 5, no. 4 (1986).

Bennett, Tony. "The Prison-House of Criticism." *New Formations,* no. 2 (1987): 127–144.

Blackburn, Regina. "In Search of the Black Female Self: Women's Autobiography and Ethnicity." In *Women's Autobiography,* ed. Estelle C. Jelinek. Bloomington: Indiana University Press, 1980.

186

Bloch, Ernst, et al. *Aesthetics and Politics.* London: New Left Books, 1977.

Bovenschen, Silvia. "Is There a Feminine Aesthetic?" In *Feminist Aesthetics,* ed. Gisela Ecker. London: The Women's Press, 1985.

Bruss, Elizabeth W. *Autobiographical Acts: The Changing Situation of a Literary Genre.* Baltimore: Johns Hopkins University Press, 1976.

Bürger, Peter. *Theory of the Avant-Garde,* trans. Michael Shaw. Minneapolis: University of Minnesota Press, 1984.

Burke, Carolyn. "Irigaray through the Looking Glass." *Feminist Studies,* 7, no. 2 (1981): 288–306.

Cameron, Deborah. *Feminism and Linguistic Theory.* London; Macmillan, 1985.

Campbell, Joseph. *The Hero with a Thousand Faces.* 2d ed. Princeton, N.J.: Princeton University Press, 1968.

Christ, Carol P. "Margaret Atwood: The Surfacing of Women's Spiritual Quest and Vision." *Signs,* 2, no. 2 (1976): 316–330.

—— *Diving Deep and Surfacing: Women Writers on Spiritual Quest.* 2d ed. Boston: Beacon, 1986.

Cixous, Hélène. "The Laugh of the Medusa," trans. Keith Cohen and Paula Cohen. *Signs,* 1, no. 4 (1976): 245–264.

—— "Castration or Decapitation?" trans. Annette Kuhn. *Signs,* 7, no. 1 (1981): 41–55.

Cixous, Hélène, and Cathérine Clément. *The Newly Born Woman,* trans. Betsy Wing. Minneapolis: University of Minnesota Press, 1986.

Cornillon, Susan Koppelman. *Images of Women in Fiction: Feminist Perspectives.* Bowling Green, Ohio: Bowling Green University Press, 1972.

Coward, Rosalind. " 'This Novel Changes Lives': Are Women's Novels Feminist Novels? A Response to Rebecca O'Rourke's Article 'Summer Reading.' " *Feminist Review,* no. 5 (1980): 53–64.

Culler, Jonathan. *Structuralist Poetics: Structuralism, Linguistics and the Study of Literature.* London: Routledge and Kegan Paul, 1975.

De Lauretis, Teresa. *Alice Doesn't: Feminism, Semiotics, Cinema.* London: Macmillan, 1984.

—— "Aesthetics and Feminist Theory: Rethinking Women's Cinema." *New German Critique,* no. 34 (1985): 154–175.

Dews, Peter. *Logics of Disintegration: Post-Structuralist Thought and the Claims of Critical Theory.* London: Verso, 1987.

Donovan, Josephine, ed. *Feminist Literary Criticism: Explorations in Theory.* Lexington: University Press of Kentucky, 1975.

Duchen, Claire. *Feminism in France: From May '68 to Mitterrand.* London: Routledge and Kegan Paul, 1986.

Du Plessis, Rachel Blau. *Writing beyond the Ending: Narrative Strategies of Twentieth-Century Women Writers.* Bloomington: Indiana University Press, 1985.

Du Plessis, Rachel Blau, and Members of Workshop 9. "For the Etruscans: Sexual Difference and Artistic Production—The Debate over a Female Aesthetic." In *The Future of Difference*, ed. Hester Eisenstein and Alice Jardine. Boston: G. K. Hall, 1980.

Eagleton, Terry. *The Rape of Clarissa: Writing, Sexuality and Class Struggle in Samuel Richardson*. Oxford: Basil Blackwell, 1982.

—— *Literary Theory: An Introduction*. Oxford: Basil Blackwell, 1983.

—— *The Function of Criticism: From "The Spectator" to Post-Structuralism*. London: Verso, 1984.

—— *Against the Grain*. London: Verso, 1986.

Ecker, Gisela, ed. *Feminist Aesthetics*. London: The Women's Press, 1985.

Ellman, Mary. *Thinking about Women*. New York: Harcourt Brace Jovanovich, 1968.

Engel, Stephanie. "Femininity as Tragedy: Re-examining the New Narcissism." *Socialist Review*, no. 53 (1980): 77–104.

Féral, Josette. "Antigone, or, The Irony of the Tribe." *Diacritics*, 8, no. 3 (September 1978): 2–14.

—— "The Powers of Difference." In *The Future of Difference*, ed. Hester Eisenstein and Alice Jardine. Boston: G. K. Hall, 1980.

Ferguson, Kathy E. *Self, Society and Womankind: The Dialectic of Liberation*. Westport, Conn.: Greenwood Press, 1980.

Ferree, Myra Marx, and Beth B. Hess. *Controversy and Coalition: The New Feminist Movement*. Boston: Twayne, 1985.

Forgacs, David. "Marxist Literary Theories." In *Modern Literary Theory: A Comparative Introduction*, ed. David Robey and Anne Jefferson. London: Batsford, 1982.

Foucault, Michel. *The History of Sexuality: An Introduction*, trans. Robert Hurley. New York: Pantheon, 1978.

Frankel, Boris. *The Post-Industrial Utopians*. Cambridge: Polity Press, 1987.

Fraser, Nancy. "What's Critical about Critical Theory? The Case of Habermas and Gender." *New German Critique*, no. 35 (1985): 97–132.

—— "On the Political and the Symbolic: Against the Metaphysics of Textuality." *Boundary 2*, 14, nos. 1, 2 (1985–86): 195–209.

—— "Towards a Discourse Ethic of Solidarity." *Praxis International*, 5, no. 4 (1986): 425–429.

—— "Social Movements vs. Disciplinary Bureaucracies." University of Minnesota: Center for Humanistic Studies, Occasional Papers no. 8, 1987.

—— "Women, Welfare and the Politics of Need Interpretation." *Thesis Eleven*, no. 17 (1987): 88–106.

Gallop, Jane. *Feminism and Psychoanalysis: The Daughter's Seduction*. London: Macmillan, 1982.

—— "*Quand nos lèvres s'écrivent*: Irigaray's Body Politic." *Romanic Review*, 74, no. 1 (1983): 77–83.

Gallop, Jane, and Carolyn Burke. "Psychoanalysis and Feminism in France." In *The Future of Difference,* ed. Hester Eisenstein and Alice Jardine. Boston: G. K. Hall, 1980.

Gardiner, Judith Kegan. "On Female Identity and Writing by Women." In *Writing and Sexual Difference,* ed. Elizabeth Abel. Brighton: Harvester, 1982.

Gerhardt, Marlis. "Wohin geht Nora? Auf der Suche nach der verlorenen Frau." *Kursbuch,* no. 47 (1977): 77–90.

—— *Stimmen und Rhythmen: Weibliche Ästhetik und Avantgarde.* Darmstadt: Luchterhand, 1986.

Giddens, Anthony. *New Rules of Sociological Method: A Positive Critique of Interpretative Sociology.* London: Hutchinson, 1976.

—— *Central Problems in Social Theory: Action, Structure and Contradiction in Social Analysis.* London: Macmillan, 1979.

Godwin, James. "Narcissus and Autobiography." *Genre,* 12 (1979): 69–92.

Grace, Sherrill E. "Quest for the Peaceable Kingdom: Urban/Rural Codes in Ray, Lawrence, and Atwood." In *Women Writers and the City: Essays in Feminist Literary Criticism,* ed. Susan Merrill Squier. Knoxville: University of Tennessee Press, 1984.

Grant, Damien. *Realism.* London: Methuen, 1970.

Grimshaw, Jean. *Feminist Philosophers: Women's Perspectives on Philosophical Traditions.* Brighton: Wheatsheaf, 1986.

Gross, Elizabeth. "Philosophy, Subjectivity and the Body: Kristeva and Irigaray." In *Feminist Challenges: Social and Political Theory,* ed. Carole Pateman and Elizabeth Gross. Sydney: Allen and Unwin, 1986.

Habermas, Jürgen. "The Public Sphere: An Encyclopaedia Article." *New German Critique,* 1, no. 3 (1974): 49–55.

—— *Die Strukturwandel der Öffentlichkeit: Untersuchungen zu einer Kategorie der bürgerlichen Gesellschaft* (1962). Reprint, Darmstadt: Luchterhand, 1984.

Hanke, Amala M. *Spatiotemporal Consciousness in English and German Romanticism: A Comparative Study of Novalis, Blake, Wordsworth and Eichendorff.* Berne: Peter Lange, 1981.

Harding, Sandra. "The Instability of the Analytical Categories of Feminist Theory." *Signs,* 11, no. 4 (1986): 645–664.

Hart, Francis. "Notes for an Anatomy of Modern Autobiography." *New Literary History,* 1 (1970): 485–511.

Haug, Frigga. "The Women's Movement in West Germany." *New Left Review,* no. 155 (1986): 50–74.

Heath, Stephen. *The Sexual Fix.* London: Macmillan, 1982.

Henriques, Julian, et al. *Changing the Subject: Psychology, Social Regulation and Subjectivity.* London: Methuen, 1984.

Hepworth, Mike, and Bryan S. Turner. *Confession: Studies in Deviance and Religion.* London: Routledge and Kegan Paul, 1982.

Hirsch, Marianne. "The Novel of Formation as Genre: Between Great Expectations and Lost Illusions." *Genre,* 12 (1979): 293–311.

—— "Spiritual *Bildung:* The Beautiful Soul as Paradigm." In *The Voyage In: Fictions of Female Development,* ed. Elizabeth Abel, Marianne Hirsch, and Elizabeth Langland. Hanover, N.H.: University Press of New England, 1983.

Hohendahl, Peter U. "Beyond Reception Aesthetics." *New German Critique,* no. 28 (1982): 108–146.

—— *The Institution of Criticism.* Ithaca: Cornell University Press, 1982.

Hollway, Wendy. "Gender Difference and the Production of Subjectivity." In Julian Henriques et al., *Changing the Subject: Psychology, Social Regulation and Subjectivity.* London: Methuen, 1984.

Hooks, Bell. *Feminist Theory: From Margin to Center.* London: Southend Press, 1984.

Huyssen, Andreas. "Mapping the Postmodern." *New German Critique,* no. 33 (1984): 5–52.

Irigaray, Luce. *This Sex Which Is Not One,* trans. Catherine Porter. Ithaca: Cornell University Press, 1985.

Jacobs, Jürgens. *Wilhelm Meister und seine Brüder: Untersuchungen zum deutschen Bildungsroman.* Munich: Fink, 1972.

Jacobus, Mary. "The Question of Language: Men of Maxims and *The Mill on the Floss.*" In *Writing and Sexual Difference,* ed. Elizabeth Abel. Brighton: Harvester, 1982.

Jaggar, Alison M. *Feminist Politics and Human Nature.* Brighton: Harvester, 1983.

Jameson, Fredric. *The Political Unconscious: Narrative as a Socially Symbolic Act.* Ithaca: Cornell University Press, 1981.

Jardine, Alice. "Pre-Texts for the Transatlantic Feminist." *Yale French Studies,* no. 62 (1981): 220–236.

—— *Gynesis: Configurations of Woman and Modernity.* Ithaca: Cornell University Press, 1985.

Jehlens, Myra. "Archimedes and the Paradox of Feminist Criticism." In *Feminist Theory: A Critique of Ideology,* ed. Nannerl O'Keohane, Michelle Z. Rosaldo, and Barbara C. Gelpi. Brighton: Harvester, 1982.

Jelinek, Estelle C. "Introduction: Women's Autobiography and the Male Tradition." In *Women's Autobiography,* ed. Estelle C. Jelinek. Bloomington: Indiana University Press, 1980.

Johnson, Pauline. "From Virginia Woolf to the Post-Moderns: Developments in a Feminist Aesthetic." *Radical Philosophy,* no. 45 (1987): 23–30.

Jones, Ann Rosalind. "Towards an Understanding of *l'écriture féminine.*" *Feminist Studies,* 7, no. 2 (1981): 264–287.

—— "Julia Kristeva on Femininity: The Limits of a Semiotic Politics." *Feminist Review,* no. 18 (1984): 56–73.

Juhasz, Suzanne. "Towards a Theory of Form in Feminist Autobiography: Kate Millett's *Flying* and *Sita;* Maxine Hong Kingston's *The Woman Warrior.*" In *Women's Autobiography,* ed. Estelle C. Jelinek. Bloomington: Indiana University Press, 1980.

Jurgensen, Manfred. *Deutsche Frauenautoren der Gegenwart.* Berne: Francke, 1983.

Kamuf, Peggy. "Replacing Feminist Criticism." *Diacritics,* 12, no. 2 (1982): 42–47.

Kaplan, Cora. "Wild Nights: Pleasure/Sexuality/Feminism." In *Sea Changes: Culture and Feminism.* London: Verso, 1986.

Kaplan, E. Ann. *Rocking around the Clock: Music Television, Postmodernism and Consumer Culture.* London: Methuen, 1987.

Keane, John. *Public Life and Late Capitalism.* Cambridge: Cambridge University Press, 1984.

Keitel, Evelyne. "Verständigungstexte: Form, Funktion, Wirkung." *German Quarterly,* 56, no. 3 (1983): 431–456.

Kenshur, Oskar. "Demystifying the Demystifiers: Metaphysical Snares of Ideological Criticism." *Critical Inquiry,* 14 (1988): 335–353.

Kolkenbrock-Netz, Jutta, and Marianne Schuller. "Frau im Spiegel: Zum Verhältnis von autobiographischer Schreibweise und feministischer Praxis." In *Entwürfe von Frauen in der Literatur des 20. Jahrhunderts,* ed. Irmela von der Lühe. Berlin: Argument, 1982.

Kristeva, Julia. *Desire in Language: A Semiotic Approach to Literature and Art,* ed. Leon S. Roudiez, trans. Thomas Gora, Alice Jardine, and Leon S. Roudiez. Oxford: Basil Blackwell, 1980.

—— "Woman Can Never Be Defined." In *New French Feminisms: An Anthology,* ed. Elaine Marks and Isabelle de Courtivron. New York: Schocken, 1981.

—— "Women's Time." In *Feminist Theory: A Critique of Ideology,* ed. Nannerl O'Keohane, Michelle Z. Rosaldo, and Barbara C. Gelpi. Brighton: Harvester, 1982.

—— *Revolution in Poetic Language,* trans. Margaret Waller. New York: Columbia University Press, 1984.

Kuhn, Annette. *Women's Pictures: Feminism and Cinema.* London: Routledge and Kegan Paul, 1982.

Lasch, Christopher. *The Culture of Narcissism: American Life in an Age of Diminishing Expectations.* New York: Norton, 1979.

—— *The Minimal Self: Psychic Survival in Troubled Times.* New York: Norton, 1984.

Lejeune, Philippe. *Le pacte autobiographique.* Paris: Seuil, 1975.

—— "The Autobiographical Contract." In *French Literary Theory Today: A Reader,* ed. Tzvetan Todorov. Cambridge: Cambridge University Press, 1982.

——— *Moi aussi*. Paris: Seuil, 1986.

Levin, Harry. *The Gates of Horn*. New York: Oxford University Press, 1963.

Lewis, Philip E. "Revolutionary Semiotics." *Diacritics*, 4 (Fall 1974): 28–37.

Lippard, Lucy. *From the Center: Feminist Essays on Women's Art*. New York: Dutton, 1976.

Lloyd, Genevieve. *The Man of Reason: 'Male' and 'Female' in Western Philosophy*. London: Methuen, 1984.

Lovell, Terry. *Pictures of Reality: Aesthetics, Politics, Pleasure*. London: British Film Institute, 1980.

——— "The Social Relations of Cultural Production: Absent Centre of a New Discourse." In Simon Clarke et al., *One-Dimensional Marxism: Althusser and the Politics of Culture*. London: Allison and Busby, 1981.

——— "Writing Like a Woman: A Question of Politics." In *The Politics of Theory*, ed. Francis Barker. Colchester: University of Essex Press, 1983.

Lunn, Eugene. *Marxism and Modernism* (1982). Reprint, London: Verso, 1985.

MacCabe, Colin. "Realism and the Cinema: Notes on Some Brechtian Theses." *Screen*, 15, no. 2 (1974): 7–27.

Macherey, Pierre. *A Theory of Literary Production*, trans. Geoffrey Wall. London: Routledge and Kegan Paul, 1978.

Makward, Christiane. "To Be or Not to Be . . . A Feminist Speaker," trans. Marlène Barsoum, Alice Jardine, and Hester Eisenstein. In *The Future of Difference*, ed. Hester Eisenstein and Alice Jardine. Boston: G. K. Hall, 1980.

Marks, Elaine. "Women and Literature in France." *Signs*, 3, no. 4 (1978): 832–842.

Martin, Biddy. "Feminism, Criticism and Foucault." *New German Critique*, no. 27 (1982): 3–30.

Martin, Wendy. "Another View of the 'City Upon a Hill': The Prophetic Vision of Adrienne Rich." In *Women Writers and the City: Essays in Feminist Literary Criticism*, ed. Susan Merrill Squier. Knoxville: University of Tennessee Press, 1984.

Marxist-Feminist Literature Collective. "Women's Writing: *Jane Eyre, Shirley, Villette, Aurora Leigh*." *Ideology and Consciousness*, no. 3 (1978).

McBurney, Blaine. "The Post-Modernist Transvaluation of Modernist Values." *Thesis Eleven*, no. 12 (1985): 94–109.

McDowell, Deborah E. "New Directions for Black Feminist Criticism." In *The New Feminist Criticism: Essays on Women, Literature and Theory*, ed. Elaine Showalter. New York: Pantheon, 1985.

Miller, Nancy K. *The Heroine's Text: Readings in the French and English Novel, 1722–1782*. New York: Columbia University Press, 1980.

——— "Women's Autobiography in France: For a Dialectics of Identification." In *Women and Language in Literature and Society*, ed. Sally McConnell-Ginet et al. New York: Praeger, 1980.

———— "Emphasis Added: Plots and Plausibilities in Women's Fiction." *PMLA*, 96, no. 1 (1981): 36–47.

———— "Changing the Subject: Authorship, Writing, and the Reader." In *Feminist Studies/Critical Studies*, ed. Teresa de Lauretis. Bloomington: Indiana University Press, 1986.

Moi, Toril. *Sexual/Textual Politics: Feminist Literary Theory*. London: Methuen, 1985.

Moretti, Franco. *The Way of the World: The Bildungsroman in European Culture*. London: Verso, 1987.

Morris, Meaghan. "Postmodernity and Lyotard's Sublime." *Art and Text*, no. 16 (1985–86): 44–67.

Morrison, Toni. "Rootedness: The Ancestor as Foundation." In *Black Women Writers: Arguments and Interviews*, ed. Mari Evans (1983). Reprint, London: Pluto, 1985.

Negt, Oskar, and Alexander Kluge. *Öffentlichkeit und Erfahrung*. Frankfurt am Main: Suhrkamp, 1972.

Niggl, Günter. *Geschichte der deutschen Autobiographie im 18. Jahrhundert: Theoretische Grundlegung und literarische Entfaltung*. Stuttgart: Metzler, 1977.

Nye, Andrea. "Woman Clothed with the Sun: Julia Kristeva and the Escape from/to Language." *Signs*, 12, no. 4 (1987): 664–686.

O'Kane, John. "Marxism, Deconstruction and Ideology: Notes Towards an Articulation." *New German Critique*, no. 33 (1984): 219–248.

Pajaczkowska, Claire. "Introduction to Kristeva." *m/f*, nos. 5, 6 (1981): 150–157.

Pascal, Roy. *Design and Truth in Autobiography*. London: Routledge and Kegan Paul, 1960.

Pateman, Carole. "Feminist Critiques of the Public/Private Dichotomy." In *Public and Private in Social Life*, ed. S. I. Benn and G. F. Gaus. London: Croom Helm, 1983.

Pearson, Carol, and Katherine Pope. *The Female Hero in American and British Literature*. New York: R. R. Bowker, 1981.

Perry, Ruth. *Women, Letters and the Novel*. New York: AMS Press, 1980.

Peyre, Henri. *Literature and Sincerity*. New Haven: Yale University Press, 1963.

Pomerlau, Cynthia S. "Quest for Community: Spiritual Autobiographies of Eighteenth-Century Quaker and Puritan Women in America." In *Women's Autobiography*, ed. Estelle C. Jelinek. Bloomington: Indiana University Press, 1980.

Pratt, Annis. *Archetypal Patterns in Women's Fiction*. Brighton: Harvester, 1982.

Register, Cheri. "American Feminist Literary Criticism: A Bibliographical Introduction." In *Feminist Literary Criticism: Explorations in Theory*, ed. Josephine Donovan. Lexington: University Press of Kentucky, 1975.

——— "Literary Criticism." *Signs*, 6, no. 2 (1980): 268–282.

Rowe, John Carlos. " 'To Live outside the Law You Must Be Honest': The Authority of the Margin in Contemporary Theory." *Cultural Critique*, no. 2 (1985–86): 35–70.

Russ, Joanna. *How to Suppress Women's Writing*. London: The Women's Press, 1984.

Ruthven, K. K. *Feminist Literary Studies: An Introduction*. Cambridge: Cambridge University Press, 1984.

Ryan, Judith. "The Vanishing Subject: Empirical Psychology and the Modern Novel." *PMLA*, 95 (1980): 857–869.

Sayre, Robert, and Michael Löwy, "Figures of Romantic Anti-Capitalism." *New German Critique*, no. 32 (1984): 42–92.

Schulte-Sasse, Jochen. "Theory of Modernism versus Theory of the Avant-Garde." Foreword to Peter Bürger, *Theory of the Avant-Garde*. Minneapolis: University of Minnesota Press, 1984.

Schur, Edwin. *The Awareness Trap: Self-Absorption Instead of Social Change*. New York: McGraw-Hill, 1976.

Schwab, Sylvia. *Autobiographik und Lebenserfahrung: Versuch einer Typologie deutschsprachigen autobiographischen Schriften zwischen 1965 und 1975*. Würzburg: Königshausen und Neumann, 1981.

Schweickart, Patrocinio. "Comments on Jehlens' 'Archimedes and the Paradox of Feminist Criticism.' " *Signs*, 8, no. 1 (1982): 170–176.

Segal, Lynne. *Is the Future Female? Troubled Thoughts on Contemporary Feminism*. London: Virago, 1987.

Sennett, Richard. *The Fall of Public Man*. New York: Knopf, 1977.

Showalter, Elaine. "Literary Criticism." *Signs*, 1, no. 2 (1975): 435–460.

——— "Feminist Criticism in the Wilderness." In *Writing and Sexual Difference*, ed. Elizabeth Abel. Brighton: Harvester, 1982.

——— *A Literature of Their Own: British Women Novelists from Brontë to Lessing*. 2d ed. London: Virago, 1982.

——— "Introduction: The Feminist Critical Revolution." In *The New Feminist Criticism: Essays on Women, Literature and Theory*, ed. Elaine Showalter. New York: Pantheon, 1985.

Smith, Barbara. "Towards a Black Feminist Criticism." In *Feminist Criticism and Social Change: Sex, Class and Race in Literature and Culture*, ed. Judith Newton and Deborah Rosenfelt. London: Methuen, 1985.

Spacks, Patricia Meyer. *The Female Imagination: A Literary and Psychological Investigation of Women's Writing*. London: Allen and Unwin, 1976.

——— *Imagining a Self: Autobiography and Novel in Eighteenth-Century England*. Cambridge, Mass.: Harvard University Press, 1976.

——— "Selves in Hiding." In *Women's Autobiography*, ed. Estelle C. Jelinek. Bloomington: Indiana University Press, 1980.

Spengemann, William C. *The Forms of Autobiography: Episodes in the History of a Literary Genre*. New Haven: Yale University Press, 1980.

Spivak, Gayatri Chakravorty. "French Feminism in an International Frame." *Yale French Studies,* no. 62 (1981): 154–184.

—— "Feminism and Critical Theory." In *In Other Worlds: Essays in Cultural Politics.* New York: Methuen, 1987.

Stanley, Julia Penelope, and Susan J. Wolfe. "Towards a Feminist Aesthetic." *Chrysalis,* 6 (1978): 57–71.

Stanton, Domna C. "Language and Revolution: The Franco-American Disconnection." In *The Future of Difference,* ed. Hester Eisenstein and Alice Jardine. Boston: G. K. Hall, 1980.

Stephan, Inge, and Sigrid Weigel. *Die verborgene Frau: Sechs Beiträge zu einer feministischen Literaturwissenschaft.* Berlin: Argument, 1985.

Stimpson, Catherine R. "Nancy Reagan Wears a Hat: Feminism and Its Cultural Consensus." *Critical Inquiry,* 14 (1988): 223–243.

Suleiman, Susan. *Authoritarian Fictions: The Ideological Novel as Literary Genre.* New York: Columbia University Press, 1983.

Swales, Martin. *The German Bildungsroman from Wieland to Hesse.* Princeton, N.J.: Princeton University Press, 1978.

Thompson, John B. *Studies in the Theory of Ideology.* Cambridge: Polity Press, 1984.

Todd, Janet. *Sensibility: An Introduction.* London: Methuen, 1986.

Tönnies, Ferdinand. *Community and Society,* trans. C. P. Loomis. London: Routledge and Kegan Paul, 1955.

Touraine, Alain. *The Post-Industrial Society,* trans. Leonard Mayhew. New York: Random House, 1971.

Weeks, Jeffrey. *Sexuality and Its Discontents: Meanings, Myths and Modern Sexualities.* London: Routledge and Kegan Paul, 1985.

Weigel, Sigrid. " 'Woman Begins Relating to Herself': Contemporary German Women's Literature (Part One)." *New German Critique,* no. 31 (1984): 53–94.

Wenzel, Hélène Vivienne. "The Text as Body/Politics: An Appreciation of Monique Wittig's Writing in Context." *Feminist Studies,* 7, no. 2 (1981): 264–287.

White, Allon. "Exposition and Critique of Julia Kristeva." Birmingham: Centre for Contemporary Cultural Studies, Special Paper no. 49.

White, Hayden. "The Question of Narrative in Contemporary Historical Theory." *History and Theory,* 23, no. 1 (1984): 1–33.

Wilden, Anthony. *System and Structure: Essays in Communication and Exchange.* 2d ed. London: Tavistock, 1980.

Williams, Raymond. *Marxism and Literature.* Oxford: Oxford University Press, 1977.

Willis, Susan. "Black Women Writers: Taking a Critical Perspective." In *Making a Difference: Feminist Literary Criticism,* ed. Gayle Greene and Coppelia Kahn. London: Methuen, 1985.

Wolff, Janet. *The Social Production of Art.* London: Macmillan, 1981.

———— *Aesthetics and the Sociology of Art*. London: Allen and Unwin, 1983.

Wolin, Richard. "The De-Aestheticization of Art: On Adorno's *Aesthetische Theorie*," *Telos*, no. 41 (1979): 105–127.

Young, Iris Marion. "Impartiality and the Civic Public: Some Implications of Feminist Critiques of Moral and Political Theory." *Praxis International*, 5, no. 4 (1986): 381–401.

Zimmerman, Bonnie. "What Has Never Been: An Overview of Lesbian Feminist Criticism." In *Making a Difference: Feminist Literary Criticism*, ed. Gayle Greene and Coppelia Kahn. London: Methuen, 1985.

Notes

Introduction

1. Toril Moi, *Sexual/Textual Politics: Feminist Literary Theory* (London: Methuen, 1985).

2. A survey of the main positions is contained in Ernst Bloch et al., *Aesthetics and Politics* (London: New Left Books, 1977). See also Eugene Lunn, *Marxism and Modernism* (1982; reprint, London: Verso, 1985).

3. Moi, *Sexual/Textual Politics,* p. 7.

4. It should be stressed, however, that the comparison can only be sustained at a purely *theoretical* level; there are fundamental historical and political differences between socialist realism as an aesthetic and political orthodoxy imposed upon artists by the state, and feminist realism as a form chosen by contemporary women writers as a means of foregrounding the representational dimension of the literary text.

5. A brief typology of various Marxist positions on the relationship between ideology and literature (e.g., the Adorno "negative knowledge" model and the Macherey "production" model) is provided by David Forgacs in "Marxist Literary Theories," in *Modern Literary Theory: A Comparative Introduction,* ed. David Robey and Anne Jefferson (London: Batsford, 1982).

6. For a discussion of similarities between poststructuralism and theories of modernism, although not specifically in relation to feminism, see Andreas Huyssen, "Mapping the Postmodern," *New German Critique,* no. 33 (1984): 36–46, and the discussion of Adorno and Derrida in Jochen Schulte-Sasse, "Theory of Modernism versus Theory of the Avant-Garde," foreword to Peter Bürger, *Theory of the Avant-Garde,* trans. Michael Shaw (Minneapolis: University of Minnesota Press, 1984).

7. Relevant texts here include: Julia Kristeva, *Desire in Language: A Semiotic Approach to Literature and Art,* ed. Leon S. Roudiez, trans. Thomas Gora,

Alice Jardine, and Leon S. Roudiez (Oxford: Basil Blackwell, 1980), and *Revolution in Poetic Language,* trans. Margaret Waller (New York: Columbia University Press, 1984); Hélène Cixous, "The Laugh of the Medusa," trans. Keith Cohen and Paula Cohen, *Signs,* 1, no. 4 (1976): 245–264, and "Castration or Decapitation?" trans. Annette Kuhn, *Signs,* 7, no. 1 (1981): 41–55; Hélène Cixous and Cathérine Clément, *The Newly Born Woman,* trans. Betsy Wing (Minneapolis: University of Minnesota Press, 1986).

8. Thus discussions of a lesbian or a black feminist aesthetic typically emphasize issues of representation and rarely make a sustained case for a unique black or lesbian literary style. See, among others, Barbara Smith, "Towards a Black Feminist Criticism," in *Feminist Criticism and Social Change: Sex, Class and Race in Literature and Culture,* ed. Judith Newton and Deborah Rosenfelt (London: Methuen, 1985); Bonnie Zimmerman, "What Has Never Been: An Overview of Lesbian Feminist Criticism," and Susan Willis, "Black Women Writers: Taking a Critical Perspective," both in *Making a Difference: Feminist Literary Criticism,* ed. Gayle Greene and Coppelia Kahn (London: Methuen, 1985); Deborah E. McDowell, "New Directions for Black Feminist Criticism," in *The New Feminist Criticism: Essays on Women, Literature and Theory,* ed. Elaine Showalter (New York: Pantheon, 1985); Barbara Christian, *Black Feminist Criticism: Perspectives on Black Women Writers* (New York: Pergamon Press, 1985).

9. Moi, *Sexual/Textual Politics,* p. 16.

10. Ibid., p. 171.

11. I borrow the phrase from an article by Nancy Fraser, "On the Political and the Symbolic: Against the Metaphysics of Textuality," *Boundary 2,* 14, nos. 1, 2 (1985–86): 195–209.

12. Bürger, *Theory of the Avant-Garde,* p. 12.

13. By suggesting that feminist positions are linked to different ideological interests, such as those of intellectuals or grass-roots activists, I do not wish to imply that the choice of a specific form of feminism can be explained simply in terms of class position. A range of complex and not always immediately discernible factors come into play in shaping the choice of a particular theoretical and ideological stance; obviously, national cultural traditions constitute another relevant factor.

14. For a discussion of Habermas's concept of communicative rationality in the context of poststructuralist debates on language, see the concluding chapter of Peter Dews, *Logics of Disintegration: Post-Structuralist Thought and the Claims of Critical Theory* (London: Verso, 1987).

15. Seyla Benhabib and Drucilla Cornell, Introduction (to a special issue on feminism), *Praxis International,* 5, no. 4 (1986): 365.

16. Alison M. Jaggar, *Feminist Politics and Human Nature* (Brighton: Harvester, 1983), p. 5.

17. Rosalind Coward, " 'This Novel Changes Lives': Are Women's

Novels Feminist Novels? A Response to Rebecca O'Rourke's Article 'Summer Reading,' " *Feminist Review,* no. 5 (1980): 57.

18. See Leslie W. Rabine's discussion of the influence of feminism on contemporary romance fiction, "Romance in the Age of Electronics: Harlequin Enterprises," in *Feminist Criticism and Social Change: Sex, Class and Race in Literature and Culture,* ed. Judith Newton and Deborah Rosenfelt (London: Methuen, 1985).

19. See, for example, Marleen Barr and Nicholas D. Smith, eds., *Women and Utopia: Critical Interpretations* (Lanham, Md.: University Press of America, 1983), and Natalie M. Rosinsky, *Feminist Futures: Contemporary Women's Speculative Fiction* (Ann Arbor: University of Michigan, 1984).

1. Against Feminist Aesthetics

1. Although my discussion focuses primarily on feminist literary theory, many of the issues raised also recur in discussions of feminist approaches to other media. See, for example, Annette Kuhn, *Women's Pictures: Feminism and Cinema* (London: Routledge and Kegan Paul, 1982); Lucy Lippard, *From the Center: Feminist Essays on Women's Art* (New York: Dutton, 1976).

2. Jane Gallop and Carolyn Burke, "Psychoanalysis and Feminism in France," in *The Future of Difference,* ed. Hester Eisenstein and Alice Jardine (Boston: G. K. Hall, 1980), p. 106.

3. See Claire Duchen, *Feminism in France: From May '68 to Mitterrand* (London: Routledge and Kegan Paul, 1986), for an account of French feminism which places the "Psych et Po" group within the context of the French women's movement as a whole. For instances of how French feminist theory does not fit the necessarily schematic overview provided in this chapter, see Cathérine Clément's contribution to Cixous and Clément, *The Newly Born Woman,* and "Variations on Common Themes," written by the editorial collective of Questions Féministes, in *New French Feminisms: An Anthology,* ed. Elaine Marks and Isabelle de Courtivron (New York: Schocken, 1981).

4. Elaine Showalter, "Feminist Criticism in the Wilderness," in *Writing and Sexual Difference,* ed. Elizabeth Abel (Brighton: Harvester, 1982), p. 16.

5. See, for example, Silvia Bovenschen, *Die imaginierte Weiblichkeit: Exemplarische Untersuchungen zu kulturgeschichtlichen und literarischen Präsentationsformen des Weiblichen* (Frankfurt am Main: Suhrkamp, 1979); Inge Stephan and Sigrid Weigel, *Die verborgene Frau: Sechs Beiträge zu einer feministischen Literaturwissenschaft* (Berlin: Argument, 1985); Susan L. Cocalis and Kay Goodman, eds., *Beyond the Eternal Feminine: Critical Essays on Women and German Literature* (Stuttgart: Hans-Dieter Heinz, 1982); Wolfgang Paulsen, ed., *Die Frau als Heldin und Autorin: Neue kritische Ansätze zur deutschen Literatur* (Berlin: Francke, 1979).

6. Gisela Ecker, ed., *Feminist Aesthetics* (London: The Women's Press, 1985).

7. The specific context of West German feminism is discussed in Edith Hoshino Altbach's article "The New German Women's Movement," in *German Feminism: Readings in Politics and Literature,* ed. Edith Hoshino Altbach et al. (Albany: State University of New York Press, 1984), pp. 3–26. See also Frigga Haug, "The Women's Movement in West Germany," *New Left Review,* no. 155 (1986): 50–74.

8. Teresa de Lauretis, "Aesthetics and Feminist Theory: Rethinking Women's Cinema," *New German Critique,* no. 34 (1985): 154.

9. Susan Koppelman Cornillon, ed., *Images of Women in Fiction: Feminist Perspectives* (Bowling Green, Ohio: Bowling Green University Press, 1972); Josephine Donovan, ed., *Feminist Literary Criticism: Explorations in Theory* (Lexington: University Press of Kentucky, 1975).

10. Elaine Showalter, "Literary Criticism," *Signs,* 1, no. 2 (1975): 435–460.

11. Elaine Showalter, "Introduction: The Feminist Critical Revolution," in *The New Feminist Criticism: Essays on Women, Literature and Theory,* ed. Elaine Showalter (New York: Pantheon, 1985), p. 6.

12. Mary Ellman, *Thinking about Women* (New York: Harcourt Brace Jovanovich, 1968); Joanna Russ, *How to Suppress Women's Writing* (London: The Women's Press, 1984).

13. See Elaine Showalter, *A Literature of Their Own: British Women Novelists from Brontë to Lessing,* 2d ed. (London: Virago, 1982), chap. 3.

14. Judith Kegan Gardiner, "On Female Identity and Writing by Women," in *Writing and Sexual Difference,* ed. Elizabeth Abel (Brighton: Harvester, 1982), p. 183.

15. Ibid., p. 187.

16. Russ, *How to Suppress Women's Writing,* p. 29.

17. Julia Penelope Stanley and Susan J. Wolfe, "Towards a Feminist Aesthetic," *Chrysalis,* 6 (1978): 57–71. Quoted in Cheri Register, "Literary Criticism," *Signs,* 6, no. 2 (1980): 272.

18. Silvia Bovenschen, "Is There a Feminine Aesthetic?" in *Feminist Aesthetics,* ed. Gisela Ecker (London: The Women's Press, 1985), p. 37.

19. Patricia Meyer Spacks, *The Female Imagination: A Literary and Psychological Investigation of Women's Writing* (London: Allen and Unwin, 1976), p. 4.

20. See, for example, Bell Hooks, *Feminist Theory: From Margin to Center* (London: South End Press, 1984); Gayatri Chakravorty Spivak, "Feminism and Critical Theory," in *In Other Worlds: Essays in Cultural Politics* (New York: Methuen, 1987).

21. Moi, *Sexual/Textual Politics,* p. 63.

22. Michèle Barrett, *Women's Oppression Today: Problems in Marxist Feminist Analysis* (London: Verso, 1980), p. 106.

23. See, for example, Christine Gledhill, "Recent Developments in Feminist Film Criticism," in *Re-Vision: Essays in Feminist Film Criticism*, ed. Mary Ann Doane et al. (Los Angeles: American Film Institute, 1983); Laura Mulvey, "Feminism, Film and the Avant-Garde," in *Women Writing and Writing about Women*, ed. Mary Jacobus (London: Croom Helm, 1979); Teresa de Lauretis, *Alice Doesn't: Feminism, Semiotics, Cinema* (London: Macmillan, 1984).

24. Theodor Adorno, "Reconciliation under Duress," in *Aesthetics and Politics*, ed. Ernst Bloch et al. (London: New Left Books, 1977), p. 160.

25. See, e.g., Rosalind Coward and John Ellis, *Language and Materialism: Developments in Semiology and the Theory of the Subject* (London: Routledge and Kegan Paul, 1977); Catherine Belsey, *Critical Practice* (London: Methuen, 1980); Colin MacCabe, "Realism and the Cinema: Notes on Some Brechtian Theses," *Screen*, 15, no. 2 (1974): 7–27.

26. Kuhn, *Women's Pictures*, p. 11.

27. Moi, *Sexual/Textual Politics*, p. 8.

28. Among the various accounts of Kristeva, the most useful, apart from Moi's discussion in *Sexual/Textual Politics*, include: Ann Rosalind Jones, "Julia Kristeva on Femininity: The Limits of a Semiotic Politics," *Feminist Review*, no. 18 (1984): 56–73; Claire Pajaczkowska, "Introduction to Kristeva," *m/f*, nos. 5, 6 (1981): 150–157; Allon White, "Exposition and Critique of Julia Kristeva" (Birmingham: Centre for Contemporary Cultural Studies, Special Paper no. 49); Andrea Nye, "Woman Clothed with the Sun: Julia Kristeva and the Escape from/to Language," *Signs*, 12, no. 4 (1987): 664–686.

29. Kristeva, *Desire in Language*, p. 133.

30. Ibid., p. 134.

31. Alice Jardine, "Pre-Texts for the Transatlantic Feminist," *Yale French Studies*, no. 62 (1981): 228.

32. Moi, *Sexual/Textual Politics*, pp. 165–166.

33. Ibid., p. 166. Elizabeth Gross has suggested that Kristeva's privileging of the avant-garde is not gender-neutral but in fact androcentric in its conceptualization of a transgressive subjectivity. See "Philosophy, Subjectivity and the Body: Kristeva and Irigaray," in *Feminist Challenges: Social and Political Theory*, ed. Carole Pateman and Elizabeth Gross (Sydney: Allen and Unwin, 1986). A related argument regarding the "masculinity" of avant-gardism is made by Marlis Gerhardt in *Stimmen und Rhythmen: Weibliche Ästhetik und Avantgarde* (Darmstadt: Luchterhand, 1986).

34. Cixous, "Castration or Decapitation?" pp. 53–54.

35. Mary Jacobus, "The Question of Language: Men of Maxims and *The Mill on the Floss*," in *Writing and Sexual Difference*, ed. Elizabeth Abel (Brighton: Harvester, 1982), p. 37.

36. Carolyn Burke, "Irigaray through the Looking Glass," *Feminist*

Studies, 7, no. 2 (1981): 288–306. See also Jane Gallop, *"Quand nos lèvres s'écrivent*: Irigaray's Body Politic," *Romanic Review,* 74, no. 1 (1983): 77–83.

37. See, e.g., Luce Irigaray, "This Sex Which Is Not One," and "The Power of Discourse and the Subordination of the Feminine," in *This Sex Which Is Not One,* trans. Catherine Porter (Ithaca: Cornell University Press, 1985). A critique of Irigaray in the context of a comprehensive analysis of the current fetishization of marginality is offered by John Carlos Rowe, " 'To Live outside the Law You Must Be Honest': The Authority of the Margin in Contemporary Theory," *Cultural Critique,* no. 2 (1985–86): 35–70.

38. Jones, "Julia Kristeva on Femininity," p. 58.

39. Recent accounts of the social construction of sexuality include: Jeffrey Weeks, *Sex, Politics and Society: The Regulation of Sexuality since 1800* (London: Longman, 1981), and *Sexuality and Its Discontents: Meanings, Myths and Modern Sexualities* (London: Routledge and Kegan Paul, 1985); Michel Foucault, *The History of Sexuality: An Introduction,* trans. Robert Hurley (New York: Pantheon, 1978). For critiques of the celebration of "feminine" sexuality, see, e.g., Janet Sayers, *Sexual Contradictions: Psychology, Psychoanalysis and Feminism* (London: Tavistock, 1984), chap. 4; Stephen Heath, *The Sexual Fix* (London: Macmillan, 1982), pp. 111–120.

40. Jones, "Julia Kristeva on Femininity," p. 60.

41. From *Revolution in Poetic Language,* quoted in Philip E. Lewis, "Revolutionary Semiotics," *Diacritics,* 4 (Fall 1974): 31.

42. See Gayatri Chakravorty Spivak, "French Feminism in an International Frame," *Yale French Studies,* no. 62 (1981): 167.

43. Elaine Marks, "Women and Literature in France," *Signs,* 3, no. 4 (1978): 835.

44. See, for example, Hélène Vivienne Wenzel, "The Text as Body/Politics: An Appreciation of Monique Wittig's Writings in Context," *Feminist Studies,* 7, no. 2 (1981): 271, for an account of Cixous's rejection of the term "feminist." A detailed critique of the "Psych et Po" group's refusal of the public sphere is offered by Duchen in *Feminism in France,* in particular chaps. 4 and 5.

45. Jones, "Julia Kristeva on Femininity," p. 63.

46. Ibid., p. 56.

47. Jane Gallop, *Feminism and Psychoanalysis: The Daughter's Seduction* (London: Macmillan, 1982), p. 97.

48. See Anthony Wilden, *System and Structure: Essays in Communication and Exchange,* 2d ed. (London: Tavistock, 1980), p. 287.

49. See Genevieve Lloyd, *The Man of Reason: 'Male' and 'Female' in Western Philosophy* (Minneapolis: University of Minnesota Press, 1984).

50. A defense of the utopian dimension of theories of feminine writing is offered by Moi in *Sexual/Textual Politics,* pp. 121–123, and by Ecker in the introduction to *Feminist Aesthetics,* p. 19.

51. Cixous, "The Laugh of the Medusa," p. 881.

52. Cixous, "Castration or Decapitation?" p. 52.

53. Julia Kristeva, "Woman Can Never Be Defined," in *New French Feminisms: An Anthology*, ed. Elaine Marks and Isabelle de Courtivron (New York: Schocken, 1981), p. 166.

54. Alice Jardine, *Gynesis: Configurations of Woman and Modernity* (Ithaca: Cornell University Press, 1985), p. 58.

55. Peggy Kamuf, "Replacing Feminist Criticism," *Diacritics*, 12, no. 2 (1982): 44–46.

56. Rachel Blau Du Plessis and Members of Workshop 9, "For the Etruscans: Sexual Difference and Artistic Production—The Debate over a Female Aesthetic," in *The Future of Difference*, ed. Hester Eisenstein and Alice Jardine (Boston: G. K. Hall, 1980), p. 149.

57. Moi, *Sexual/Textual Politics*, p. 166.

58. Christiane Makward, "To Be or Not to Be . . . a Feminist Speaker," trans. Marlène Barsoum, Alice Jardine, and Hester Eisenstein, in *The Future of Difference*, ed. Hester Eisenstein and Alice Jardine (Boston: G. K. Hall, 1980), p. 97.

59. See "What is Literature?" in Terry Eagleton, *Literary Theory: An Introduction* (Oxford: Basil Blackwell, 1983), pp. 1–16.

2. Subjectivity and Feminism

1. John B. Thompson, *Studies in the Theory of Ideology* (Cambridge: Polity Press, 1984), p. 148.

2. Julian Henriques et al., *Changing the Subject: Psychology, Social Regulation and Subjectivity* (London: Methuen, 1984), p. 7.

3. See, for example, Jardine's *Gynesis*, in particular the chapter entitled "The Demise of Experience." For a brief discussion of some of the tensions between feminist politics and poststructuralist theory, see Michèle Barrett, "The Concept of Difference," *Feminist Review*, no. 26 (1987), esp. pp. 34–36.

4. Anthony Giddens, *Central Problems in Social Theory: Action, Structure and Contradiction in Social Analysis* (London: Macmillan, 1979), p. 69.

5. Anthony Giddens, *New Rules of Sociological Method: A Positive Critique of Interpretative Sociology* (London: Hutchinson, 1976), p. 121.

6. Giddens, *Central Problems in Social Theory*, p. 5.

7. Ibid., p. 7.

8. Ibid., p. 40.

9. Ibid., p. 58.

10. Wendy Hollway, "Gender Difference and the Production of Subjectivity," in Julian Henriques et al., *Changing the Subject: Psychology, Social Regulation and Subjectivity* (London: Methuen, 1984), p. 278.

11. See, e.g., Nancy Fraser, "Women, Welfare and the Politics of Need Interpretation," *Thesis Eleven,* no. 17 (1987): 88–106. For a more optimistic view of changes to women's socioeconomic status since the reemergence of feminism, see Pippa Norris, *Politics and Sexual Equality: The Comparative Position of Women in Western Democracies* (Brighton: Wheatsheaf, 1987).

12. Giddens, *Central Problems in Social Theory,* p. 70.

13. Ibid., p. 71.

14. Deborah Cameron, *Feminism and Linguistic Theory* (London: Macmillan, 1985), p. 153.

15. Kristeva, "Woman Can Never Be Defined," p. 137.

16. See, among others, Jonathan Arac et al., *The Yale Critics: Deconstruction in America* (Minneapolis: University of Minnesota Press, 1983); Michael Fisher, *Does Deconstruction Make Any Difference? Poststructuralism and the Defense of Poetry in Modern Criticism* (Bloomington: Indiana University Press, 1985).

17. Oscar Kenshur, "Demystifying the Demystifiers: Metaphysical Snares of Ideological Criticism," *Critical Inquiry,* 14 (1988): 346.

18. Giddens, *Central Problems in Social Theory,* p. 4.

19. See Terry Eagleton, "Wittgenstein's Friends," in *Against the Grain* (London: Verso, 1986), pp. 99–111.

20. See, among others, Iris Marion Young, "Impartiality and the Civic Public: Some Implications of Feminist Critiques of Moral and Political Theory," *Praxis International,* 5, no. 4 (1986): 381–401; Nancy Fraser, "Towards a Discourse Ethic of Solidarity," *Praxis International,* 5, no. 4 (1986): 425–429.

21. Huyssen, "Mapping the Postmodern," p. 44.

22. Carole Pateman, "Feminist Critiques of the Public/Private Dichotomy," in *Public and Private in Social Life,* ed. S. I. Benn and G. F. Gaus (London: Croom Helm, 1983), p. 281.

23. Fraser, "Towards a Discourse Ethic of Solidarity," p. 428.

24. Jardine, *Gynesis,* p. 154.

25. Ibid., p. 89.

26. Josette Féral, "Antigone, or, The Irony of the Tribe," *Diacritics,* 8, no. 3 (1978): 12. See also Féral's "The Powers of Difference," in *The Future of Difference,* ed. Hester Eisenstein and Alice Jardine (Boston: G. K. Hall, 1980).

27. See, for example, Meaghan Morris, "Postmodernity and Lyotard's Sublime," *Art and Text,* no. 16 (1985–86); Christopher Norris, "Philosophy as a Kind of Narrative: Rorty on Post-Modern Liberal Culture," in *The Contest of Faculties: Philosophy and Theory after Deconstruction* (London: Methuen, 1985).

28. See Nancy K. Miller, "Changing the Subject: Authorship, Writing, and the Reader," in *Feminist Studies/Critical Studies,* ed. Teresa de Lauretis (Bloomington: Indiana University Press, 1986), p. 106.

29. Young, "Impartiality and the Civic Public," p. 382.

30. See Sandra Harding, "The Instability of the Analytical Categories of Feminist Theory," *Signs,* 11, no. 4 (1986): 645–664. For an alternative view, see Jane Flax, "Postmodernism and Gender Relations in Feminist Theory," *Signs,* 12, no. 4 (1987): 621–643.

31. Boris Frankel, *The Post-Industrial Utopians* (Cambridge: Polity Press, 1987), p. 184.

32. Young, "Impartiality and the Civic Public," p. 397.

33. Ibid., p. 383.

34. Kathy E. Ferguson, *Self, Society and Womankind: The Dialectic of Liberation* (Westport, Conn.: Greenwood Press, 1980), p. 12.

35. A critical survey of current theories of "masculine" rationality and "feminine" mutuality is offered by Christopher Lasch in *The Minimal Self: Psychic Survival in Troubled Times* (New York: Norton, 1984), in particular pp. 244–253.

36. It must be acknowledged, however, that a critique of essentialism does not imply that biology can be simply dissolved into a category of discourse. As Sandra Harding points out, human beings exist as embodied creatures, not disembodied egos, and women's physiological experiences (menstruation, childbirth, etc.) differ fundamentally from those of men. At the same time, of course, the experience of the body is always already symbolically encoded, so that the biological can never be separated from the social, with which it is dialectically interrelated. See Harding, "The Instability of the Analytical Categories of Feminist Theory," pp. 661–662, and, for a more comprehensive discussion of the limitations of nature/culture dualisms, Lynda Birke, *Women, Feminism and Biology: The Feminist Challenge* (Brighton: Wheatsheaf, 1986).

37. See Edwin Schur, *The Awareness Trap: Self-Absorption Instead of Social Change* (New York: McGraw-Hill, 1976).

38. Stanley Aronowitz, "On Narcissism," *Telos,* no. 44 (1980): 75.

39. Schulte-Sasse, "Theory of Modernism versus Theory of the Avant-Garde," p. xxvi.

40. Duranty quoted in Harry Levin, *The Gates of Horn* (New York: Oxford University Press, 1966), p. 69.

41. Judith Ryan, "The Vanishing Subject: Empirical Psychology and the Modern Novel," *PMLA,* 95 (1980): 858.

42. Henri Peyre, *Literature and Sincerity* (New Haven: Yale University Press, 1963), p. 2.

43. "General usage . . . still intends by realism the close rendering of ordinary experience." Damien Grant, *Realism* (London: Methuen, 1970), p. 72.

44. Jonathan Culler, *Structuralist Poetics: Structuralism, Linguistics and the Study of Literature* (London: Routledge and Kegan Paul, 1975), p. 147.

45. See Fredric Jameson, *The Political Unconscious: Narrative as a Socially Symbolic Act* (Ithaca: Cornell University Press, 1981), pp. 107–110.
46. Ibid., p. 151.
47. Raymond Williams, *Marxism and Literature* (Oxford: Oxford University Press, 1977)', pp. 180–185.
48. Jameson, *The Political Unconscious,* p. 106.

3. On Confession

1. Christopher Lasch, *The Culture of Narcissism: American Life in an Age of Diminishing Expectations* (New York: Norton, 1978), p. 71.
2. Cynthia S. Pomerlau, "Quest for Community: Spiritual Autobiographies of Eighteenth-Century Quaker and Puritan Women in America," in *Women's Autobiography,* ed. Estelle C. Jelinek (Bloomington: Indiana University Press, 1980), p. 37.
3. Estelle C. Jelinek, "Introduction: Women's Autobiography and the Male Tradition," in Jelinek, ed., *Women's Autobiography,* p. 19.
4. William C. Spengemann, *The Forms of Autobiography: Episodes in the History of a Literary Genre* (New Haven: Yale University Press, 1980). The concluding "Bibliographical Essay" traces the changing critical status of autobiography as a genre.
5. Francis Hart, "Notes for an Anatomy of Modern Autobiography," *New Literary History,* 1 (1970): 491.
6. In the case of texts written in a language other than English, I have cited translations whenever these are readily available. All other translations are my own.
7. Jelinek, "Women's Autobiography and the Male Tradition," p. 10.
8. Richard Sennett, *The Fall of Public Man* (New York: Knopf, 1977), p. 267.
9. Roy Pascal, *Design and Truth in Autobiography* (London: Routledge and Kegan Paul, 1960).
10. Elizabeth W. Bruss, *Autobiographical Acts: The Changing Situation of a Literary Genre* (Baltimore: Johns Hopkins University Press, 1976), p. 10.
11. Ibid., p. 12.
12. Ibid., p. 11.
13. Philippe Lejeune, "The Autobiographical Contract," in *French Literary Theory Today: A Reader,* ed. Tzvetan Todorov (Cambridge: Cambridge University Press, 1982), p. 193. This is the translation of the first chapter of *Le pacte autobiographique* (Paris: Seuil, 1975).
14. Ibid., p. 202.
15. Nancy K. Miller, "Women's Autobiography in France: For a Dialectics of Identification," in *Women and Language in Literature and Society,* ed. Sally McConnell-Ginet et al. (New York: Praeger, 1980). Lejeune's most recent work contains a reassessment and critique of his own earlier theoretical position; see *Moi aussi* (Paris: Seuil, 1986), esp. pp. 9–35.

16. It must be noted, however, that in two cases (Merian, Offenbach) the author's name is a pseudonym. The effect here is to *intensify* rather than decrease the aura of authenticity generated by the text, the implication being that the author has been forced to resort to a pseudonym precisely because she is disclosing the most intimate and revealing details of her private life.

17. Marie Cardinal, *The Words to Say It,* trans. Pat Goodheart (Cambridge, Mass.: Van Vactor and Goodheart, 1983), p. 248. Originally published as *Les mots pour le dire* (Paris: Grasset et Fasquelle, 1975).

18. Ann Oakley, *Taking It Like a Woman* (London: Jonathan Cape, 1984), p. xi.

19. See, e.g., Manfred Jurgensen, *Deutsche Frauenautoren der Gegenwart* (Berne: Francke, 1983), p. 215.

20. Evelyne Keitel, "Verständigungstexte—Form, Funktion, Wirkung," *German Quarterly,* 56, no. 3 (1983): 439.

21. See the back cover of the Fontana 1985 paperback edition.

22. Keitel, "Verständigungstexte," p. 431.

23. Ibid., p. 436.

24. Oakley, *Taking It Like a Woman,* p. 2.

25. Keitel, "Verständigungstexte," p. 447.

26. Suzanne Juhasz, "Towards a Theory of Form in Feminist Autobiography: Kate Millet's *Flying* and *Sita; Maxine* Hong Kingston's *The Woman Warrior,*" in *Women's Autobiography,* ed. Estelle C. Jelinek (Bloomington: Indiana University Press, 1980), p. 237.

27. Kate Millett, *Sita* (London: Virago, 1977), p. 250.

28. Ibid., p. 253.

29. Judith Offenbach, *Sonja: Eine Melancholie für Fortgeschrittene* (Frankfurt am Main: Suhrkamp, 1980), p. 215.

30. Kate Millett, *Flying* (1974; reprint, London: Hart-Davis, MacGibbon, 1975), p. 338.

31. Karin Struck, *Kindheits Ende: Journal einer Krise* (Frankfurt am Main: Suhrkamp, 1982), p. 497.

32. Juhasz, "Theory of Form," p. 224.

33. Oakley, *Taking It Like a Woman,* p. 179.

34. Svende Merian, *Der Tod des Märchenprinzen* (1980; reprint, Reinbek: Rowohlt, 1983), p. 323.

35. Audre Lorde, *The Cancer Journals* (1980; reprint, London: Sheba Feminist Publishers, 1985), p. 14.

36. Offenbach, *Sonja,* pp. 152–153.

37. Millett, *Flying,* pp. 82–83.

38. Karin Struck, *Klassenliebe* (Frankfurt am Main: Suhrkamp, 1973), p. 209.

39. Terry Eagleton, *The Rape of Clarissa: Writing, Sexuality and Class Struggle in Samuel Richardson* (Oxford: Basil Blackwell, 1982), p. 14.

40. Ibid., p. 13.

41. Jürgen Habermas, *Die Strukturwandel der Öffentlichkeit: Untersuchungen zu einer Kategorie der bürgerlichen Gesellschaft* (1962; reprint, Darmstadt: Luchterhand, 1984), pp. 66–67.

42. Ruth Perry, *Women, Letters and the Novel* (New York: AMS Press, 1980), p. 76.

43. Schleiermacher quoted in Günter Niggl, *Geschichte der deutschen Autobiographie im 18. Jahrhundert: Theoretische Grundlegung und literarische Entfaltung* (Stuttgart: Metzler, 1977), p. 106.

44. Foucault, *The History of Sexuality*, p. 60.

45. James Goodwin, "Narcissus and Autobiography," *Genre*, 12 (1979): 82.

46. Mike Hepworth and Bryan S. Turner, *Confession: Studies in Deviance and Religion* (London: Routledge and Kegan Paul, 1982), p. 8.

47. Oakley, *Taking It Like a Woman*, p. 57.

48. Lorde, *The Cancer Journals*, p. 65.

49. Regina Blackburn, "In Search of the Black Female Self: African-American Women's Autobiographies and Ethnicity," in *Women's Autobiography*, ed. Estelle C. Jelinek (Bloomington: Indiana University Press, 1980), pp. 149–162.

50. Patricia Meyer Spacks, "Selves in Hiding," in Jelinek, ed., *Women's Autobiography*, p. 132.

51. Millett, *Sita*, p. 136.

52. Offenbach, *Sonja*, p. 264.

53. Ibid., p. 236.

54. Struck, *Kindheits Ende*, p. 387.

55. Ibid., p. 297.

56. An overview of the eighteenth-century cult of sentiment is contained in Janet Todd's *Sensibility: An Introduction* (London: Methuen, 1986).

57. Sennett, *The Fall of Public Man*, p. 30.

58. See Aronowitz, "On Narcissism," and the other articles in the special issue on narcissism in *Telos*, no. 44 (1980), for defenses and critiques of Lasch's thesis. Further critical responses can be found in a symposium entitled *The Culture of Narcissism*, published in *Salmagundi*, 46 (1979). A feminist critique of Lasch is offered by Stephanie Engel, "Femininity as Tragedy: Re-examining the New Narcissism," *Socialist Review*, no. 53 (1980): 77–104. For a discussion of the gender blindness of Sennett's *Fall of Public Man* and of theories of modernity in general, see Janet Wolff, "The Invisible Flaneuse: Women and the Literature of Modernity," *Theory, Culture and Society*, 2, no. 3 (1985): 37–48.

59. Offenbach, *Sonja*, p. 304.

60. Oakley, *Taking It Like a Woman*, p. 55.

61. Ibid., p. 54.

62. Alice Koller, *An Unknown Woman: A Journey to Self-Discovery* (1982; reprint, New York: Bantam, 1983), p. 69.

63. Struck, *Kindheits Ende,* p. 141.
64. Lasch, *The Culture of Narcissism,* p. 35.
65. Offenbach, *Sonja,* p. 291.
66. Perry, *Women, Letters and the Novel,* p. 125.
67. Offenbach, *Sonja,* p. 181.
68. Goodwin, "Narcissus and Autobiography," p. 90.
69. Struck, *Kindheits Ende,* p. 91.
70. Patricia Meyer Spacks, *Imagining a Self: Autobiography and Novel in Eighteenth-Century England* (Cambridge, Mass.: Harvard University Press, 1976), p. 22.
71. Millett, *Sita,* p. 137.
72. Ibid.
73. Eagleton, *The Rape of Clarissa,* p. 44.
74. Millett, *Sita,* pp. 272–273.
75. Sennett, *The Fall of Public Man,* p. 334.
76. Wendy Martin, "Another View of the 'City upon a Hill': The Prophetic Vision of Adrienne Rich," in *Women Writers and the City: Essays in Feminist Literary Criticism,* ed. Susan Merrill Squier (Knoxville: University of Tennessee Press, 1984), p. 261.
77. Offenbach, *Sonja,* p. 98.
78. Schur, *The Awareness Trap,* pp. 139–142.
79. Anja Meulenbelt, *The Shame Is Over: A Political Life Story,* trans. Ann Oosthuizen (London: The Women's Press, 1980), p. 137.
80. Merian, *Der Tod des Märchenprinzen,* p. 87.
81. Oakley, *Taking It Like a Woman,* p. 2.
82. Lorde, *The Cancer Journals,* p. 1.
83. Sigrid Weigel, " 'Woman Begins Relating to Herself': Contemporary German Women's Literature (Part One)," *New German Critique,* no. 31 (1984): 82. See also Jutta Kolkenbrock-Netz and Marianne Schuller, "Frau im Spiegel: Zum Verhältnis von autobiographischer Schreibweise und feministischer Praxis," in *Entwürfe von Frauen in der Literatur des 20. Jahrhunderts,* ed. Irmela von der Lühe (Berlin: Argument, 1982).
84. Cardinal, *The Words to Say It,* p. 164.
85. Weeks, *Sexuality and Its Discontents,* p. 209. See also the concluding pages of Simon Watney, "The Banality of Gender," *Oxford Literary Review,* 8, nos. 1, 2 (1986): 13–21.
86. Weeks, *Sexuality and Its Discontents,* p. 189.

4. The Novel of Self-Discovery

1. Introduction, in *The Voyage In: Fictions of Female Development,* ed. Elizabeth Abel, Marianne Hirsch, and Elizabeth Langland (Hanover, N.H.: University Press of New England, 1983), pp. 6–7.

2. See Marianne Hirsch, "Spiritual *Bildung:* The Beautiful Soul as Paradigm," in Abel, Hirsch, and Langland, eds., *The Voyage In.*

3. E.g., Annis Pratt, *Archetypal Patterns in Women's Fiction* (Brighton: Harvester, 1982).

4. Nancy K. Miller, *The Heroine's Text: Readings in the French and English Novel, 1722–1782* (New York: Columbia University Press, 1980), p. xi.

5. Todd, *Sensibility,* p. 4.

6. See Tony Tanner, *Adultery and the Novel: Contract and Transgression* (Baltimore: Johns Hopkins University Press, 1979).

7. See Rachel Blau Du Plessis, *Writing beyond the Ending: Narrative Strategies of Twentieth-Century Women Writers* (Bloomington: Indiana University Press, 1985), pp. 6–15.

8. Hirsch, "Spiritual *Bildung,*" p. 27.

9. See Du Plessis, *Writing beyond the Ending,* pp. 16–19, and Eagleton, *The Rape of Clarissa,* pp. 72–77.

10. See, e.g., Hayden White, "The Question of Narrative in Contemporary Historical Theory," *History and Theory,* 23, no. 1 (1984): 1–33.

11. Doris Lessing, *The Summer before the Dark* (London: Jonathan Cape, 1973), p. 176.

12. Stefan, *Häutungen* (Munich: Frauenoffensive, 1975), p. 62.

13. Joan Barfoot, *Gaining Ground* (1978; reprint, London: The Women's Press, 1980), p. 27.

14. Ibid., p. 69.

15. Margaret Atwood, *Surfacing* (London: André Deutsch, 1972), p. 11.

16. Lessing, *The Summer before the Dark,* p. 158.

17. Atwood, *Surfacing,* p. 106.

18. Barfoot, *Gaining Ground,* p. 88.

19. Carol Christ, "Margaret Atwood: The Surfacing of Women's Spiritual Quest and Vision," *Signs,* 2, no. 2 (1976): 325.

20. Barfoot, *Gaining Ground,* p. 43.

21. Marilyn French, *The Women's Room* (New York: Summit, 1977), p. 458.

22. Stefan, *Häutungen,* p. 106.

23. Introduction, in Abel, Hirsch, and Langland, eds., *The Voyage In,* p. 13.

24. Ibid.

25. The quotation is from Wilhelm Dilthey, *Das Erlebnis und die Dichtung,* cited in Martin Swales, *The German Bildungsroman from Wieland to Hesse* (Princeton, N.J.: Princeton University Press, 1978), p. 3. See also Jürgen Jacobs, *Wilhelm Meister und seine Brüder: Untersuchungen zum deutschen Bildungsroman* (Munich: Fink, 1972). Franco Moretti's just published study, *The Way of the World: The Bildungsroman in European Culture* (London: Verso, 1987), is a useful contribution to the comparative study of the *Bildungsroman*

in a nineteenth-century European context, although it is marred by a severe case of gender-blindness.

26. My argument here draws upon Marianne Hirsch, "The Novel of Formation as Genre: Between Great Expectations and Lost Illusions," *Genre,* 12 (1979): 293–311.

27. Lessing, *The Summer before the Dark,* p. 12.

28. Fay Weldon, *Praxis* (London: Hodder and Stoughton, 1978), p. 269.

29. See Susan Suleiman, *Authoritarian Fictions: The Ideological Novel as Literary Genre* (New York: Columbia University Press, 1983), for a structuralist analysis of the *Bildungsroman* as a didactic genre.

30. Lessing, *The Summer before the Dark,* p. 21.

31. Moretti, *The Way of the World,* pp. 1–13.

32. French, *The Women's Room,* p. 368.

33. See, for example, Janet Todd, *Women's Friendship in Literature* (New York: Columbia University Press, 1980).

34. For a discussion of the theme of community in the work of black women writers, see Willis, "Black Women Writers," and Toni Morrison, "Rootedness: The Ancestor as Foundation," in *Black Women Writers: Arguments and Interviews,* ed. Mari Evans (1983; reprint, London: Pluto, 1985).

35. Ferdinand Tönnies, *Community and Society,* trans. C. P. Loomis (London: Routledge and Kegan Paul, 1955).

36. For example, Margot Schroeder's *Der Schlachter empfiehlt noch immer Herz* (Munich: Frauenbuchverlag, 1976) reveals clearly the vast gulf which separates the feminist radical from the women for whom she claims to speak. See, for instance, p. 57: "This ruined consciousness. A commodity is sitting in front of you"; p. 81: "They fascinated me, because they shocked me. Frenzied consumer addicts"; p. 119: "In the movement I sometimes forget, that the majority of women have no awareness of themselves."

37. I borrow the term from Carol P. Christ, *Diving Deep and Surfacing: Women Writers on Spiritual Quest,* 2d ed. (Boston: Beacon Press, 1986), p. 18. It is used in a rather different context by Susan J. Rosowski to designate the nineteenth-century novel of female destiny as an "awakening to limitations." See "The Novel of Awakening," in *The Voyage In: Fictions of Female Development,* ed. Elizabeth Abel, Marianne Hirsch, and Elizabeth Langland (Hanover, N.H.: University Press of New England, 1983).

38. Stefan, *Häutungen,* p. 43.

39. Atwood, *Surfacing,* pp. 105–106.

40. Ibid., p. 191.

41. Ibid., p. 189.

42. See Joseph Campbell, *The Hero with a Thousand Faces,* 2d ed. (Princeton, N.J.: Princeton University Press, 1968), for a comprehensive discussion of the quest as archetypal narrative. An application of Campbell's analysis to woman-centered literature is contained within Carol Pearson and

Katherine Pope, *The Female Hero in American and British Literature* (New York: R. R. Bowker, 1981).

43. The typical thematic and structural features of the feminist "novel of awakening" bear obvious points of resemblance to the literature of Romanticism. See, e.g., M. H. Abrams, *Natural Supernaturalisms: Tradition and Revolution in Romantic Literature* (New York: Norton, 1971), esp. chap. 4, "The Circuitous Journey: Through Alienation to Reintegration"; Amala M. Hanke, *Spatiotemporal Consciousness in English and German Romanticism: A Comparative Study of Novalis, Blake, Wordsworth and Eichendorff* (Berne: Peter Lange, 1981).

44. Barfoot, *Gaining Ground*, p. 86.

45. Ibid., p. 105.

46. Paule Marshall, *Praisesong for the Widow* (London: Virago, 1983), p. 151.

47. Ibid., p. 254.

48. Robert Sayre and Michael Löwy, "Figures of Romantic Anti-Capitalism," *New German Critique*, no. 32 (1984): 55–57.

49. Atwood, *Surfacing*, p. 129.

50. Ibid., p. 184.

51. Ibid., p. 159.

52. Ibid., p. 108.

53. Barfoot, *Gaining Ground*, p. 149.

54. Atwood, *Surfacing*, p. 169.

55. Ibid., p. 168.

56. Barfoot, *Gaining Ground*, pp. 146–147.

57. Atwood, *Surfacing*, pp. 161–162.

58. Barfoot, *Gaining Ground*, p. 91.

59. Atwood, *Surfacing*, p. 181.

60. Stefan, *Häutungen*, p. 61.

61. Barfoot, *Gaining Ground*, p. 168.

62. Atwood, *Surfacing*, p. 176.

63. "As a woman thinking, I experience no such division in my own being between nature and culture, between my female body and my conscious thought." Adrienne Rich, *Of Woman Born: Motherhood as Experience and Institution* (1976; reprint, London: Virago, 1977), p. 95. See Cora Kaplan's critique of Rich's conception of a benign female nature in "Wild Nights: Pleasure/Sexuality/Feminism," in *Sea Changes: Culture and Feminism* (London: Verso, 1986), pp. 50–56.

64. See Jean Grimshaw, *Feminist Philosophers: Women's Perspectives on Philosophical Traditions* (Brighton: Wheatsheaf, 1986), p. 135. Grimshaw's book offers a valuable critique of appeals to "female experience" as the basis for feminist theory.

65. See Sherrill E. Grace, "Quest for the Peaceable Kingdom: Urban/

Rural Codes in Ray, Lawrence and Atwood," in *Women Writers and the City: Essays in Feminist Literary Criticism,* ed. Susan Merrill Squier (Knoxville: University of Tennessee Press, 1984). A discussion of the "nature as monster" theme is contained within Margaret Atwood, *Survival: A Thematic Guide to Canadian Literature* (Toronto: Anansi, 1972), chap. 2.

66. Marlis Gerhardt, "Wohin geht Nora? Auf der Suche nach der verlorenen Frau," *Kursbuch,* no. 47 (1977): 53.

67. For an overview, see Leslie Adelson, "Subjectivity Reconsidered: Botho Strauss and Contemporary West German Prose," *New German Critique,* no. 30 (1983): 3–59.

68. Marshall, *Praisesong for the Widow,* p. 255.

69. Julia Kristeva, "Women's Time," in *Feminist Theory: A Critique of Ideology,* ed. Nannerl O'Keohane, Michelle Z. Rosaldo, and Barbara C. Gelpi (Brighton: Harvester, 1982), pp. 36–38.

5. Politics, Aesthetics, and the Feminist Public Sphere

1. See Roland Barthes, *S/Z,* trans. Richard Miller (London: Cape, 1975).

2. For a critical account of the influence of Althusser on English cultural studies, see Terry Lovell, "The Social Relations of Cultural Production: Absent Centre of a New Discourse," in Simon Clarke et al., *One Dimensional Marxism: Althusser and the Politics of Culture* (London: Allison and Busby, 1980).

3. MacCabe, "Realism and the Cinema," p. 16.

4. Belsey, *Critical Practice,* p. 51.

5. Coward, "Are Women's Novels Feminist Novels?" p. 60.

6. MacCabe, "Realism and the Cinema," p. 16.

7. Pierre Macherey, *A Theory of Literary Production,* trans. Geoffrey Wall (London: Routledge and Kegan Paul, 1978), p. 55.

8. Blaine McBurney, "The Post-Modernist Transvaluation of Modernist Values," *Thesis Eleven,* no. 12 (1985): 100–101.

9. Lunn, *Marxism and Modernism,* pp. 216–217.

10. Bürger, *Theory of the Avant-Garde,* pp. 52–53.

11. Ibid., pp. 86–87.

12. Huyssen, "Mapping the Postmodern," p. 9. For an early formulation of the dilemmas facing modern art in a post–avant-garde era, see Hans Magnus Enzensberger, "The Aporias of the Avant-garde," in *The Consciousness Industry: On Literature, Politics and the Media,* ed. Michael Roloff (New York: Seabury Press, 1974). A recent critique of the "bureaucratization of the avant-garde" undertaken from a more conservative position is Suzi Gablik, *Has Modernism Failed?* (New York: Thames and Hudson, 1984).

13. Huyssen, "Mapping the Postmodern," p. 41.

14. E. Ann Kaplan, *Rocking around the Clock: Music Television, Postmod-*

ernism and Consumer Culture (London: Methuen, 1987), esp. chap. 3. For one version of the argument that late capitalism has deconstructed the unified subject more efficiently than *écriture*, see Terry Eagleton, "Capitalism, Modernism, Postmodernism," in *Against the Grain* (London: Verso, 1986).

15. Pauline Johnson, "From Virginia Woolf to the Post-Moderns: Developments in a Feminist Aesthetic," *Radical Philosophy*, no. 45 (1987): 29.

16. E.g., Perry Anderson, *Considerations on Western Marxism* (London: New Left Books, 1976).

17. For a helpful overview of Adorno's defense of modernism, see Richard Wolin, "The De-Aestheticization of Art: On Adorno's *Aesthetische Theorie*," *Telos*, no. 41 (1979): 105–127.

18. Jürgen Habermas, "The Public Sphere: An Encyclopaedia Article," *New German Critique*, 1, no. 3 (1974): 49.

19. Habermas, *Strukturwandel der Öffentlichkeit*, p. 52.

20. See Oskar Negt and Alexander Kluge, *Öffentlichkeit und Erfahrung* (Frankfurt am Main: Suhrkamp, 1972); John Keane, *Public Life and Late Capitalism: Towards a Socialist Theory of Democracy* (Cambridge: Cambridge University Press, 1984). For an overview of some of the debates generated by Habermas's model of the public sphere, see Peter U. Hohendahl, *The Institution of Criticism* (Ithaca: Cornell University Press, 1982), chap. 7, "Critical Theory, Public Sphere and Culture: Jürgen Habermas and His Critics."

21. Keane, *Public Life and Late Capitalism*, p. 29.

22. Terry Eagleton, *The Function of Criticism* (London: Verso, 1986), p. 118.

23. Hooks, *Feminist Theory: From Margin to Center*, p. 3. See also Sheila Radford-Hill, "Considering Feminism as a Model for Social Change," in *Feminist Studies/Critical Studies*, ed. Teresa de Lauretis (Bloomington: Indiana University Press, 1986).

24. See Catherine R. Stimpson, "Nancy Reagan Wears a Hat: Feminism and Its Cultural Consensus," *Critical Inquiry*, 14 (1988): 223–243.

25. Myra Marx Ferree and Beth B. Hess, *Controversy and Coalition: The New Feminist Movement* (Boston: Twayne, 1985), p. 49.

26. I borrow the term from Duchen, *Feminism in France*, p. 122.

27. My argument here draws on Tony Bennett's "The Prison-House of Criticism," *New Formations*, no. 2 (1987), in particular pp. 135–140.

28. Nancy Fraser, "Social Movements vs. Disciplinary Bureaucracies: The Discourses of Social Needs" (University of Minnesota: Center for Humanistic Studies, Occasional Papers no. 8, 1987).

29. Peter U. Hohendahl, "Beyond Reception Aesthetics," *New German Critique*, no. 28 (1982): 134.

30. See Gablik, *Has Modernism Failed?*

31. Some of the most valuable of these include: Tania Modleski, *Loving with a Vengeance: Mass-Produced Fantasies for Women* (New York: Methuen,

1984); Janice Radway, *Reading the Romance: Women, Patriarchy and Popular Literature* (Chapel Hill: University of North Carolina Press, 1984); Rosalind Coward, *Female Desire: Women's Sexuality Today* (London: Paladin, 1984). For a discussion of the association of mass culture with the "feminine," see Andreas Huyssen, "Mass Culture as Woman: Modernism's Other," in *Studies in Entertainment: Critical Approaches to Mass Culture,* ed. Tania Modleski (Bloomington: Indiana University Press, 1986), and Tania Modleski, "Femininity as Mas(s)querade: A Feminist Approach to Mass Culture," in *High Theory, Low Culture,* ed. Colin MacCabe (Manchester: Manchester University Press, 1986).

32. Michèle Barrett, "Feminism and the Definition of Cultural Politics," in *Feminism, Culture and Politics,* ed. Rosalind Brunt and Caroline Rowan (London: Lawrence and Wishart, 1982), p. 55. See also Terry Lovell, "Writing Like a Woman: A Question of Politics," in *The Politics of Theory,* ed. Francis Barker et al. (Colchester: University of Essex Press, 1983).

33. Janet Wolff, *Aesthetics and the Sociology of Art* (London: Allen and Unwin, 1983), p. 11.

34. See Macherey, *Theory of Literary Production,* pp. 51–55.

35. See Janet Wolff, *The Social Production of Art* (London: Macmillan, 1981), esp. chap. 2.

36. Nina Baym, *Women's Fiction: A Guide to Novels by and about Women in America, 1820–1870* (Ithaca: Cornell University Press, 1978), p. 14.

37. Barrett, "Feminism and the Definition of Cultural Politics," p. 50.

38. See Williams, *Marxism and Literature,* pp. 155–156.

39. Patrocinio Schweickart, "Comments on Jehlens' 'Archimedes and the Paradox of Feminist Criticism,' " *Signs,* 8, no. 1 (1982): 175.

40. Bürger, *Theory of the Avant-Garde,* pp. 53–54.

41. See, e.g., Lynne Segal, *Is the Future Female? Troubled Thoughts on Contemporary Feminism* (London: Virago, 1987), and Judith Stacey, "The New Conservative Feminism," *Feminist Studies,* 9, no. 3 (1983): 559–584.

Index

Abel, Elizabeth, *The Voyage In,* 123
Acker, Kathy, 15
Adorno, Theodor, 31, 39; modernism in, 4, 33, 159, 163
Aesthetics: political status of, 2–7, 8–12, 30–40, 46–48, 156–164, 175–182; realist, 3–4, 152, 155, 156–158, 161–162; ideology and, 8–9, 20–21, 31–32, 79, 154, 156–157, 161–162, 176–178; relative autonomy of, 9, 28–30, 158–159, 175–179; functionalist, 10, 175–176; gender bias in, 23, 24, 44–48, 176–177; reflectionist, 26–30; negative, 31–32, 40–48, 155. *See also* American feminist aesthetics; Feminist aesthetics; French feminism; Marxist aesthetics; Reception
Agency, 52–53, 55–62, 65, 66–67
Althusser, Louis, 61, 156
American feminist aesthetics: instrumentalism of, 3, 6–7; reflectionist model in, 3, 9, 26, 27–28, 30; content-based, 4, 23–24, 29–30; subjectivity in, 20–21, 22, 29–30, 50; ideology in, 27–28; female experience in, 22, 25–26, 27–29; authorial consciousness in, 26, 30; literariness in, 28–29.
Aronowitz, Stanley, 78
Art. *See* Aesthetics; Feminist aesthetics; Literature
Artaud, Antonin, 33, 34
Atwood, Margaret, *Surfacing,* 13, 122, 130, 131, 143, 145, 146, 147, 149, 180
Augustine, Saint, 103

Authenticity, 22, 136; obsession with, 88–89, 106–108, 112–113; and representation, 94–96, 147; ideological dimensions of, 104–108. *See also* Autonomy; Identity; Subjectivity
Autobiography, 15–17, 25; and fiction, 25, 91–96, 97–98; in oppositional subcultures, 25, 94–96; authenticity in, 79, 81–82, 94–96, 100–103; traditional, 85, 86–87; definition of, 89–91; truth of, 90, 93–95, 97, 100, 112–113; male bourgeois, 91, 93–94, 101–103, 115; representation in, 94–96; eighteenth-century, 101–102, 103–104, 110, 115; gender identity in, 118–119, 154. *See also* Confession
Autonomy, 68, 77, 131, 150–151. *See also* Authenticity; Identity; Subjectivity
Avant-garde: and experimental literature, 5, 15–16, 32, 34, 38, 39, 43–44, 174; death of, 159–161, 174. *See also* Experimental literature

Balzac, Honoré de, 81
Barfoot, Joan, *Gaining Ground,* 13, 122, 129–130, 131, 142, 144, 146, 147, 149
Barrett, Michèle, 17, 28, 177
Barthes, Roland, 63, 68–69, 156
Bartram, Grace, *Peeling,* 122, 138
Baym, Nina, 177
Belsey, Catherine, 156–157
Benhabib, Seyla, 12

Index

Index

Index

Jong, Erica, 14
Joyce, James, 33, 47
Juhasz, Suzanne, 96, 98

Kafka, Franz, 181
Kamuf, Peggy, 45
Kaplan, E. Ann, 160–161
Keitel, Evelyne, 93, 94–95
Kelly, Mary, *Post-Partum Document,* 174
Kenshur, Oscar, 64
Koller, Alice, 92; *An Unknown Woman,* 88, 98, 109, 115, 119
Kristeva, Julia, 2, 6, 40, 43, 62, 63, 150, 159; semiotic in, 5, 33–35, 38–39
Kuhn, Annette, 32

Lacan, Jacques, 20, 22, 38, 52, 58, 60, 157; phallocentrism of language in, 5, 35, 58, 60; language acquisition in, 40–41; mirror stage in, 111
Langland, Elizabeth, *The Voyage In,* 123
Language: gendered nature of, 5, 22, 23, 26, 36–44, 62–66; phallocentrism of, 22, 23, 36, 40–44, 59, 61–62; overdetermination of, 37–38; social functions of, 38–39, 41, 52, 65–66; acquisition of, 40–41; politics of, 41–42, 63–66; and subjectivity, 52–53, 55–62; ideological function of, 63–66; suspicion of, 146–147. *See also* Discourse; Ideology; Literature
Lasch, Christopher, 86, 107, 109–110, 113
Lautréamont, Comte de, 33
Lejeune, Philippe, 90–91, 92
Lesbianism, 6, 72, 119, 167; as theme in feminist literature, 105, 118, 131, 138. *See also* Homosexuality
Lessing, Doris, *The Summer before the Dark,* 122, 129, 135, 136, 138
Lévi-Strauss, Claude, 58
Lewis, Philip, 39
Liberalism, bourgeois, 67–68, 72. *See also* Individualism, bourgeois
Liberation: political, 2, 6–7, 12–13, 39–40, 51, 57, 126–128, 150–153; psychological, 148, 150–153
Lispector, Claire, 15
Literary meaning, 9, 27, 48–50, 175, 180. *See also* Literature

Literary theory. *See* Aesthetics; American feminist aesthetics; Feminist aesthetics; Feminist literary theory; French feminism
Literature: production of, 1, 8, 10, 48–50; social function of, 2, 3–4, 6–7, 19, 21, 31, 127–128, 157–158, 175–176; political status of, 2–7, 8–9, 30–40, 46–48, 127–128, 152, 156–164, 175–182; as oppositional discourse, 4–5, 8, 30–33, 38–40, 178; relative autonomy of, 9, 28–30, 50, 158–159, 175–179; as historical category, 175–176. *See also* Autobiography; Avant-garde; *Bildungsroman,* feminist; *Bildungsroman,* male; Confession; Experimental literature; Feminist literature; Novel of self-discovery; Women's literature
Logocentrism, 63
Lorde, Audre, 100, 105; *The Cancer Journals,* 88, 96, 116, 119
Löwy, Michael, 145
Lukács, Georg, 3, 31, 80, 159
Lunn, Eugene, 159
Lyotard, Jean-François, 69

MacCabe, Colin, 156, 157
Macherey, Pierre, 156, 176
Makward, Christiane, 48
Mallarmé, Stéphane, 33, 34
Marcuse, Herbert, 95, 163
Marks, Elaine, 39
Marriage, 115–116, 124, 128–129, 138
Marshall, Paule, *Praisesong for the Widow,* 122, 130, 144–145, 146, 150
Martin, Wendy, 114
Marxism, 9, 13, 17, 18, 21, 45, 52, 72, 128, 151–152
Marxist aesthetics, 2, 3, 4, 7, 21, 31, 33, 159, 163, 178, 179
Marxist feminism, 20, 21, 26. *See also* Socialist feminism
Mass culture, 18, 121, 160, 163, 165, 166, 173–174, 181
McCarthy, Mary, 88
Merian, Svende, 92, 98, 99–100, 115; *Der Tod des Märchenprinzen,* 88, 93, 96, 109, 116–117, 118–119

Index

Meulenbelt, Anja, 92, 115; *The Shame Is Over*, 88, 98–99
Miller, Nancy, 91, 124
Millett, Kate, 98, 105, 112, 113; *Flying*, 88, 96, 100, 112; *Sexual Politics*, 24, 96; *Sita*, 88, 96, 97, 109, 118
Modernism, 3, 4, 5, 13, 94, 147, 152; limitations of, 5–6, 38, 47, 157–164; in critical theory, 33, 163; ideology of, 155; revolutionary potential of, 154, 159–162, 163; and realism, 155, 156–158, 161; in feminist aesthetics, 156–159, 161–163; historical status of, 158–159
Modernity, 5, 18, 47, 55, 69, 76, 127, 128, 132, 138, 140, 141, 147, 148, 149, 152, 169
Moi, Toril, 2, 3, 6, 7, 8, 27, 29, 32, 35
Moretti, Franco, 138
Musil, Robert, 81
Myth, 128, 148, 149

Narcissism, 106–108, 109, 110, 111, 115
Narrative: phallocentrism of, 42–43; historical status of, 123–126; ubiquitousness of, 127; in self-discovery novel, 128–132; political value of, 152, 154–155
Nature: in novel of self-discovery, 127, 132, 142–150; in Canadian writing, 149; in German writing, 149
Novel of awakening, 127, 141–150
Novel of self-discovery, 13, 17, 88; social implications of, 123–126, 128, 132–133, 134, 135–138, 140–141, 150–153; marriage in, 124, 128–129; separation in, 124–125, 126, 141, 142–144; identity in, 124–126, 150–153; *Bildungsroman* form, 126–127, 132, 133–141, 142, 143, 152; nature in, 127, 132, 142–150; "awakening" form, 127, 141–150; psychological transformation in, 129, 130–133, 134–138, 142–145, 150–153; female community in, 132, 138–141, 150; society in, 132–133, 142–144, 145–148; irony in, 136, 143; nostalgia in, 143, 145; Romanticism in, 145–150, 152–153

Oakley, Ann, 92, 94, 99, 105, 109, 115, 116; *Taking It Like a Woman*, 13, 88, 92, 95, 98–99

Offenbach, Judith, 100, 105, 109, 110, 112–113, 114; *Sonja*, 88, 96, 97, 109, 110–111, 118
Olsen, Tillie, 15
Oppression, 74–75, 169. *See also* Feminist politics; Liberation

Pascal, Roy, *Design and Truth in Autobiography*, 89
Pateman, Carole, 67
Patriarchy: and bourgeois humanism, 4–5, 27–28; ideology of, 5, 22, 23, 27–28, 56, 179. *See also* Phallocentrism
Perry, Ruth, 101, 110
Peyre, Henri, 81
Phallocentrism, 20, 22, 23; in language, 5, 36–37, 40–43
Piercy, Marge: *Fly away Home*, 122, 135; *Small Changes*, 122, 141
Politics. *See* Feminist politics
Pomerlau, Cynthia, 86
Postmodernism, 55, 70, 71, 155, 162–163
Poststructuralism, 4, 11, 20–21, 52, 53, 54–55
Private sphere, 107, 115; women in, 72–73, 75, 129, 150
Psychoanalysis, 11, 13, 20, 23, 39–40, 57–58, 118
Public sphere, bourgeois: emergence of, 164–165; critical function of, 165–166; disintegration of, 165–166; ideal and real status of, 168–169. *See also* Feminist public sphere
Public sphere, feminist. *See* Feminist public sphere

Radical feminism, 12–13, 127
Rationality, 12, 165. *See also* Reason
Realism: in Marxist theory, 3, 31, 156; in feminist literature, 15–17, 29, 44, 78–82, 152, 155, 161–162; ideological complicity of, 31, 79, 154, 156–157, 161–162; and modernism, 155, 156–162
Reason: in feminism, 70–71, 72
Reception: of feminist literature, 8, 10, 21, 93, 116–117, 160; collective, 93; and aesthetic conventions, 157–158, 174; ideologies of, 159–162
Reinig, Christa, 15

Index

Rich, Adrienne, 114, 147
Romanticism, 106, 128; in feminism, 76, 82, 127, 128, 145–150; political significance of, 148–150; in self-discovery novel, 145–150, 152–153
Rorty, Richard, 69
Rousseau, Jean-Jacques, *Confessions*, 89, 103
Russ, Joanna, 24, 25
Ryan, Judith, 81

Sand, George, 48
Sarraute, Nathalie, 88
Sayre, Robert, 145
Schleiermacher, Friedrich, 102
Schroeder, Margot, *Der Schlachter empfiehlt noch immer Herz*, 122, 138
Schulte-Sasse, Jochen, 78–79
Schur, Edwin, 115
Schwaiger, Brigitte, *Wie kommt das Salz ins Meer*, 13, 122, 129, 130
Schweickart, Patrocinio, 179
Screen, 31
Self. *See* Authenticity; Autonomy; Identity; Subjectivity
Sennett, Richard, 88–89, 106–108, 113
Sexuality, female, 35–36, 37, 40, 57–58, 60, 116, 167. *See also* Feminine, the
Showalter, Elaine, 20, 22, 24, 26, 29; *A Literature of Their Own*, 24
Shumaker, Wayne, 86
Socialist feminism, 20, 26–27, 127, 148. *See also* Marxist feminism
Society, 139–140. *See also* Community
Spacks, Patricia Meyer, 26, 105, 112
Spengemann, William, 87
Spirituality, 127, 128, 149
Stanley, Julia Penelope, 26
Stefan, Verena, 115, 129; *Häutungen*, 13, 83, 88, 92, 100, 116–117, 118, 122, 129, 131, 142, 144, 146, 149
Struck, Karin, 97, 100, 105, 109, 114; *Die Mutter*, 92; *Kindheits Ende*, 88, 92–93, 105; *Klassenliebe*, 88, 92–93, 96; *Lieben*, 92
Structuration theory, 55–57, 60–61, 64–65, 75

Subjectivity: gender of, 14, 20–21, 22, 44–45, 59–60, 70–71, 75–78, 94–95, 118–119, 132, 142, 154–155; death of, 22, 44, 55, 57–58, 68–70, 169; male bourgeois, 22, 67, 68, 101–103, 106, 107–108, 155; as a function of language, 22–23, 44, 52–53, 55, 57, 68–69; in feminist politics, 36–40, 51, 66–71, 72–75, 83–84, 115–121, 154–155; and truth, 52, 69–70, 113–114; in structuration theory, 55–57, 75; ideological formation of, 56, 58–59, 67, 72–74, 76, 82, 104–105, 106–108, 156, 169; social formation of, 60, 75, 77–78, 91–96, 104–106, 139, 168–169; and individualism, 68, 93, 151, 155. *See also* Authenticity; Autonomy; Identity

Teresa, Saint, 103
Thompson, John B., 52
Tönnies, Ferdinand, 140
Turner, Bryan, 104

Utopian socialism, 140

Virago Press, 15
Voluntarism, 58

Walker, Alice: *The Color Purple*, 122, 139; *Meridian*, 122, 129
Weeks, Jeffrey, 119–120
Weigel, Sigrid, 118, 119
Weintraub, Karl, 86
Weldon, Fay, *Praxis*, 122, 136–137
Williams, Raymond, 85
Wittgenstein, Ludwig, 65
Wittig, Monique, 16, 80
Wolf, Christa, 17
Wolfe, Susan J., 26
Wolff, Janet, 17, 176
Women's literature, 1, 13–14, 19, 25. *See also* Feminist literature
Women's Press, The, 15
Woolf, Virginia, 6, 29, 81, 161, 162, 180, 181

Young, Iris Marion, 18, 70, 72, 76

223